RAND McNALLY

Classroom Atlas

Editor
Brett R. Gover

Research and Writing
Elizabeth Leppman, PhD

Cartographic Coordination
Nina Lusterman, Marzee Eckhoff

Cartography
Gregory P. Babiak, Rob Ferry, Marc Kugel

Design
Rand McNally Design

Photo Credits
l = left, c = center, r = right, t = top, b = bottom

Cover photo ©Image Source/Superstock, art ©istockphoto; p. 6 ©Richard I'Anson/Lonely Planet Images; p. 8 all ©Photodisc; p. 16 t ©Photodisc, (l to r) ©Photodisc, ©Photodisc, ©Photodisc, ©Corbis, ©Photodisc; p. 17 (l to r) ©Brand X/Getty Images, ©Photodisc, ©Photodisc, ©DigitalVison/Getty Images, ©Photodisc; p. 18 all ©Photodisc; p. 19 (l to r) ©Photodisc, © Photodisc, © Photodisc, ©Maso Florence/Lonely Planet Images, ©Corbis; p. 20 (l to r) ©Photodisc, ©Corbis, ©Richard I'Anson/Lonely Planet Images. Photodisc, ©Lindsay Brown/Lonely Planet Images; p. 21 (l to r) ©Photodisc, ©Photodisc, ©Photodisc, ©Digital Vision/Getty images, ©Photodisc; p. 24 ©Photodisc/Getty Images; p. 25 ©Photodisc/Getty Images; p. 26 l ©Gareth McCormack/Lonely Planet Images, r ©Getty Images; p. 28 t ©Photodisc; p. 28-29 (l to r) ©Cheryl Conlon/Lonely Planet Images, ©Photodisc, ©Photodisc, ©Rob Blakers/Lonely Planet Images, ©Photodisc, ©Jeffrey Becom/Lonely Planet Images, ©Jim Wark/Lonely Planet Images, ©Jon Davidson/Lonely Planet Images; p. 28-29 (timeline l to r) © Brian Brockman/iStockphoto.com, ©Corbis, ©Richard I'Anson/Lonely Planet Images, ©Comstock/Getty Images, ©Comstock/Getty Images, ©Richard I'Anson/Lonely Planet Images, ©Stockbyte/Getty images, ©Photodisc; p. 32-33 (l to r) ©Photodisc, ©Ray Laskowitz/Lonely Planet Images, ©Jerry Alexander/Lonely Planet Images, ©John Elk III/Lonely Planet Images, ©Corbis, ©Eric L. Wheater/Lonely Planet Images; p. 33 tl ©Photodisc, tr ©Photodisc, c ©Richard I'Anson/Lonely Planet Image b ©Photodisc; p. 34 tall ©Photodisc; p. 35 t ©Brand /Getty Images, bl ©©Michael Aw/Lonely Planet Images, br ©Photodisc; p. 41 (t to b) ©Ann Cecil/Lonely Planet Images, ©Corel, ©Photodisc, ©Gareth McCormack/Lonely Planet Images, ©Rick Gerharter/Lonely Planet Images; p. 43 tl ©Getty images, tr ©Photodisc, (bl to br) ©Ionas Kaltenbach/Lonely Planet Images, ©Photodisc, ©Photodisc, ©Photodisc, ©Digital Vision, ©Photodisc; p. 46 tl ©Mark Newman/Lonely Planet Images, tr ,bl, bc, br ©Photodisc; p. 47 tl ©Photodisc, tr ©Richard Cummins/Lonely Planet Images, bl ©iStockphoto.com/SochAnam, bc ©Photodisc, br ©Visions of America/Joe Sohm/PunchStock; p. 48 tl ©putmanphoto/istockphoto, tr ©Photodisc, b (l to r) ©Photodisc, ©Witold Skrypczak/Lonely Planet Images, ©Richard I'Anson/Lonely Planet Images, ©Lee Foster/Lonely Planet Images; p. 49 tl ©Photodisc, tr ©Photodisc, bl ©XKarDoc/istockphoto, bc ©DigitalVision/Getty Images, br ©Purdue9394/istockphoto; p. 50 tl ©DigitalVision/Getty Images, tr ©John Elk III/Lonely Planet Images, b (l to r) ©David Frazier/Corbis, ©Stephen Saks/Lonely Planet Images, ©David Frazier/Corbis, ©Angela Mrotek/Rand McNally; p. 51 tl ©Witold Skrypczak/Lonely Planet Images, tr ©Olivier Cirendin/Lonely Planet Images, bl ©Pdfield/istockphoto, bc ©dlewis33/istockphoto, br ©earleliason/istockphoto; p. 52 tl ©Punchstock, tr ©Richard Cummins/Lonely Planet Images, bl ©Jupiter Images/Thinkstock/Alamy, bc ©Photodisc, br ©Photodisc; p. 53 tl ©Photodisc, tr ©Photodisc, bl ©Photodisc, bc ©Steve Bly/Alam br ©Travel Klamath; p 54 tl ©ArtBoyMB/istockphoto, tr ©Ernest Manewal/Lonely Planet Images, bl ©Photodisc, bc ©brytta/istockphoto, br ©DigitalVision/ Getty Images; p. 55 tl ©fotoarek/istockphot tr ©Douglas Peebles Photography/Alamy, bl ©Photodisc, bc ©Rpsycho/istockphoto, br © LaoFu/istockphoto; p. 60 both ©Photodisc; p. 61 t ©Photodisc, c ©Phillip & Karen Smith/Lonely Planet Images b (l to r) ©Photodisc, ©Photodisc, ©Glenn van der Knijff/Lonely Planet Images; p. 66 ©Richard I'Anson/Lonely Planet Images; p. 67 l ©Photodisc, c ©Tom Boyden/Lonely Planet Images, r ©Photodisc; p. 68-69 (timeline l to r) ©Ryan Fox/Lonely Planet Images, ©Photodisc, ©Comstock, ©Photodisc, ©Photodisc, ©Photodisc, ©Photodisc, ©Eric L. Wheater/Lonely Planet Images; p. 68 l ©Judy Bellah/Lonely Planet Images, c ©Photodisc, r ©Jeff Greenberg/Lonely Planet Images; p. 69 (l to r) ©Photodisc, ©Ryan Fox/Lonely Planet Images, ©Photodisc, ©Photodisc; p. 72 l ©Photodisc, r ©Photodisc; p. 73 tl ©Photodisc, tr ©Bruce Yuan-Yue/Lonely Planet Images, inset ©Paul Bernhardt/Lonely Planet Images, cl ©Bruce Yuan-Yue/Lonely Planet Images, cr ©Photodisc, b ©Sayarikuna/istockphoto; p. 74 t @Getty Images; p 74-75 (l to r) ©Digital Vision, ©Photodisc, ©Photodisc, ©Corbis, ©Photodisc, ©Photodisc, ©Jean-Bernard Carillet/Lonely Planet Images, ©Digital Vision, (timeline l to r) ©Photodisc, ©Photodisc, ©Photodisc, ©Brand X, last four ©Photodisc; p. 80 t ©Paul Bigland/Lonely Planet Images, c ©Getty Images, b ©Photodisc; p. 81 t ©Photodisc, b ©Getty Image; p. 82 (t to b) ©Donald C. Priscilla Alexander Eastman/Lonely Planet Images, ©Christopher Wood/Lonely Planet Images, ©Getty Images, ©Digital Vision/Getty Images, ©Photodisc; p. 83 (t to b) ©Wade Eakle/Lonely Planet Image ©Grant Dixon/Lonely Planet Images, ©Gareth McCormack/Lonely Planet Images, ©Getty Images; p. 84 t ©Photodisc, c ©Matt Fletcher/Lonely Planet Images, p. 85 (l to r) ©Photodisc, ©Ariadne Van Zandbergen/Lonely Planet Images, ©Tom Cockrem/Lonely Planet Images , ©Photodisc, p. 84-85 (timeline l to r) ©Photodisc, ©Patrick Horton/Lonely Planet Images, ©Photodisc, ©Ariadne Van Zandber gen/Lonely Planet Images, ©Corbis, ©Corbis, ©Corbis, ©Louise Gubb/Corbis Saba; p. 88 t ©Photodisc, tl ©Photodisc, tc ©Photodisc, tr ©Jane Sweeney/Lonely Planet Images, bl ©Tony Wheeler/Lonel Planet Images, bc ©Photodisc, br ©Christine Osborne/Lonely Planet Images; p. 89 tl ©Digital Vision, tr ©Photodisc, cl ©Digital Vision, cr ©Digital Vision, bl ©Alex Dissanayake/Lonely Planet Images, br ©Digital Vision; p. 90 t ©Wayne Walton/Lonely Planet Images, bl ©Photodisc, ©Getty Images; p. 91 all ©Photodisc; p. 92 t ©Photodisc; p. 92-93 (l to r) ©Bob Charlton/Lonely Planet Images, ©Pho disc, ©Corbis, ©Jane Sweeney/Lonely Planet Images, ©Olivier Cirendini/Lonely Planet Images, ©Photodisc, ©Mark Newman/Lonely Planet Images, ©Martin Moos/Lonely Planet Images, ©Photodisc; p.92-93 (timeline l to r) ©Jane Sweeney/Lonely Planet Images, ©Photodisc, ©Bill Wassman/Lonely Planet Images, ©Photodisc, ©Photodisc, ©Corbis, ©Corbis, ©Photodisc; p. 94 (t to b) ©Photodisc, ©John Elk III/Lonely Planet Images, © pomortzeff/istockphoto, ©Corbis; p. 96 (t to b) ©Gregory Adams/Lonely Planet Images, ©Phil M. Weymouth/Lonely Planet Images, ©Anthony Plummer/Lonely Planet Images, ©Digital Vision/Getty Images; p. 104 (t to b) ©Photodisc, ©Juliet Coombe/Lonely Planet Images, ©Patrick Ben Luke Snyder/Lonely Planet Images, ©Digital Vision/Getty Images; p. 105 (to b) ©Photodisc, ©Richard I'Anson/Lonely Planet Images, © photomorphic/istockphoto; p. 106 (t to b) ©Photodisc, ©Richard I'Anson/Lonely Planet Images, ©Anders Blomqvist/Lonely Planet Images, ©Paul Greenway/Lonely Planet Images; p. 107 t ©Digital Vision/Getty Images, bl & br ©Corbis; p. 108 ©Chris Mellor/Lonely Planet Images; p. 108-109 (l to r) ©Photodisc, ©Fergus Blakiston/Lonely Planet Images, last four ©Photodisc; p. 108-109 (timeline l to r) ©Photodisc, ©Getty Images, last six ©Photodisc; p. 112 tl & tr ©Bernard Napthine/Lonely Planet Images, c ©Photodisc, bl ©Paul Sincla Lonely Planet Images, bc ©Russell Mountford/Lonely Planet Images, br ©David Wall/Lonely Planet Images; p. 113 t ©Digital Vision/Getty Images, c ©Peter Hendrie/Lonely Planet Images , bl ©Robert Halstead/Lonely Planet Images, bc ©Leonard Douglas Zell/Lonely Planet Images, br ©Michael Aw/Lonely Planet Images; p. 116 t ©Juliet Coombe/Lonely Planet Images, cl ©Corbis, cr ©Scott Darsney/Lonely Planet Images; p. 117 t ©Mlenny/istockphoto, c ©staphy/istockphoto, (l to r) first three ©Corbis, ©Photodisc; p. 116-117 (timeline l to r) ©Chris Barton/Lonely Planet Images, kkaplin/istockpho ©Holger Leue/Lonely Planet Images, ©Thinkstock, ©Antrey/istockphoto, ©Brand X, ©Corbis

Manufactured by Rand McNally
Skokie, Illinois 60077

Printed in Madison, WI, U.S.A.
September 2011
1st printing
PO# 5095
ISBN: 528-00458-1
ISBN-13: 978-0-528-00458-2

For information about ordering the *Classroom Atlas* or the *Classroom Atlas Teacher's Guide*, call 1-800-678-RAND (-7263) or visit our website at **www.randmcnally.com/education**.

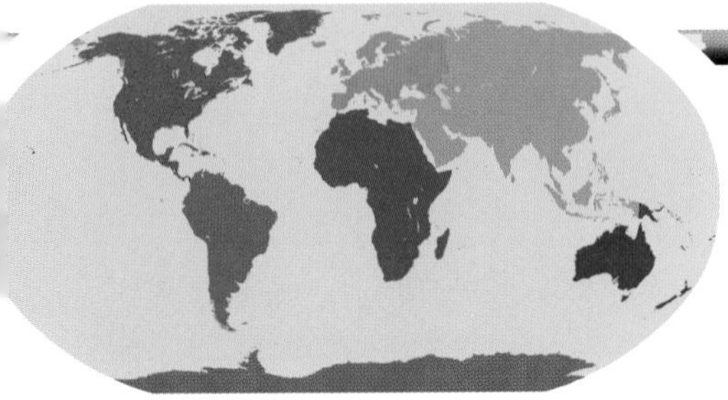

Table of Contents

How to Use the Atlas

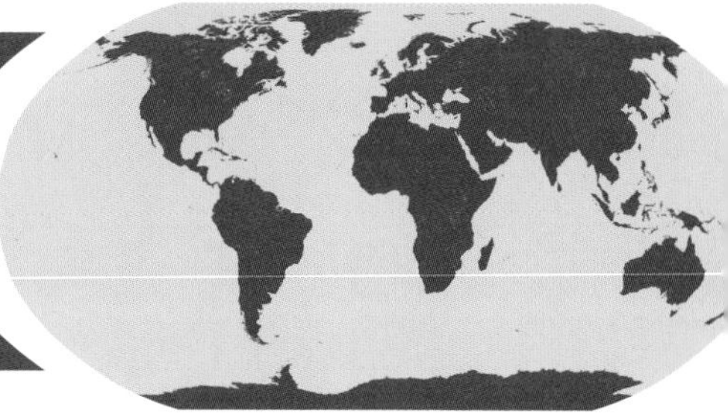

Getting to Know Your World

An atlas is a collection of maps. This atlas is a collection of more than 90 physical, political, and thematic maps. It also includes photographs, charts, graphs, and other special features.

Physical Maps

On the physical maps, different **land elevations** and **ocean depths** are shown by different colors. Major **physical features**, such as the Rocky Mountains in North America, and major rivers, such as the Colorado River, are named. Countries and some cities are also named.

Political Maps

The political maps show **political units**—areas under one government, such as countries, states, provinces, territories, and cities. Countries, states, and provinces are shown in different colors so that you can recognize them more easily. Cities are shown in different sizes of type and have different symbols to show their populations.

Map Legends

The **legend** of a map explains the symbols used on the map. It helps you "decode" the information. In this atlas, the legends on the physical and political maps explain much of the map information. To keep the legends on the individual maps from getting too large, these legends include only a few key symbols. The complete legend for all information on the physical and political maps is on page 7. Take some time to get familiar with these symbols so that you can recognize them on the individual maps.

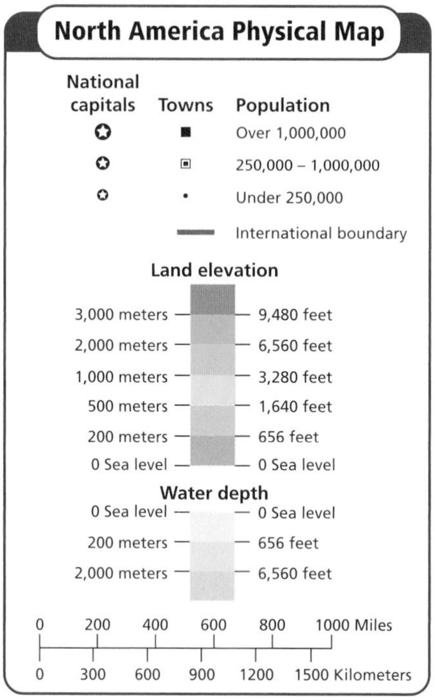

The **scale bar** in the legend tells how much smaller the map is than the real area it represents. The scale bar below is from the North America Political Map. To see how the scale bar works, place your ruler on the bar. You will see that one inch represents about 650 miles (one centimeter represents about 400 kilometers). Find two cities on the map that are about one inch apart (or two cities that are about one centimeter apart) on the North America Political Map. In the real world, these places are about 650 miles (or 400 kilometers) apart.

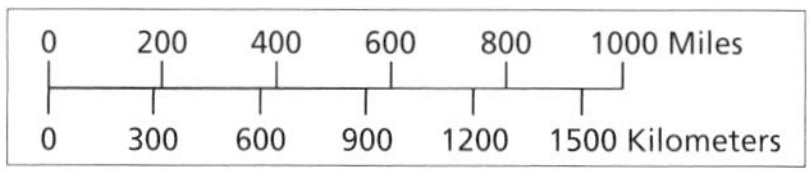

Directional Arrows

The physical and political maps in this atlas have directional arrows. The four arrows together are called a **compass rose**. The letters on the compass rose stand for **N**orth, **S**outh, **E**ast, and **W**est. On the map, the North arrow always points toward the North Pole. The South arrow always points toward the South Pole.

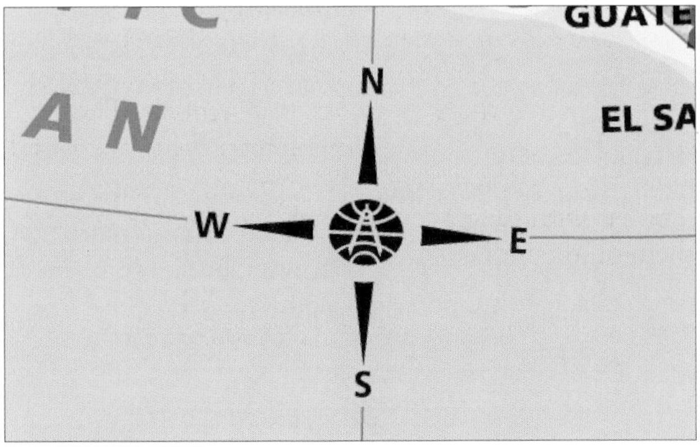

Map Grids

The blue lines drawn east-west across the maps are **lines of latitude**, or parallels. The blue lines drawn north-south are **lines of longitude**, or meridians. The lines of latitude and longitude create **grids** on the maps.

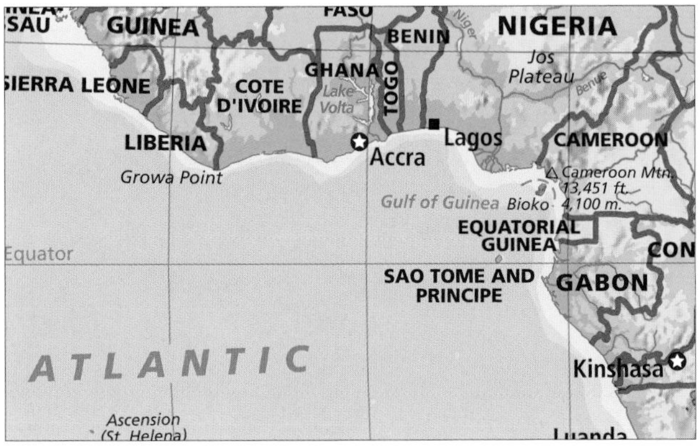

The physical and political maps have red letters along both sides and red numbers along the top and bottom. These letters and numbers are one way of giving names to these grids.

Look at the political map of Africa on page 87. Put your left index finger on the **E** at the left side of the map, and your right index finger on the **4** at the top of the map. Trace both fingers across the map until they meet at the grid square where the city of Lagos, Nigeria, is located.

Lagos is in the **E4** square of the grid on the map. The lines of latitude north and south of the E and the lines of longitude on either side of the 4 create the E4 square. (See the areas highlighted in purple on the map below.) E4 is the map key, or alpha-numeric grid location, for Lagos. What other cities are in the E4 square?

The city of Mogadishu in Somalia is in the E8 square. In what square do you find the country of Sierra Leone?

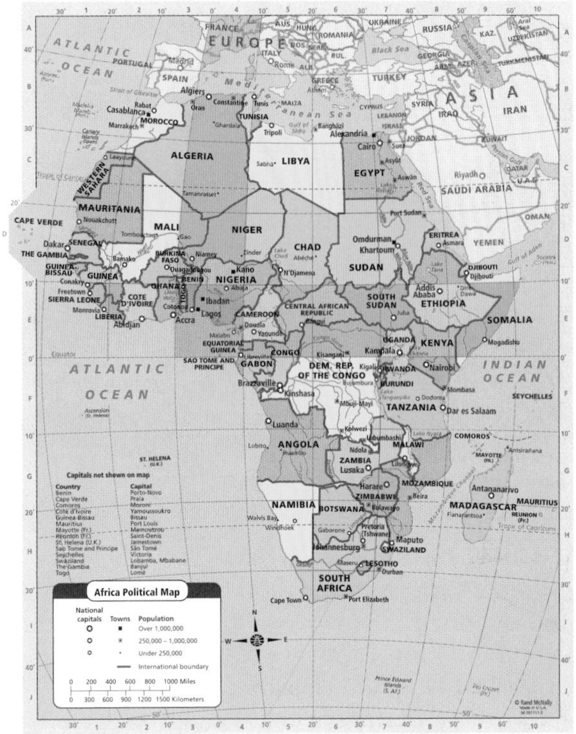

Index

The index is **a list in alphabetical order** of most of the places that appear on the maps. Each place entry in the index is followed by its map key, or alpha-numeric grid location, and the number of the page on which it appears.

Place	Map Key	Page
A		
Aberdeen, *South Dakota*	B6	**38**
Abidjan, *cap. Cote d'Ivoire, Afr.*	E3	**87**
Abilene, *Texas*	E6	**38**
Absaroka Range, *U.S.*	B3	**36**
Abu Dhabi, *cap. U.A.E., Asia*	C5	**99**
Abuja, *cap. Nigeria, Afr.*	E4	**87**
Acapulco, *Guerrero, Mexico*	C3	**64**
Accra, *cap. Ghana, Afr.*	E3	**87**
Aconcagua, *Cerro, highest peak, S.A.*	G4	**70**
Adana, *Turkey*	B3	**98**
Ad-Dammām, *Saudi Arabia*	C5	**98**
Addis Ababa, *cap. Ethiopia, Afr.*	E7	**87**
Adelaide, *cap. South Australia, Austr.*	D2	**111**

Place
Amundsen Sea, *A*
Amur River, *Asia*
Anchorage, *Alask*
Andaman Islands,
Andes, *mts., S.A.*
Andorra, *country,*
Angara River, *Rus*
Angarsk, *Russia*
Angel Falls, *S.A.*
Angola, *country,*
Anguilla, *dep., N.*
Anhui, *province,*
Ankara, *cap. Turk*
Ann Arbor, *Michi*
Annapolis, *cap. M*
Anshan, *China*

Did you know?

Each "Did You Know?" presents an interesting fact about th world.

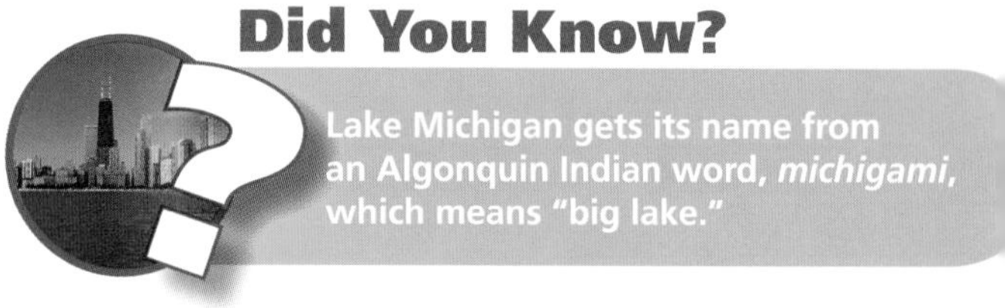

Did You Know?
Lake Michigan gets its name from an Algonquin Indian word, *michigami*, which means "big lake."

What If?

Each "What If?" asks you to use information from the atlas and other sources to answer a critical thinking question. There are no right or wrong answers, but be sure you can present facts to support your opinions.

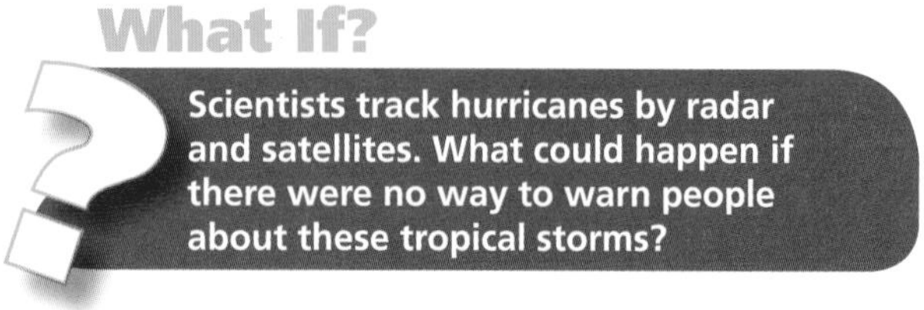

What If?
Scientists track hurricanes by radar and satellites. What could happen if there were no way to warn people about these tropical storms?

Thematic Maps

Have you ever seen a weather map on television that uses different colors to show places with different temperatures? That map is a thematic map. It shows information about **a specific topic** and where a particular condition is found. The thematic maps in this atlas give you information about specific topics or themes.

This atlas has ten world thematic maps. These maps let you compare the same kinds of information for areas around the world. For example, you could use the World Climate Map to see what places in the world have a climate similar to the climate where you live.

This atlas also has thematic maps in the sections about each of the continents. Several different thematic maps often appear on the same page. This allows you to compare different topics for the same area. For example, if you compare a climate map and a population density map for Africa, what do you think you might discover?

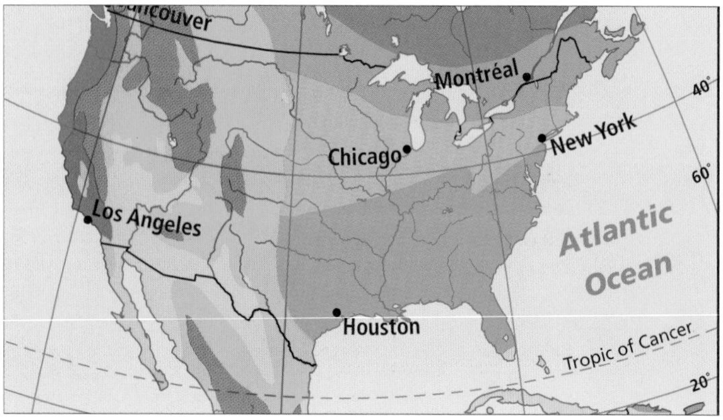

Graphs, Charts, and Photographs

The graphs, charts, and photographs in the atlas help illustrate information from the maps. They may help you se the same information in a different way. They may also provide additional information about the themes of the map The photographs will show you how the features shown on the map look in the real world.

World Lumber Exports

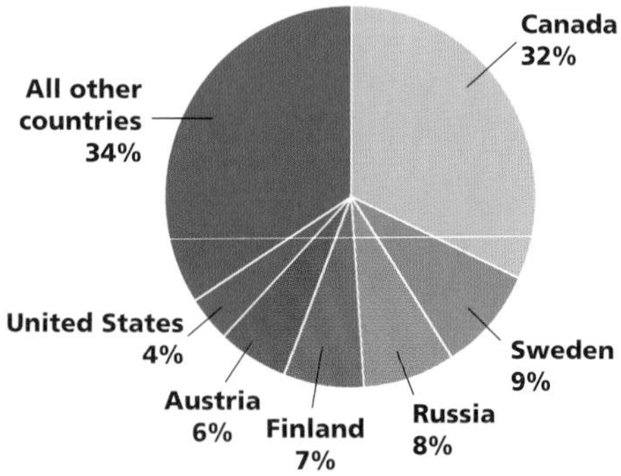

Canada 32%
All other countries 34%
United States 4%
Austria 6%
Finland 7%
Russia 8%
Sweden 9%

Automobiles per 1,000 people

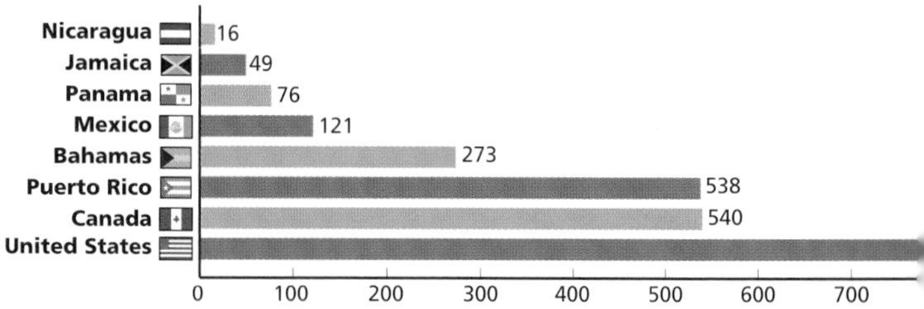

Nicaragua 16
Jamaica 49
Panama 76
Mexico 121
Bahamas 273
Puerto Rico 538
Canada 540
United States
0
100
200
300
400
500
600
700

Legend for Physical and Political Maps

Water Features

ATLANTIC OCEAN	Ocean or sea
	Lake (physical map)
	Lake (political map)
	Salt lake (physical map)
	Salt lake (political map)
	Seasonal lake
Nile	River
Niagara Falls	Waterfall

Land Features

ASIA	Continent
Mt. Mitchell 6,684 ft. 2,037 m. △	Mountain peak
Kilimanjaro 19,340 ft. 5,895 m. ▲	Highest mountain peak
Alps	Physical feature (mountain range, desert, plateau, etc.)
Borneo	Island

Cultural Features

	International boundary
	State, province, or territory boundary
EGYPT	Country
KANSAS	State, province, or territory
PUERTO RICO (U.S.)	Dependency

Population Centers

National capital	State, province, or territory capital	Town	Population
			Over 1,000,000
			250,000 — 1,000,000
			Under 250,000

Land Elevations and Ocean Depths

Land elevation

3,000 meters	9,840 feet
2,000 meters	6,560 feet
1,000 meters	3,280 feet
500 meters	1,640 feet
200 meters	656 feet
0 Sea level	0 Sea level

Water depth

0 Sea level	0 Sea level
200 meters	656 feet
2,000 meters	6,560 feet

Geographical Terms

The large illustration to the right is a view of an imaginary place. It shows many of Earth's different types of landforms, bodies of water, and political features. The following vocabulary list defines many of the features on the map.*

See if you can find an example of each feature on the maps in the atlas.

Archipelago:
A group of islands.

Canyon:
A deep, narrow valley with high, steep sides.

Coast:
Land along a large lake, a sea, or an ocean.

Desert:
A large land area that receives very little rainfall.

Forest:
A large area covered with trees.

Gulf:
A large part of an ocean or a sea that lies within a curved coastline. A gulf is larger than a bay.

Harbor:
A sheltered body of water where ships can safely anchor.

Hill:
A small area of land that is higher than the land around it.

Island:
A piece of land that is surrounded by water.

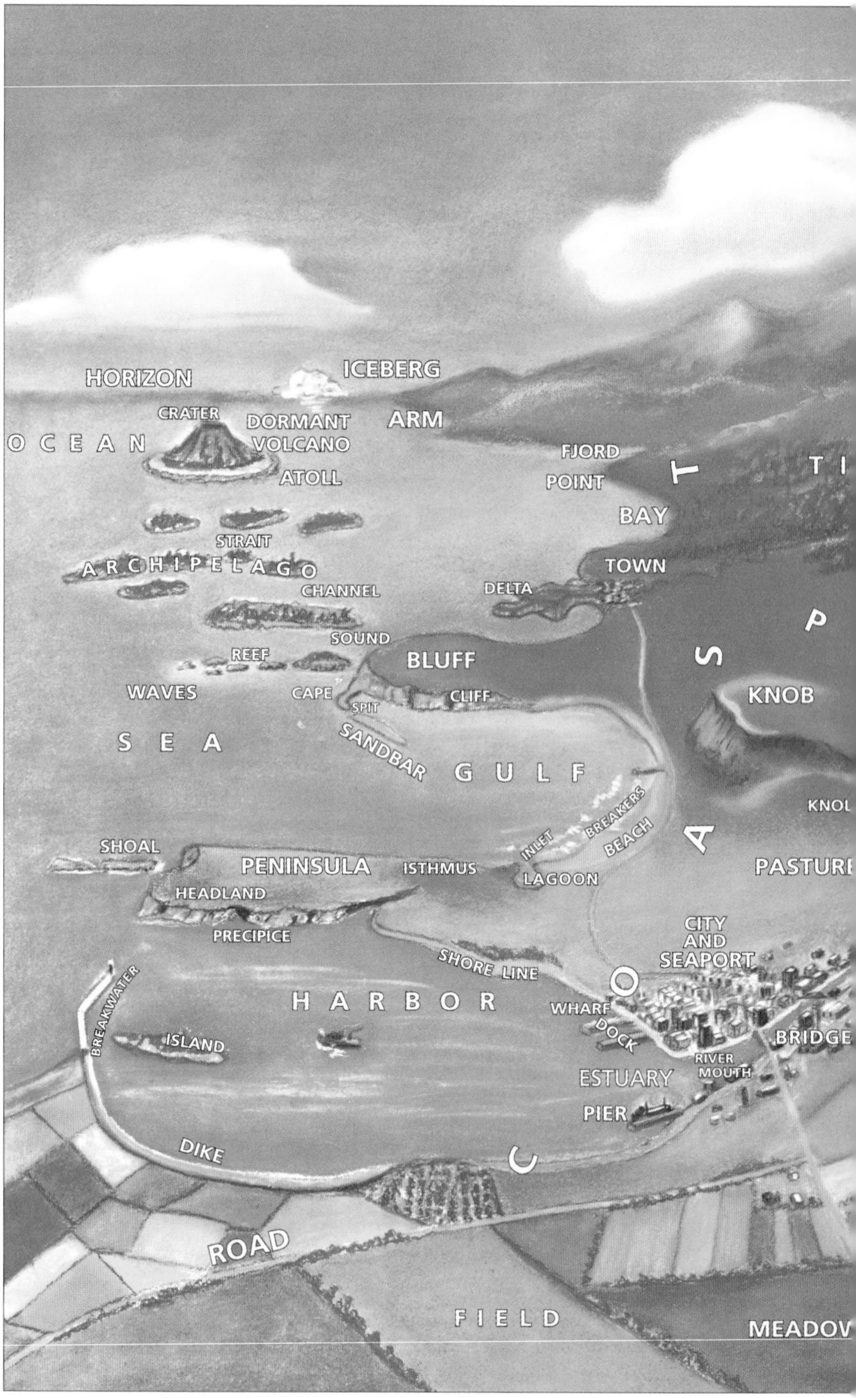

Isthmus:
A narrow piece of land that joins two larger areas of land.

Lake:
A body of water completely surrounded by land.

Mountain:
Land that rises much higher than the land around it.

MIT
GLACIER
SNOWLINE
PEAK
PASS
TIMBERLINE
MOUNTAIN RANGE
ACTIVE VOLCANO
FOOTHILLS
HILL
CANYON
GULCH
CINDER CONE
TABLELAND
PLATEAU
BRINK
VILLAGE
PIEDMONT
VALLEY
FOREST
STREAM
DIVIDE
WATERFALL
RESERVOIR
BROOK
RAPIDS
CHASM
LAKE
MARSH
DAM
POWER PLANT
RIVER
BAYOU
BRANCH
WOODS
TUNNEL
CANAL
IRRIGATED LAND
RIGHT BANK
RAILROAD
LEFT BANK
LOCKS
GORGE
OASIS
RIDGE
IVATED LAND
CRAG
DUNE
MESA
IRPORT
SLOPE
POND
LEDGE
DESERT

The Rand McNally Geographical Terms Desk Map (order number 005-13156-1) includes definitions for all of the terms that appear on the map illustration.

ountain range:
row of mountains that are joined together.

cean:
ne of Earth's largest bodies of water.

ain:
large, flat land area.

ateau:
large area of land where the highest elevation is generally e same. A plateau may have deep valleys.

River:
A body of fresh water that flows from higher to lower land. A river usually flows into another river, a lake, a sea, or an ocean.

Sea:
A large body of salt water nearly or partly surrounded by land. A sea is much smaller than an ocean.

Valley:
Lower land between hills or mountains.

World Physical Map

This map shows the world's land elevations and ocean depths.

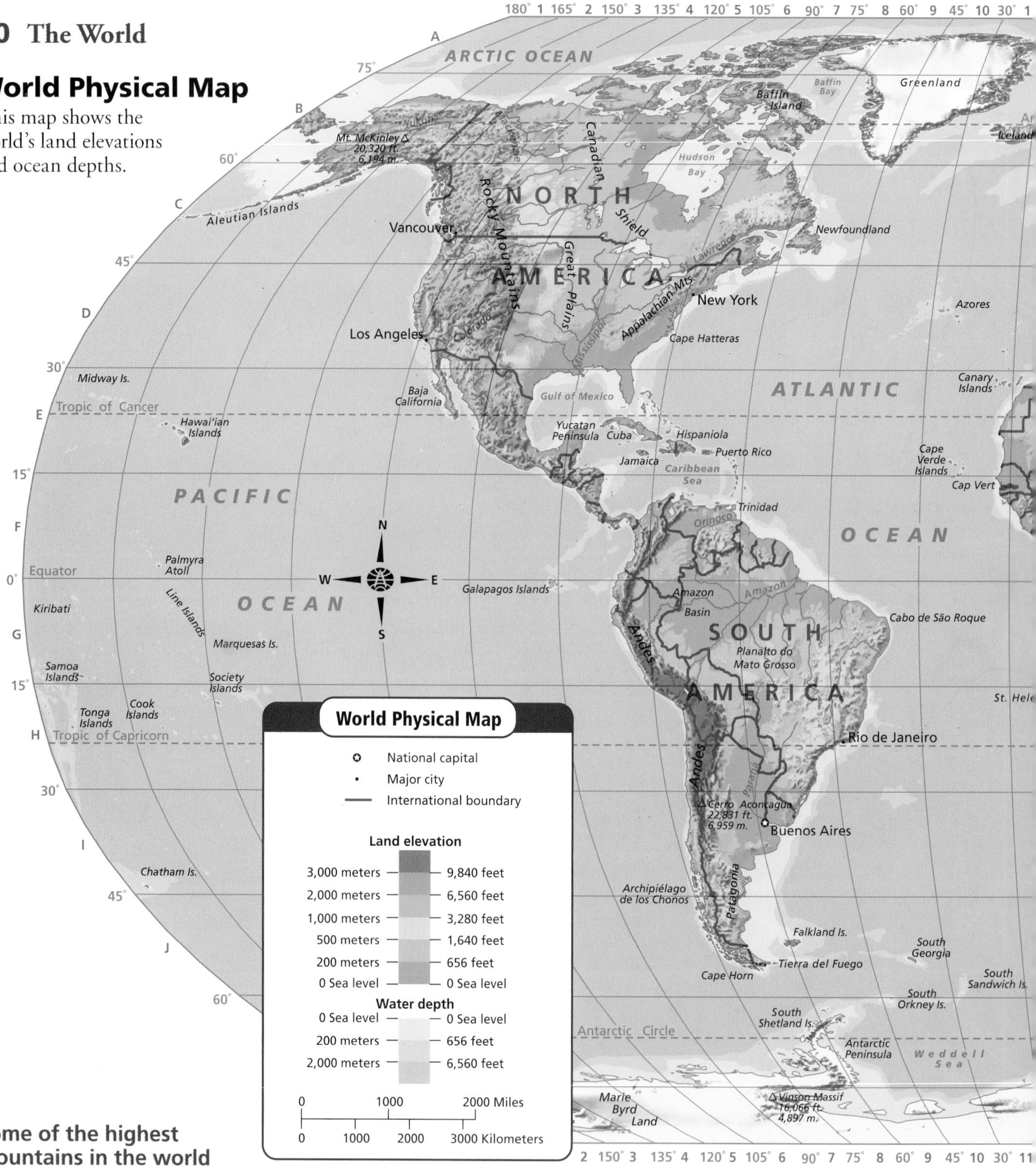

Some of the highest mountains in the world

ARCTIC OCEAN
Franz Josef Land
Novaya Zemlya
Nordkapp
Yenisey
Ob
Lena
Siberia
Ural Mts
Volga
Moscow
Don
Sea of Okhotsk
Bering Sea
Kamchatka Peninsula
Sakhalin
Amur
Altai Mts
Aral Sea
Caucasus
Gora El'brus 18,510 ft. 5,642 m.
Balkan Peninsula
Black Sea
ASIA
Gobi Desert
Beijing
Hokkaidō
Honshū
Sea of Japan
Pamir
Sicily
Crete
Cyprus
Plateau of Tibet
Himalayas
Zagros Mts
Indus
Ganges
Huang
Yangtze
East China Sea
Kyūshū
Cairo
Nile
Mt. Everest 29,028 ft. 8,848 m.
PACIFIC
Tropic of Cancer
Taiwan
Arabian Peninsula
Red Sea
Mumbai (Bombay)
Deccan
Mekong
Hainan Dao
Mariana Islands
Wake Island
Luzon
South China Sea
Arabian Sea
Bay of Bengal
Guam
Socotra
Lakshadweep
Mindanao
OCEAN
Ethiopian Plateau
Sri Lanka
Malay Peninsula
Palau Islands
Caroline Islands
Marshall Islands
Congo
Congo Basin
Rift Valley
Maldive Islands
Equator
Borneo
Celebes
New Guinea
Kilimanjaro 19,340 ft. 5,895 m.
Seychelles
Sumatra
Solomon Islands
Java
INDIAN
Cocos Islands
Zambezi
Madagascar
Coral Sea
New Hebrides
Great Sandy Desert
New Caledonia
Fiji Is.
Mauritius
Reunion
Kalahari Desert
Tropic of Capricorn
AUSTRALIA
Great Dividing Range
Johannesburg
OCEAN
Darling
Sydney
Cape Leeuwin
North Island
Aoraki (Mt. Cook) 12,316 ft. 3,754 m.
Tasmania
South Island
Îles Kerguélen
OCEAN
Antarctic Circle
Enderby Land
Wilkes Land
Victoria Land
NTARCTICA
© Rand McNally
Made in U.S.A.
M-101117-3

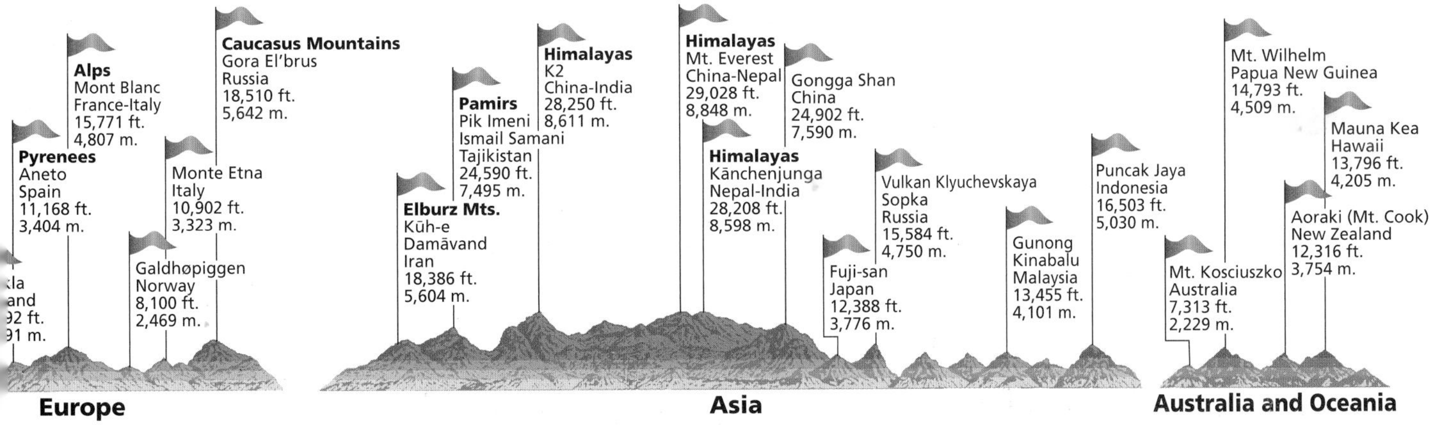
Alps
Mont Blanc
France-Italy
15,771 ft.
4,807 m.
Caucasus Mountains
Gora El'brus
Russia
18,510 ft.
5,642 m.
Pyrenees
Aneto
Spain
11,168 ft.
3,404 m.
Monte Etna
Italy
10,902 ft.
3,323 m.
Galdhøpiggen
Norway
8,100 ft.
2,469 m.
Himalayas
K2
China-India
28,250 ft.
8,611 m.
Pamirs
Pik Imeni
Ismail Samani
Tajikistan
24,590 ft.
7,495 m.
Elburz Mts.
Kūh-e
Damāvand
Iran
18,386 ft.
5,604 m.
Himalayas
Mt. Everest
China-Nepal
29,028 ft.
8,848 m.
Gongga Shan
China
24,902 ft.
7,590 m.
Himalayas
Kānchenjunga
Nepal-India
28,208 ft.
8,598 m.
Vulkan Klyuchevskaya
Sopka
Russia
15,584 ft.
4,750 m.
Fuji-san
Japan
12,388 ft.
3,776 m.
Gunong
Kinabalu
Malaysia
13,455 ft.
4,101 m.
Puncak Jaya
Indonesia
16,503 ft.
5,030 m.
Mt. Wilhelm
Papua New Guinea
14,793 ft.
4,509 m.
Mauna Kea
Hawaii
13,796 ft.
4,205 m.
Aoraki (Mt. Cook)
New Zealand
12,316 ft.
3,754 m.
Mt. Kosciuszko
Australia
7,313 ft.
2,229 m.
Europe
Asia
Australia and Oceania

World Political Map

People have divided up Earth's land into almost 200 countries. A few of these countries are more than a thousand years old, but most have been formed in the last 200 years.

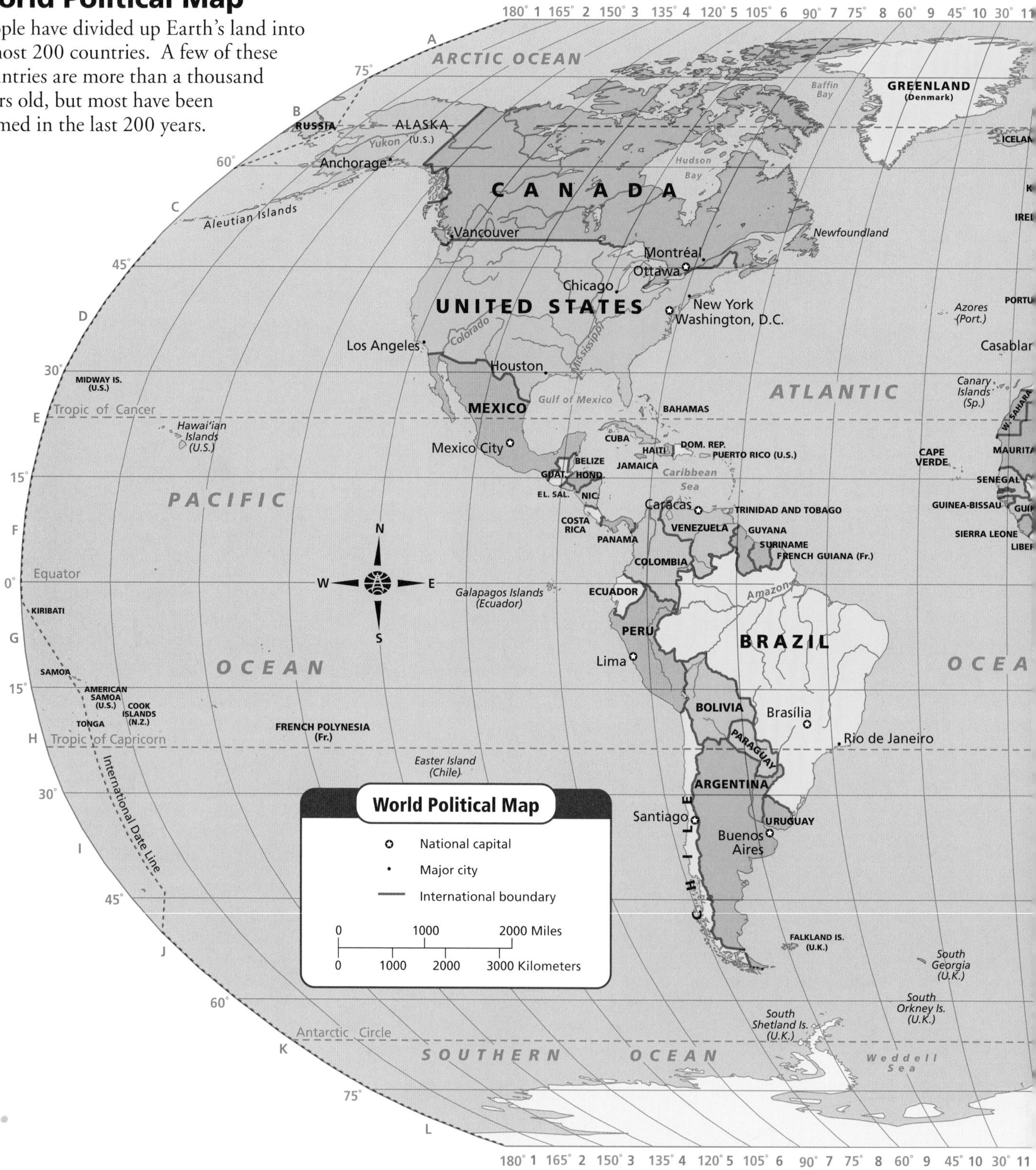
World Political Map
National capital
Major city
International boundary
0 1000 2000 Miles
0 1000 2000 3000 Kilometers
ARCTIC OCEAN
GREENLAND (Denmark)
Baffin Bay
RUSSIA
ALASKA (U.S.)
Yukon
Anchorage
Aleutian Islands
CANADA
Hudson Bay
Vancouver
Newfoundland
Montréal
Ottawa
Chicago
UNITED STATES
New York
Washington, D.C.
Colorado
Mississippi
Los Angeles
Houston
Gulf of Mexico
MEXICO
Mexico City
MIDWAY IS. (U.S.)
Tropic of Cancer
Hawai'ian Islands (U.S.)
BAHAMAS
CUBA
HAITI
DOM. REP.
PUERTO RICO (U.S.)
JAMAICA
BELIZE
GUAT.
HOND.
EL SAL.
NIC.
COSTA RICA
PANAMA
Caribbean Sea
Caracas
TRINIDAD AND TOBAGO
VENEZUELA
GUYANA
SURINAME
FRENCH GUIANA (Fr.)
COLOMBIA
ECUADOR
Galapagos Islands (Ecuador)
PERU
Lima
BRAZIL
Amazon
BOLIVIA
Brasília
PARAGUAY
Rio de Janeiro
ARGENTINA
URUGUAY
Santiago
Buenos Aires
CHILE
FALKLAND IS. (U.K.)
PACIFIC
OCEAN
ATLANTIC
OCEA
Equator
KIRIBATI
SAMOA
AMERICAN SAMOA (U.S.)
COOK ISLANDS (N.Z.)
TONGA
Tropic of Capricorn
International Date Line
FRENCH POLYNESIA (Fr.)
Easter Island (Chile)
Azores (Port.)
PORTU
Casablar
Canary Islands (Sp.)
W. SAHARA
MAURITA
CAPE VERDE
SENEGAL
GUINEA-BISSAU
GUI
SIERRA LEONE
LIBEF
ICELAN
IREL
South Georgia (U.K.)
South Orkney Is. (U.K.)
South Shetland Is. (U.K.)
Weddell Sea
Antarctic Circle
SOUTHERN
OCEAN
N
S
E
W
180° 1 165° 2 150° 3 135° 4 120° 5 105° 6 90° 7 75° 8 60° 9 45° 10 30° 11
75° 60° 45° 30° 15° 0° 15° 30° 45° 60° 75°
A B C D E F G H I J K L

14 30° 15 45° 16 60° 17 75° 18 90° 19 105° 20 120° 21 135° 22 150° 23 165° 24 180°
Franz Josef Land
ARCTIC OCEAN
Novaya Zemlya
Yenisey
Lena
Ob
RUSSIA
FINLAND
SWEDEN
EST.
LAT.
LITH.
Volga
Moscow
Novosibirsk
Bering Sea
Sea of Okhotsk
POLAND
BELARUS
UKRAINE
CZ.
SLVK.
AUS.
HUNG.
MOLD.
ROM.
CRO.
BOS.
SERB.
KAZAKHSTAN
MONGOLIA
Black Sea
BUL.
MT.
KS.
ALB.
MA.
GREECE
GEO.
ARM.
AZER.
UZBEKISTAN
KYRG.
TURKMENISTAN
TAJIK.
TURKEY
NORTH KOREA
Beijing
Sea of Japan
SOUTH KOREA
Seoul
JAPAN
Tōkyō
Crete
CYPRUS
SYRIA
LEB.
ISRAEL
IRAQ
Tehrān
IRAN
AFGHANISTAN
CHINA
Mediterranean Sea
TUNISIA
Cairo
JORDAN
KUWAIT
PAKISTAN
Yangtze
Shanghai
International Date Line
LIBYA
EGYPT
SAUDI ARABIA
QATAR
U.A.E.
Karāchi
NEPAL
BHU.
Ganges
Kolkata (Calcutta)
BNGL.
TAIWAN
PACIFIC
Tropic of Cancer
Hong Kong
Mumbai (Bombay)
INDIA
MYANMAR
LAOS
NORTHERN MARIANA ISLANDS (U.S.)
WAKE ISLAND (U.S.)
Red Sea
Nile
OMAN
ERITREA
CHAD
SUDAN
YEMEN
Arabian Sea
Bay of Bengal
THAILAND
South China Sea
PHILIPPINES
GUAM (U.S.)
Addis Ababa
DJIBOUTI
Bangkok
CAMBODIA
VIETNAM
Manila
OCEAN
CENTRAL AFRICAN REPUBLIC
SOUTH SUDAN
ETHIOPIA
SOMALIA
SRI LANKA
PALAU
FED. STATES OF MICRONESIA
MARSHALL ISLANDS
CAMEROON
Congo
UGANDA
KENYA
MALDIVES
BRUNEI
MALAYSIA
SINGAPORE
Borneo
New Guinea
Equator
GABON
CONGO
RWANDA
DEM. REP. OF THE CONGO
BURUNDI
Sumatra
Jakarta
INDONESIA
PAPUA NEW GUINEA
SOLOMON ISLANDS
SEYCHELLES
TANZANIA
Java
TIMOR-LESTE
COMOROS
INDIAN
ANGOLA
ZAMBIA
MALAWI
MOZAMBIQUE
Coral Sea
VANUATU
FIJI
MADAGASCAR
MAURITIUS
NEW CALEDONIA (Fr.)
NAMIBIA
ZIMBABWE
BOTSWANA
REUNION (Fr.)
Tropic of Capricorn
Johannesburg
SWAZILAND
OCEAN
AUSTRALIA
Brisbane
SOUTH AFRICA
LESOTHO
Darling
Perth
Sydney
Melbourne
Auckland
NEW ZEALAND
Tasmania
Îles Kerguélen (Fr.)
SOUTHERN OCEAN
Antarctic Circle
ANTARCTICA
© Rand McNally
Made in U.S.A.
M-101116-2
A
B
C
D
E
F
G
H
I
J
K
L
75°
60°
45°
30°
15°
0°
15°
30°
45°
60°
75°

World Climate Map

This map shows climate conditions throughout the world. Climate is the average **weather** conditions over a long period of time. Temperature and precipitation together make up climate.

Climate Graphs

Each of the climate graphs below shows the average temperature and precipitation for every month of the year. The 12 letters below each graph are the first letters of the twelve months, beginning with January (J) and ending with December (D). There is one climate graph for every type of climate region in the world.

Curved lines on the graphs show temperatures in degrees Celsius and degrees Fahrenheit. The numbers are to the left of the graphs.

Vertical bars on the graphs show monthly precipitation in inches and centimeters. The numbers are to the right of the graphs.

Colors on the graphs match colors on the map. The cities for the graphs are also shown on the map.

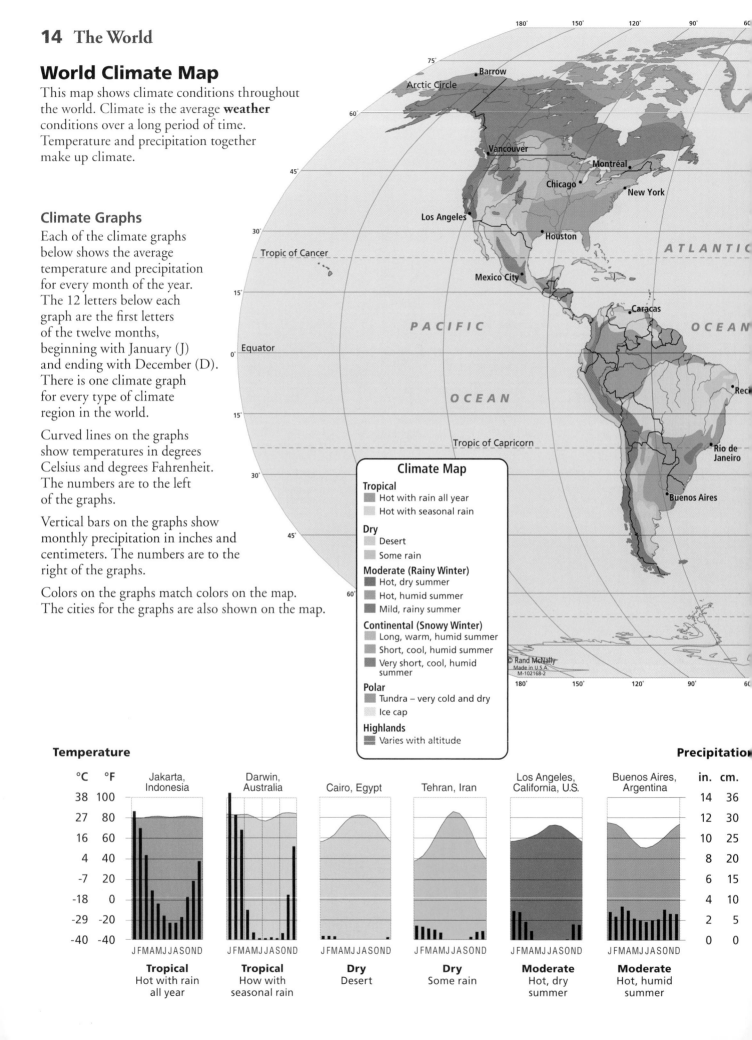

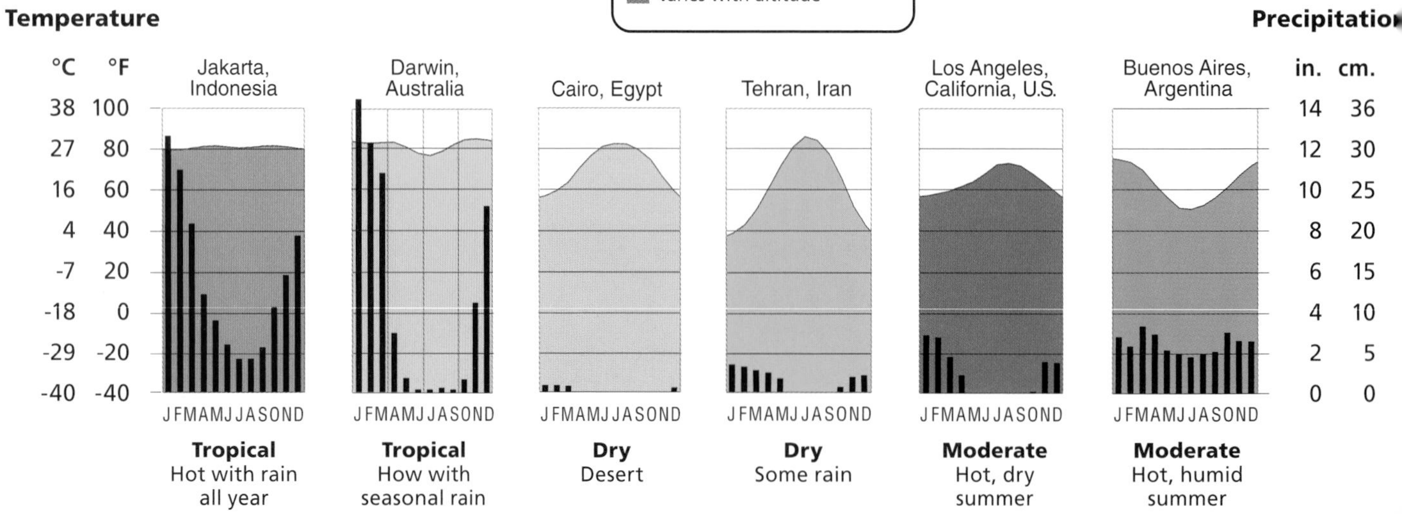

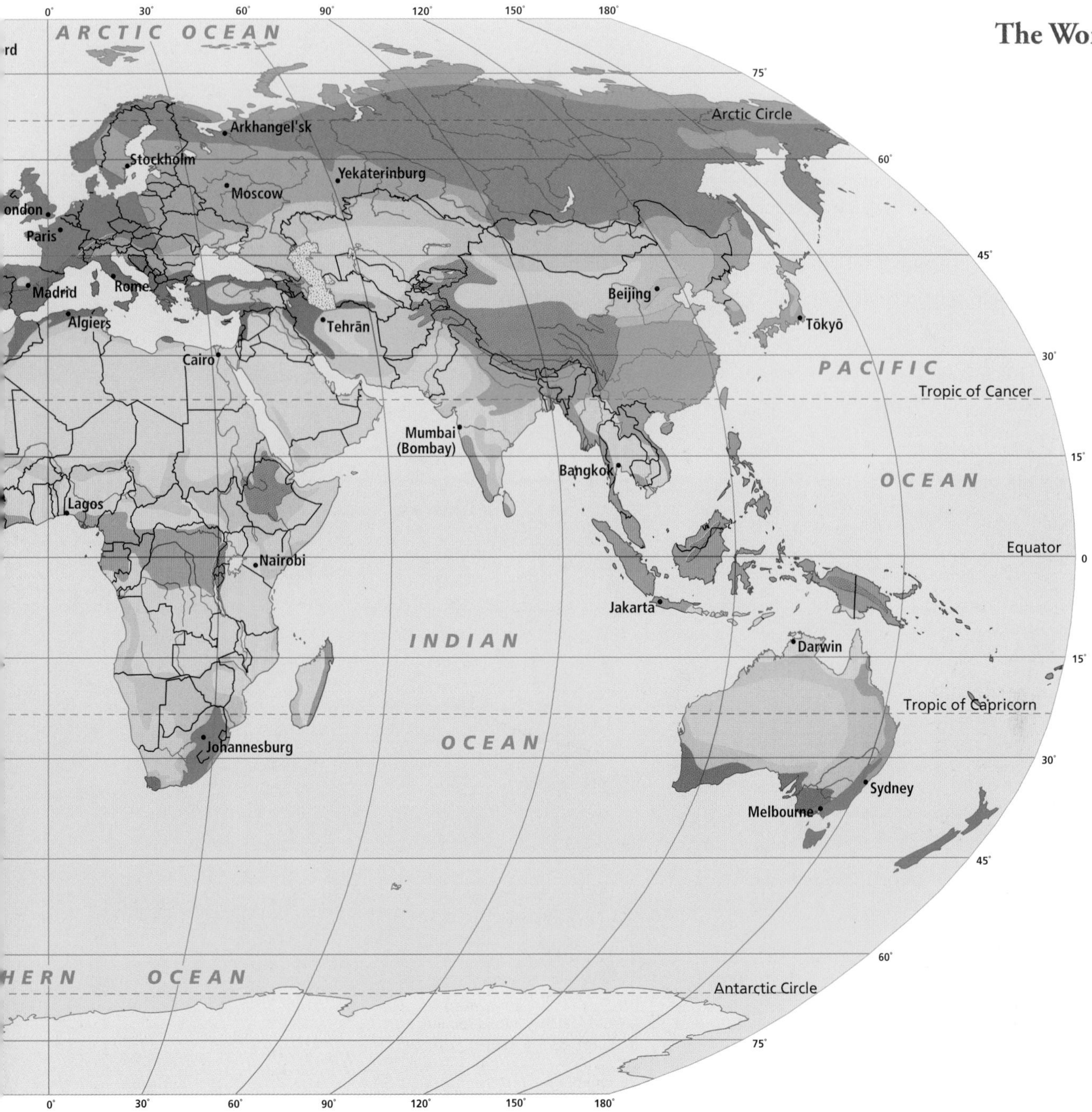
ARCTIC OCEAN
Arkhangel'sk
Stockholm
Yekaterinburg
Moscow
London
Paris
Madrid
Rome
Algiers
Tehrān
Beijing
Tōkyō
Cairo
PACIFIC
Tropic of Cancer
Mumbai (Bombay)
Bangkok
OCEAN
Lagos
Nairobi
Equator
Jakarta
INDIAN
Darwin
Tropic of Capricorn
OCEAN
Johannesburg
Sydney
Melbourne
OCEAN
Antarctic Circle
Arctic Circle
0°
30°
60°
90°
120°
150°
180°
75°
60°
45°
30°
15°
0
15°
30°
45°
60°
75°

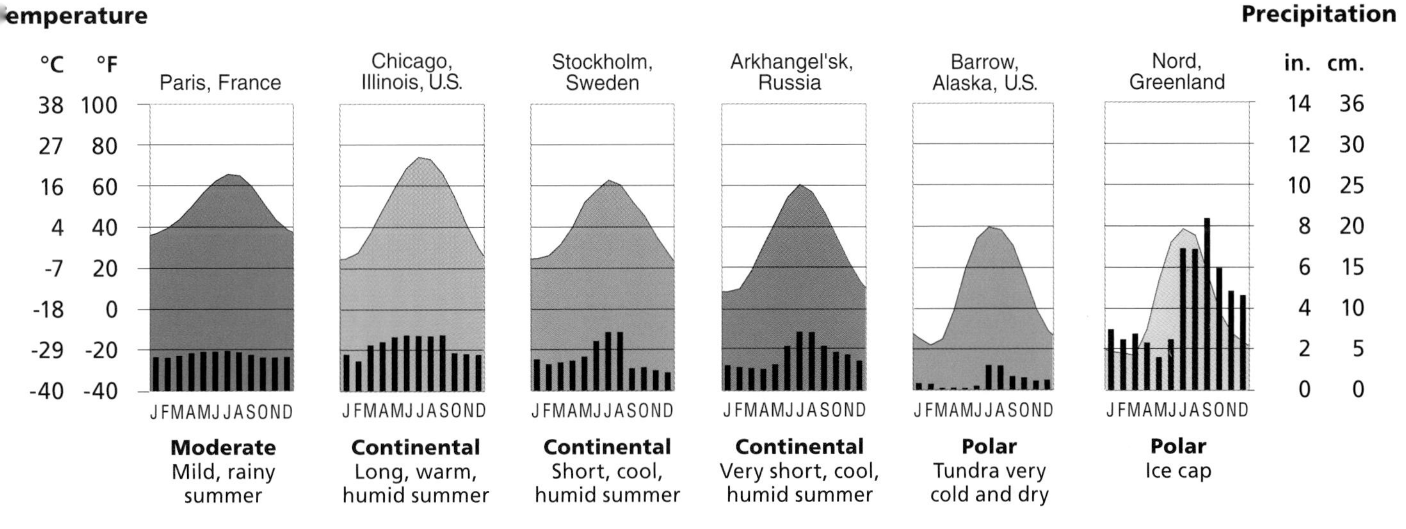
Temperature
Precipitation
°C °F
in. cm.
Paris, France
Chicago, Illinois, U.S.
Stockholm, Sweden
Arkhangel'sk, Russia
Barrow, Alaska, U.S.
Nord, Greenland
38 100
27 80
16 60
4 40
-7 20
-18 0
-29 -20
-40 -40
14 36
12 30
10 25
8 20
6 15
4 10
2 5
0 0
JFMAMJJASOND
Moderate
Mild, rainy summer
Continental
Long, warm, humid summer
Continental
Short, cool, humid summer
Continental
Very short, cool, humid summer
Polar
Tundra very cold and dry
Polar
Ice cap

World Environments Map

This map shows different environments throughout the world. The environment of a place is its physical setting and conditions. Some environments, such as forest and tundra, are natural. Other environments, such as cropland and urban areas, have been created by humans. This map shows many of the world's largest urban areas.

The theme of this map is land environments, but 75% of Earth's surface is covered by water. This causes Earth to look blue from space. For this reason, Earth is sometimes called the Blue Planet. Only 3% of the water on Earth is fresh water. The other 97% of Earth's water is salt water.

Forest

Swamp

Crop and woodland

Cropland

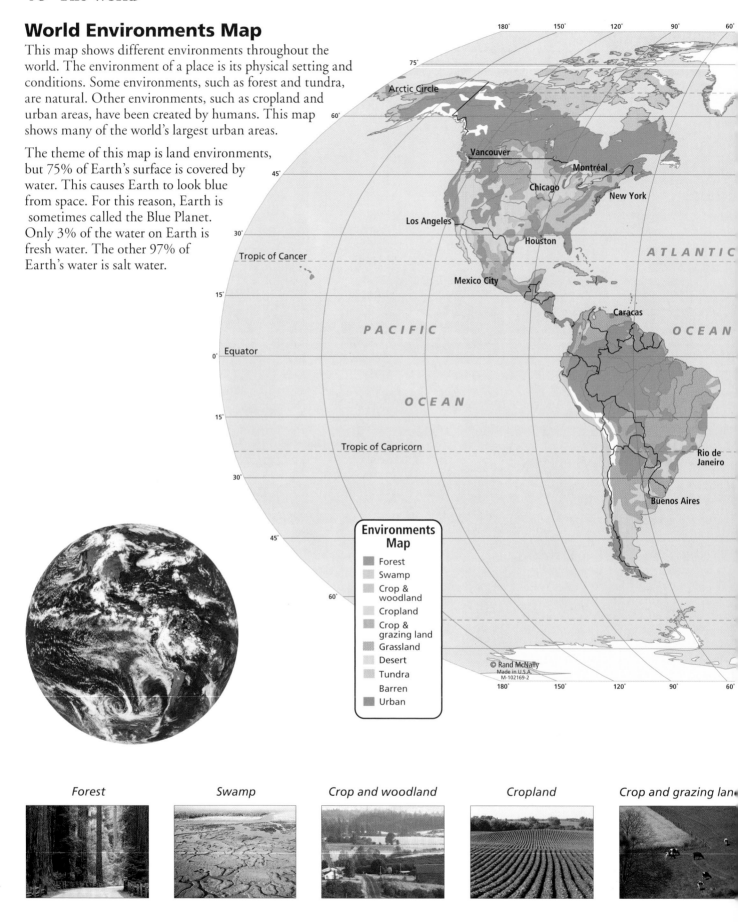

Crop and grazing lan

Grassland

Desert

Tundra

Barren

Urban

World Population Density Map

This map shows which parts of the world have many people and which have few people. The largest areas of dense population are in East Asia, South Asia, and Europe. Vast areas of the world are too cold, too dry, or too mountainous for dense population.

Population Density Map

People per sq. mile
(People per sq. km)

- Over 1,250 *(Over 500)*
- 250 – 1,250 *(100 – 500)*
- 62.5 – 250 *(25 – 100)*
- 25 – 62.5 *(10 – 25)*
- 2.5 – 25 *(1 – 10)*
- Under 2.5 *(Under 1)*

© Rand McNally
Made in U.S.A.
M-102170-2

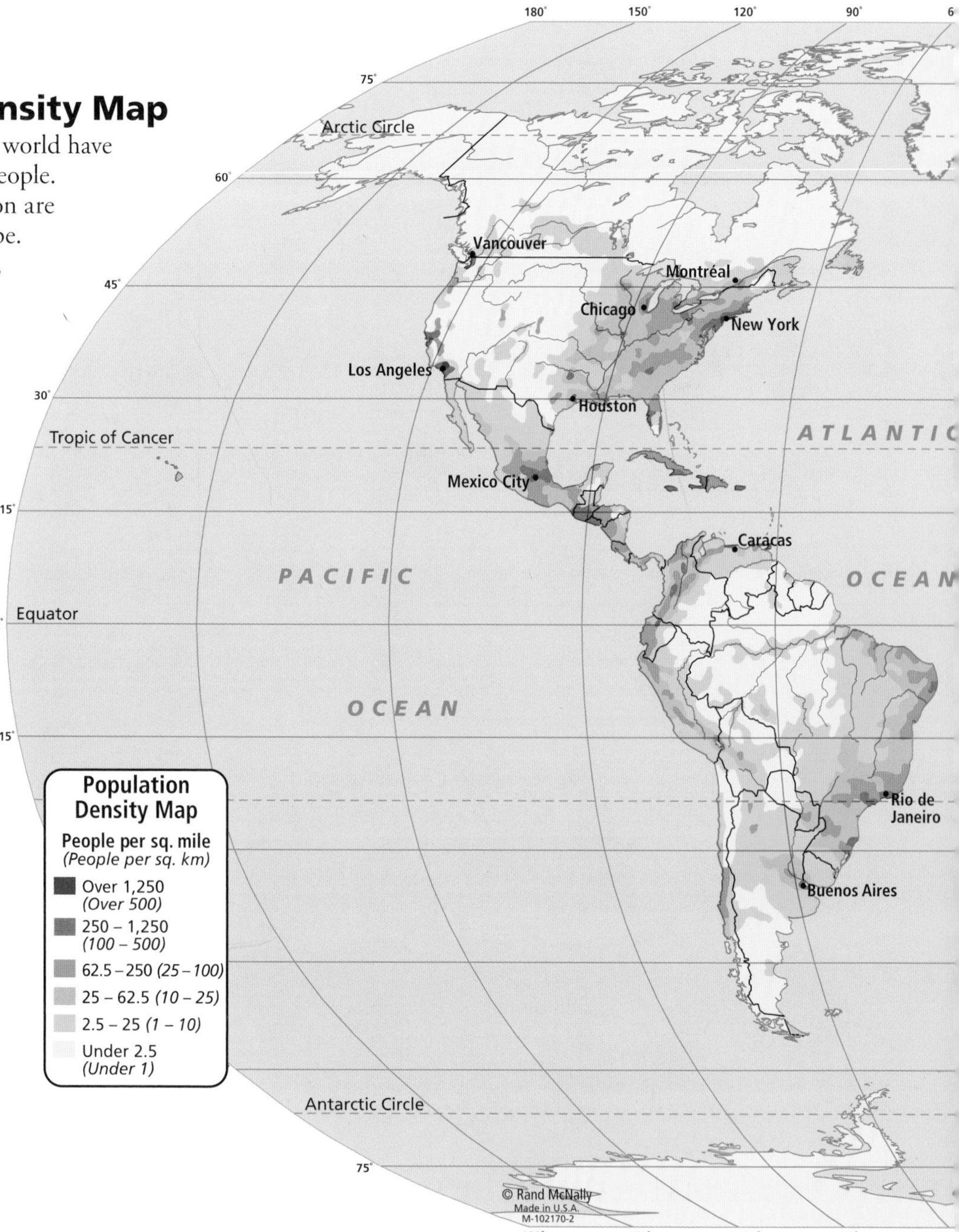

Children Around the World

North America

North America

Middle America

South America

Europe

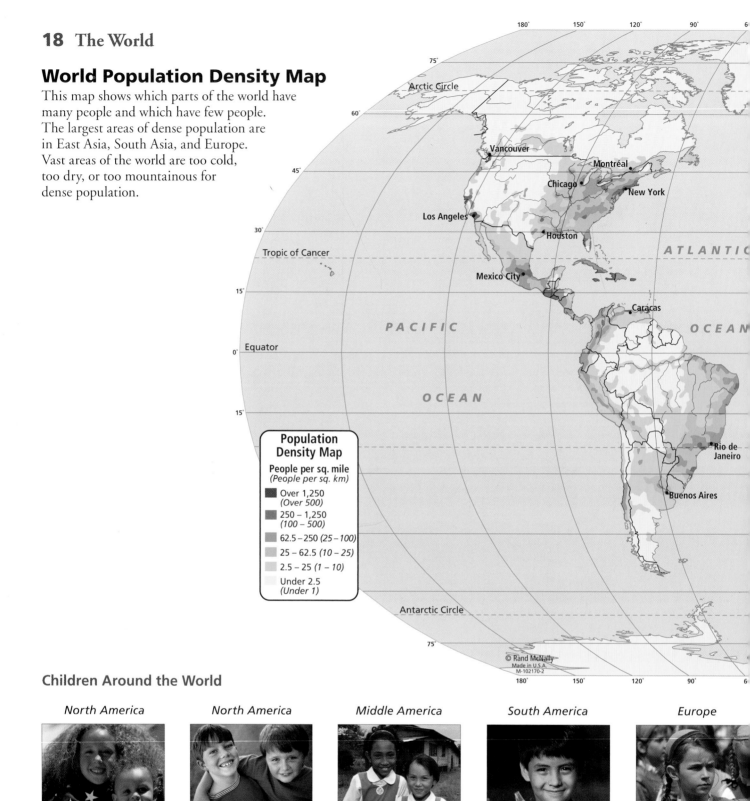

World Population Growth

For most of human history, the world's population grew very slowly. About 250 years ago, it began to grow faster as people learned to control illnesses. Now people in many parts of the world are having smaller families, and the rate of growth may be slowing down.

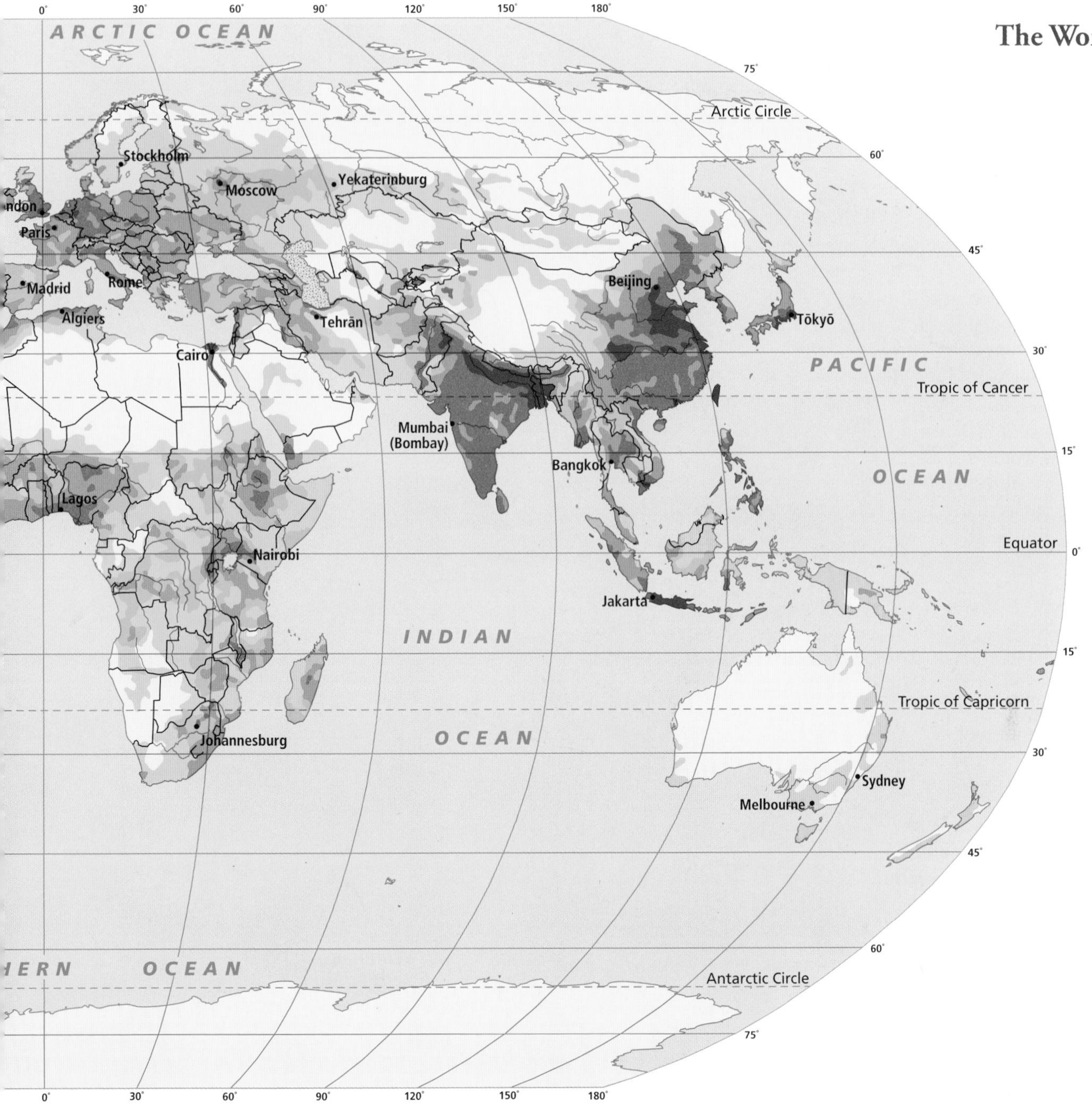
0°
30°
60°
90°
120°
150°
180°
ARCTIC OCEAN
75°
Arctic Circle
60°
Stockholm
Moscow
Yekaterinburg
ndon
Paris
45°
Madrid
Rome
Beijing
Algiers
Tehrān
Tōkyō
Cairo
30°
PACIFIC
Tropic of Cancer
Mumbai
(Bombay)
15°
Bangkok
OCEAN
Lagos
Equator
0°
Nairobi
Jakarta
INDIAN
15°
Tropic of Capricorn
Johannesburg
OCEAN
30°
Sydney
Melbourne
45°
60°
HERN
OCEAN
Antarctic Circle
75°

Africa

Middle East

Asia

Asia

Australia

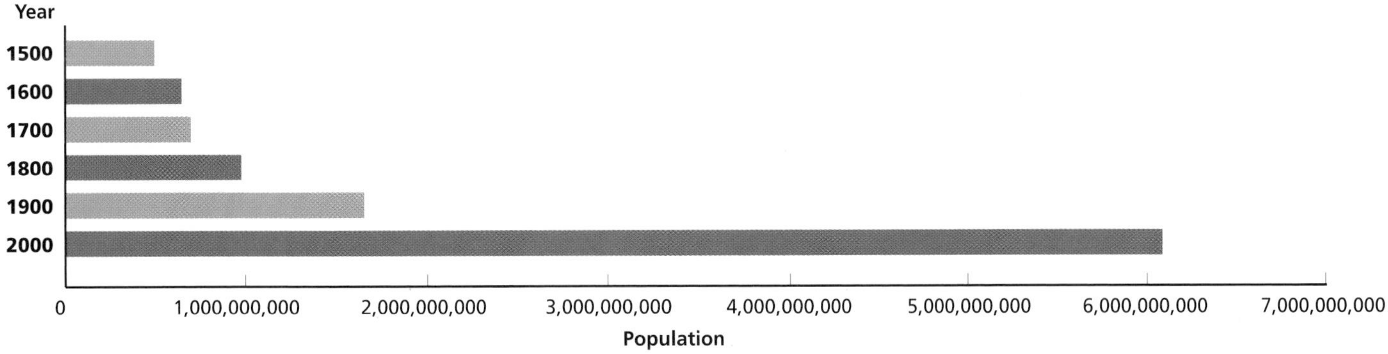
Year
1500
1600
1700
1800
1900
2000
0
1,000,000,000
2,000,000,000
3,000,000,000
4,000,000,000
5,000,000,000
6,000,000,000
7,000,000,000
Population

World Patterns of Economic Activity

This map shows how people around the world make a living. Each color on the map shows the most important economic activity for that area.

Look at the bright yellow area of Canada and the United States. According to the map legend, agriculture is the most important economic activity there. If you went to this area, you would see farm fields, orchards, and farm animals such as dairy cows and pigs. You probably would see grain elevators, feed stores, and other businesses that support farming. Of course, you would see banks, office buildings, stores, and factories, but not as many as you would see in the areas colored red.

According to the map legend, the most important economic activities in the red areas are manufacturing and commerce. Manufacturing is making goods. Automobiles, computers, clothing, and skateboards are examples of goods.

Commerce is the buying and selling of goods. Commerce also includes the buying and selling of services. Medical care, banking, education, and cable television are examples of service industries. In Canada, the United States, Europe, and Japan more people work in service industries than in manufacturing or agriculture. If you went to the areas shown in red, you would see a concentration of banks, office buildings, factories, and stores. Many of the world's largest manufacturing and commerce areas are shown on this map.

According to the map legend, hunting, forestry, and subsistence farming are the most important economic activities in the brown areas. In these areas you would find people working on small farms, growing food for themselves and their families. You would find people hunting and fishing to get food for themselves and their families.

Nomadic herding

Hunting

Subsistence farming

Forestry

Agriculture

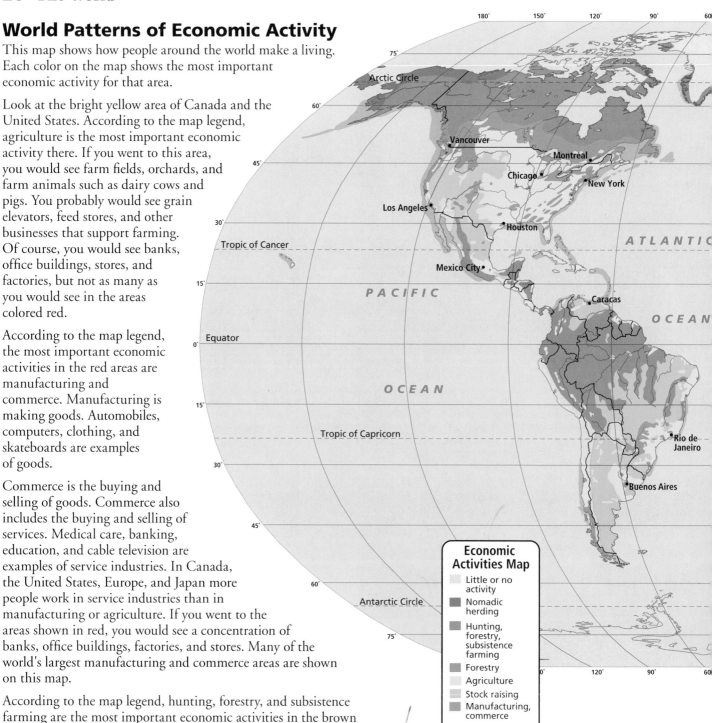

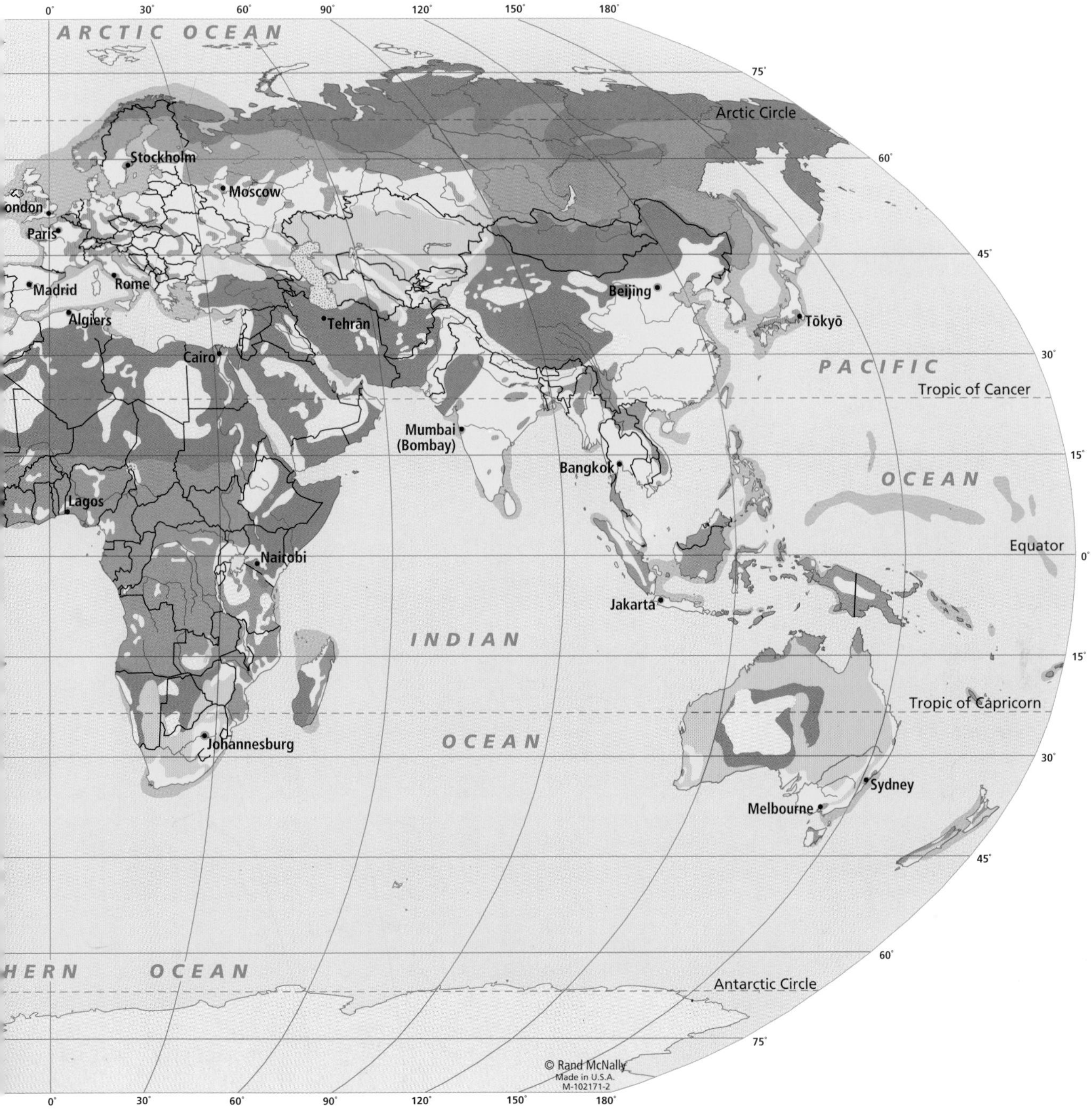

Agriculture

Stock raising

Manufacturing

Commerce

Fishing

World Mineral Fuel Deposits

Deposits of coal, petroleum, and natural gas are found in very limited parts of the world. The United States is fortunate to have significant deposits of all three.

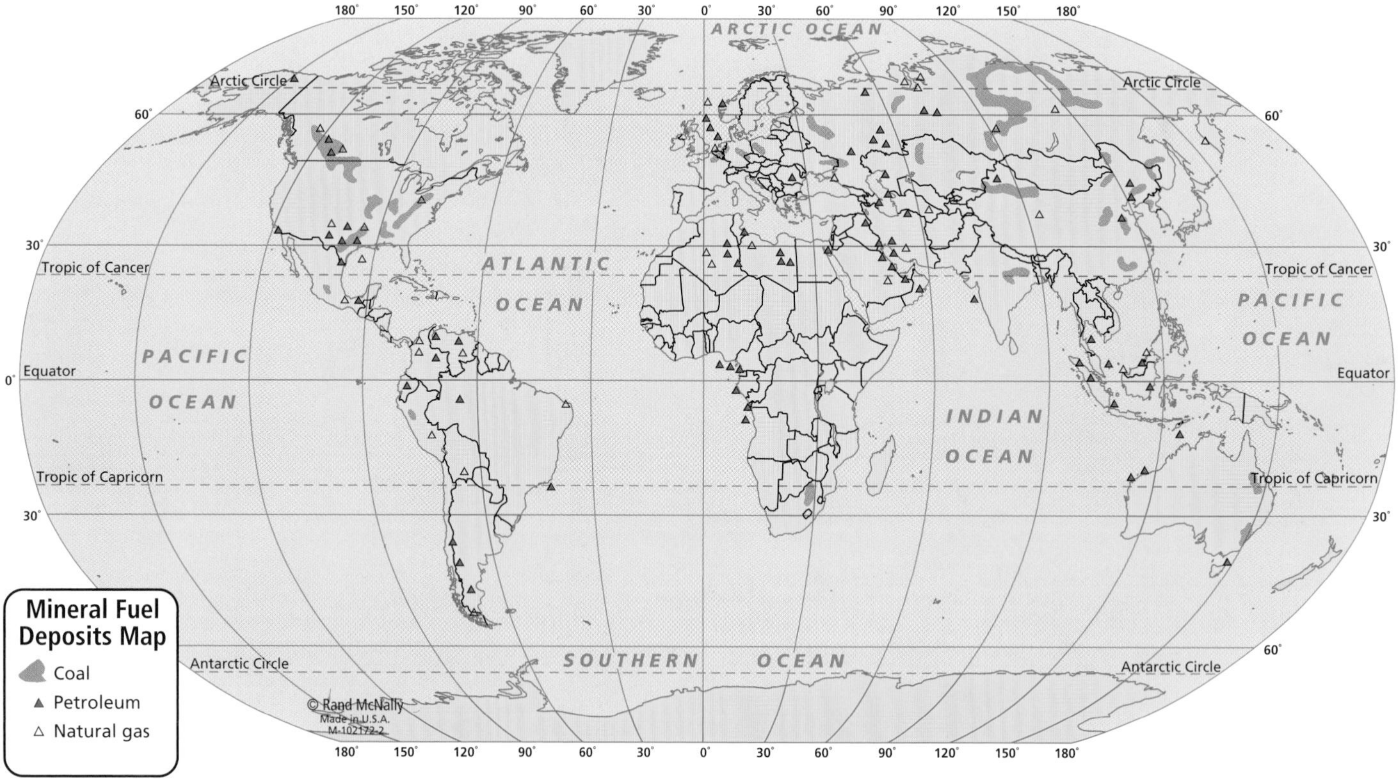

World Coal Production

China and the United States, which have extensive deposits of coal, lead the world in coal production.

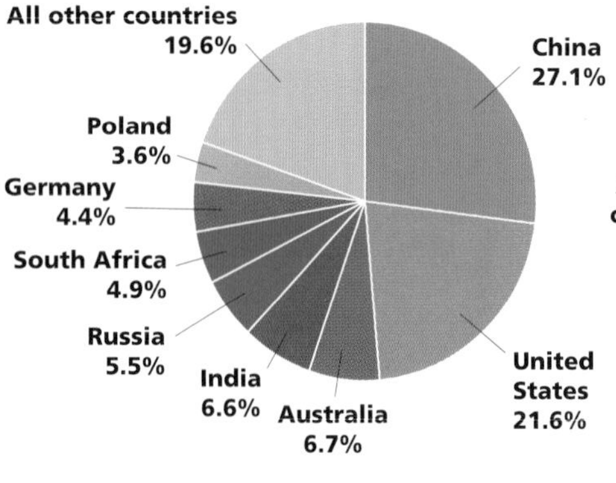
China 27.1%
United States 21.6%
Australia 6.7%
India 6.6%
Russia 5.5%
South Africa 4.9%
Germany 4.4%
Poland 3.6%
All other countries 19.6%

World Petroleum Production

Saudi Arabia, Russia, and the United States produce nearly one-third of the world's oil.

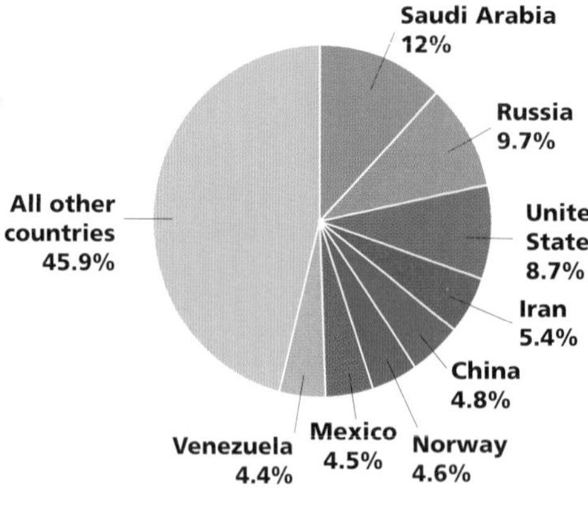
Saudi Arabia 12%
Russia 9.7%
United States 8.7%
Iran 5.4%
China 4.8%
Norway 4.6%
Mexico 4.5%
Venezuela 4.4%
All other countries 45.9%

World Uranium Production

Canada and Australia lead the world in production of uranium, which is used as a fuel in nuclear energy plants.

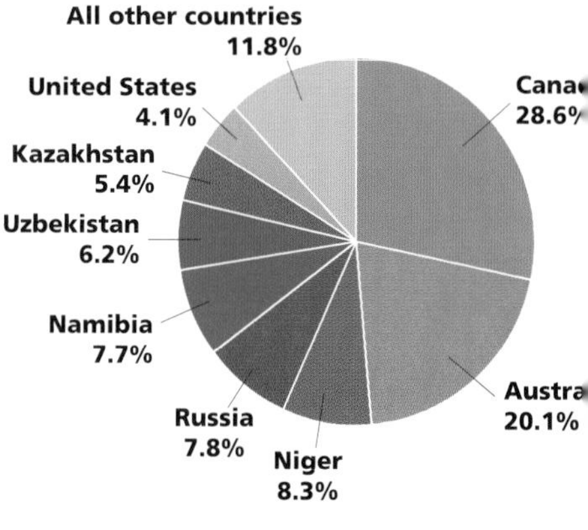
Cana
28.6%
Austra
20.1%
Niger 8.3%
Russia 7.8%
Namibia 7.7%
Uzbekistan 6.2%
Kazakhstan 5.4%
United States 4.1%
All other countries 11.8%

World Energy Consumption

anufacturing, heating, and transportation are the three main ways that people use ergy. This explains why the largest users of energy are industrialized countries that ve large populations and relatively cold climates.

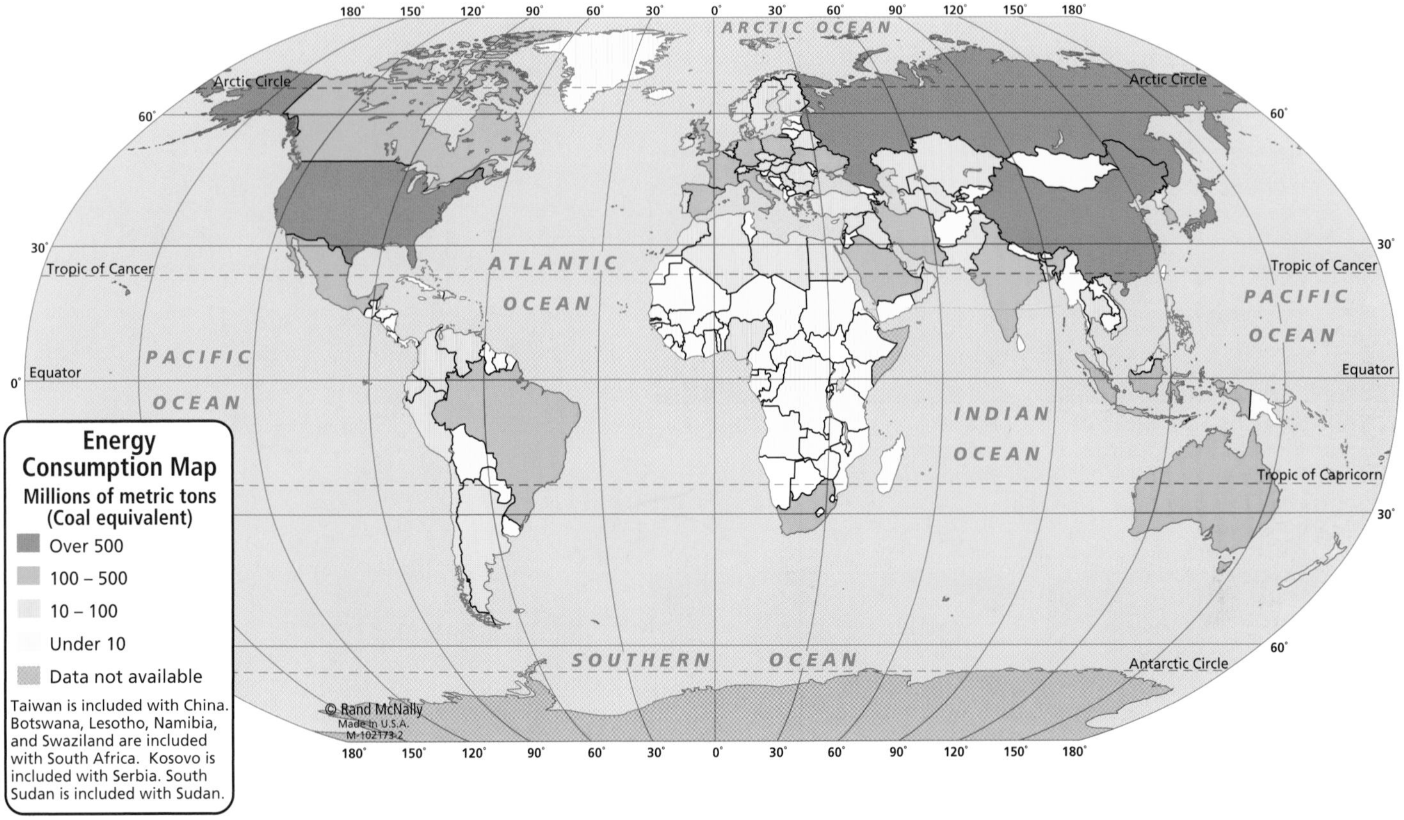

Energy Terms

Coal:
A rock created from ancient plant life under enormous pressure. It is burned to produce heat and create steam for running machines or making electricity. Most coal, when burned, emits sulfur, a major component of acid rain.

Geothermal power:
Uses water heated naturally beneath the earth's surface. The steam that results powers engines that create electricity. Geothermal power is a clean source of energy, but it is available only in very limited areas.

Fossil fuels:
Formed from remains of plants and animals over millions of years. Fossil fuels are not renewable sources of energy because it takes vast amounts of time to create them. Coal, oil, and natural gas are fossil fuels.

Hydroelectricity:
Generated by fast-moving water that is used to power generators. Dams on rivers provide sources of rapidly moving water. Hydroelectricity is a clean source of power, but the dams can have negative effects on their surroundings.

Natural gas:
A form of petroleum, this flammable gas is used mainly as fuel for stoves, furnaces, and hot-water heaters. Natural gas is a clean-burning fuel.

Nuclear energy:
Created by splitting atoms. The energy is used to heat water that makes steam to drive electricity generators. The safety of nuclear plants and the hazardous wastes they create are of great concern.

Petroleum:
A liquid, also called oil. Petroleum is the most widely used source of energy in the world. It is used to produce gasoline, kerosene, and fuel oil. It is also used to manufacture plastics and other products.

Wind power and solar energy:
Two sources of renewable energy. They are not in wide use today, but in some places the use of wind to make electricity is increasing.

Plate Tectonics

According to the theory of plate tectonics, the earth's surface is divided into more than a dozen plates. These plates move very slowly—just a few inches a year. As they move, they collide or grind past each other. Most of the world's volcanoes and earthquakes occur at the places where plates meet.

Many plates collide with or grind past the Pacific Plate. The Ring of Fire is the name given to the band of earthquakes and volcanic activity around the Pacific Ocean.

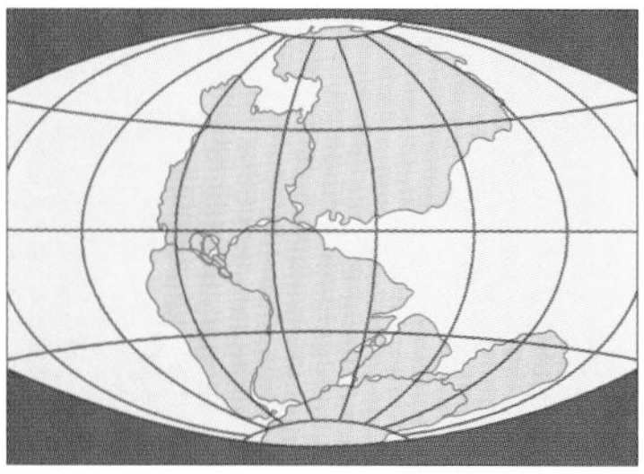

225 million years ago: Most of the world's land was together in a single "supercontinent." Scientists call this giant continent Pangaea.

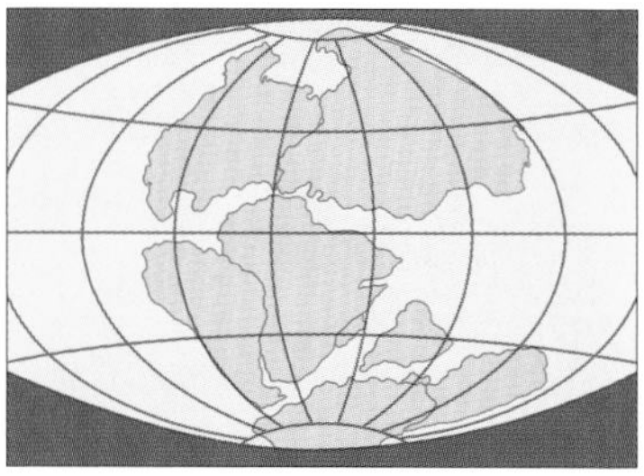

180 million years ago: Pangaea split up into separate landmasses.

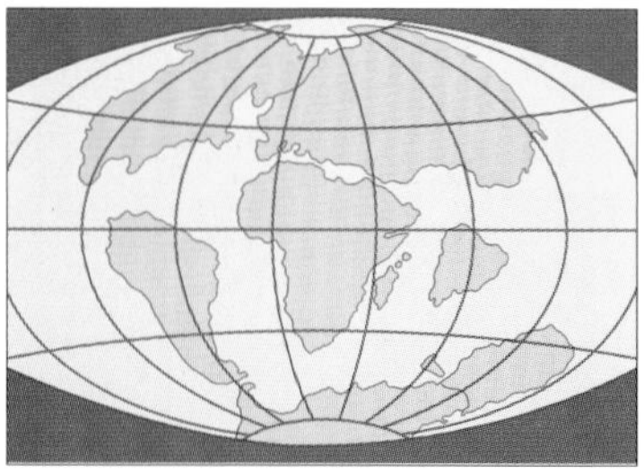

65 million years ago: The oceans as we know them today began to take shape. South America and India moved away from Africa.

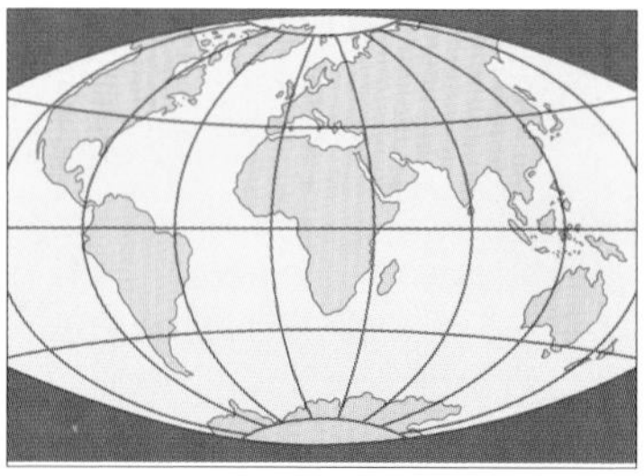

The present day: India has joined with Asia, Australia has moved away from Antarctica, and North America has separated from Europe.

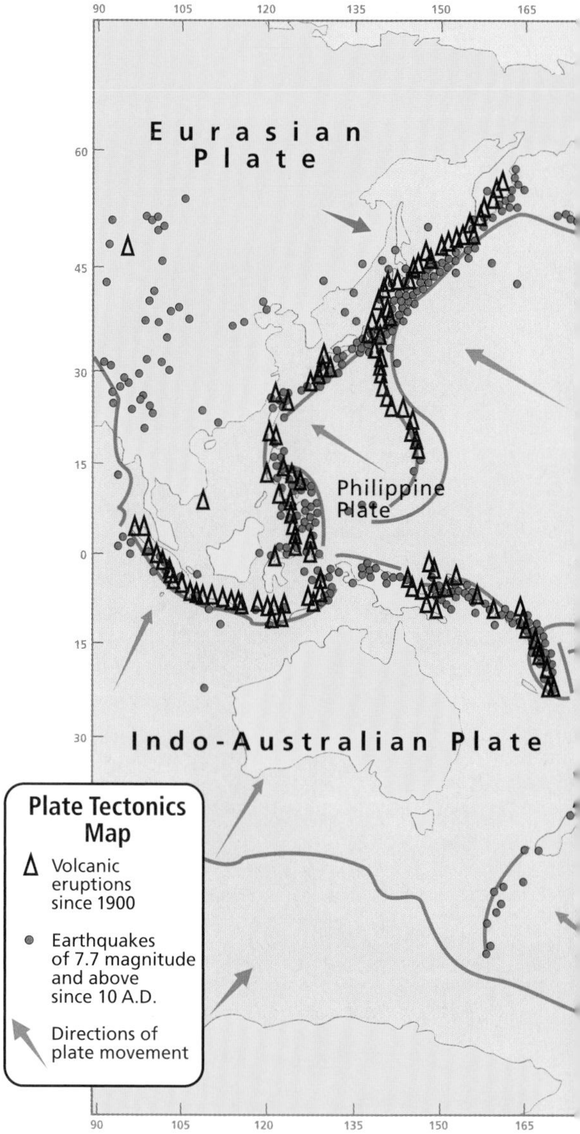

Some Notable Earthquakes

Year	Magnitude (Richter Scale)	Place	Estimated Deaths
2004	9.0	Sumatra, Indonesia	280,000 killed by earthquake and tsunami
1990	7.7	Iran	50,000 killed by earthquake and landslides
1976	7.5	Tangshan, China	255,000
1970	7.9	Peru	66,000
1964	9.2	Prince William Sound, AK	125 killed by earthquake and tsunami
1948	7.3	Turkmenistan	110,000
1927	7.9	Qinghai, China	200,000
1923	7.9	Japan	143,000 killed by earthquake and fire
1908	7.2	Italy	100,000 killed by earthquake and tsunami
1906	7.8	San Francisco, CA	3,000 killed by earthquake and fire

Damage from the 1906 San Francisco earthquake

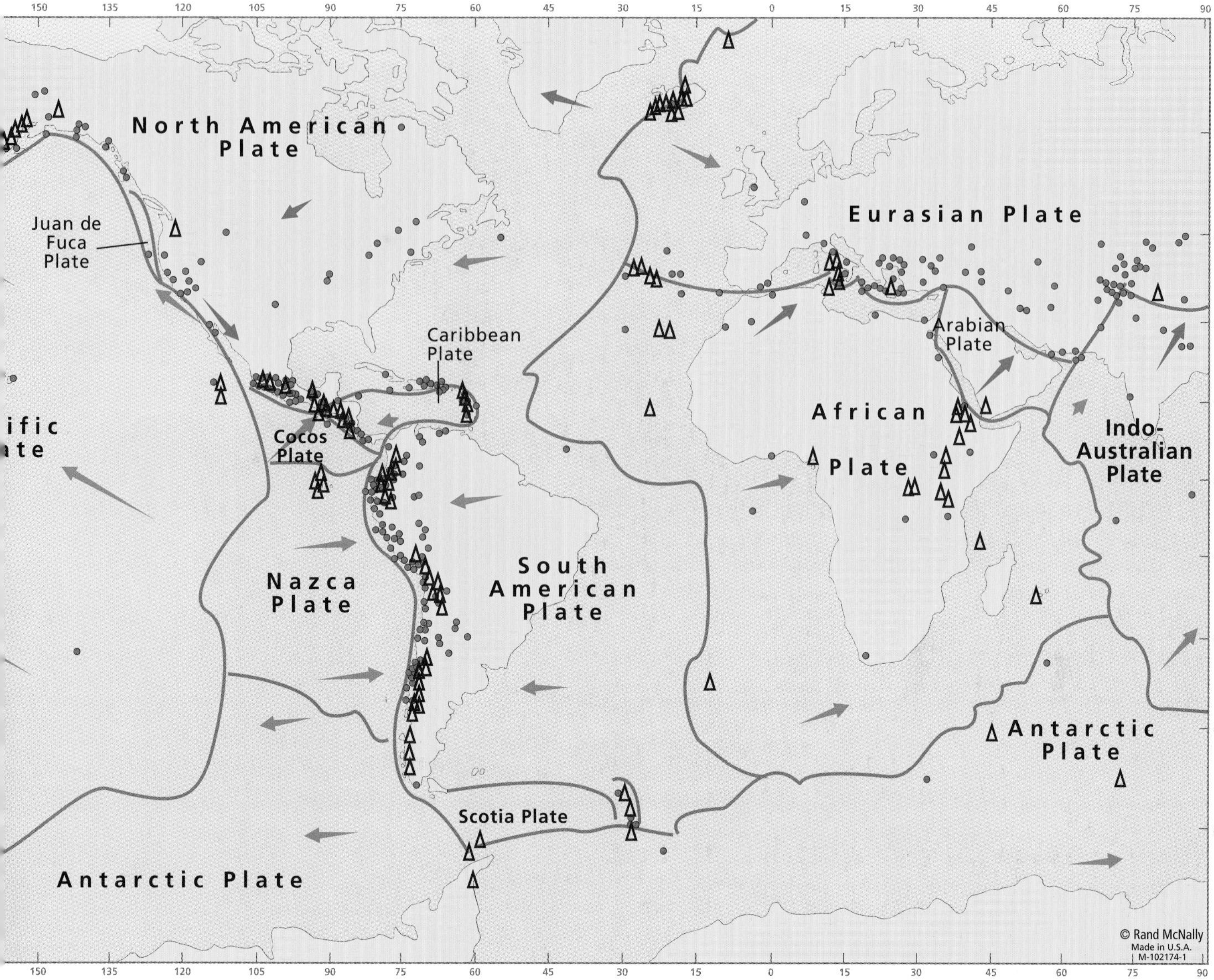

ome Notable Volcanic Eruptions

ear	Magnitude Explosivity Index (VEI)	Name (location)	Estimated Deaths
1991	6	Mt. Pinatubo (Philippines)	350
1985	3	Nevado del Ruiz (Colombia)	25,000
1980	5	Mt. St. Helens (Washington, U.S.)	57
1963	3	Surtsey (Iceland)	Volcano creates new island
1902	4	Mt. Pelée (Martinique)	30,000
1883	6	Krakatoa (Indonesia)	36,000 killed, most by tsunami
1815	7	Gunung Tambora (Indonesia)	92,000
79	5	Vesuvius (Italy)	3,000 killed in Pompeii and Herculaneum

Eruption of Mt. St. Helens in 1980.

World Time Zones

The world is divided into 24 standard time zones. As Earth turns on its axis each day, the sun is overhead at different places at different times. Each time zone is based on the place where the sun is overhead at noon. The boundaries are adjusted so that people whose activities are connected live in the same time zone.

You can determine the standard time for any time zone in the world. Add one hour for each time zone you count as you go east. Subtract one hour for each time zone you count as you go west.

Prime Meridian

The Prime Meridian is also called the Greenwich Meridian because it is centered on the Royal Greenwich Observatory near London in the United Kingdom. It represents 0° longitude. Time around the world is counted from this meridian.

International Date Line

The International Date Line is halfway around the world from the Prime Meridian, at 180° longitude. Like time zone boundaries, the International Date Line is adjusted from 180° so that people in the same country have the same day. The time is the same on both sides of the International Date Line, but the day is different. West of the International Date Line it is one day later than it is east of the International Date Line.

New Zealand, which lies just west of the International Date Line, is one of the first places in the world to greet each new day.

The precise location of the Prime Meridian is marked at the Royal Greenwich Observatory near London.

Examples of Time Changes

Auckland, New Zealand

12 midnight June 26

Los Angeles, California, United States

4 a.m. June 25

Montréal, Québec, Canada

7 a.m. June 25

Rio de Janeiro, Brazil

9 a.m. June 25

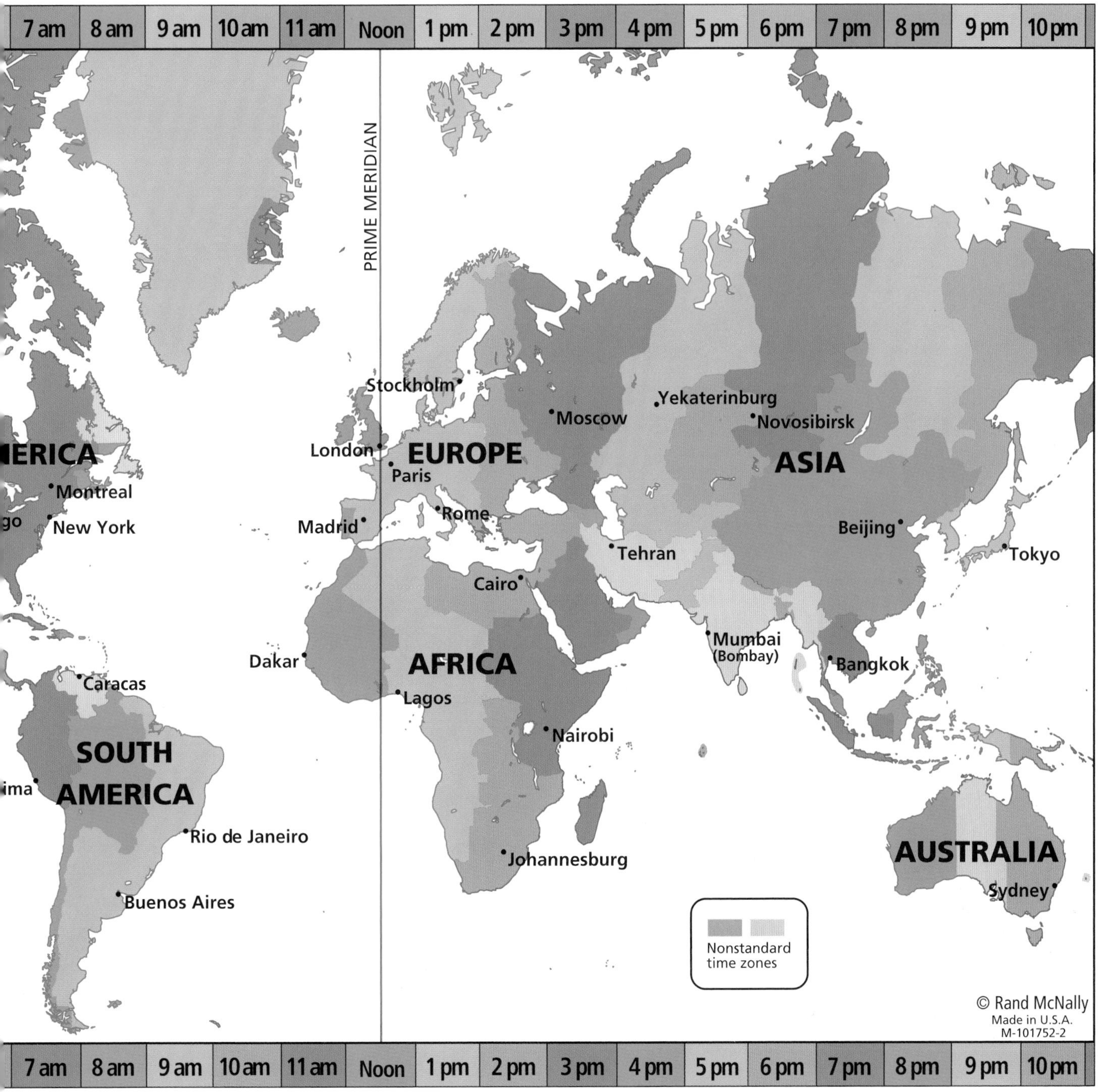
7 am
8 am
9 am
10 am
11 am
Noon
1 pm
2 pm
3 pm
4 pm
5 pm
6 pm
7 pm
8 pm
9 pm
10 pm
PRIME MERIDIAN
ERICA
Montreal
New York
SOUTH AMERICA
Caracas
Rio de Janeiro
Buenos Aires
EUROPE
Stockholm
London
Paris
Madrid
Rome
Moscow
AFRICA
Dakar
Cairo
Lagos
Nairobi
Johannesburg
ASIA
Yekaterinburg
Novosibirsk
Tehran
Mumbai
(Bombay)
Bangkok
Beijing
Tokyo
AUSTRALIA
Sydney
Nonstandard time zones
© Rand McNally
Made in U.S.A.
M-101752-2

Paris, France

1 p.m.
June 25

Moscow, Russia

3 p.m.
June 25

Novosibirsk, Russia

6 p.m.
June 25

Tokyo, Japan

9 p.m.
June 25

North America

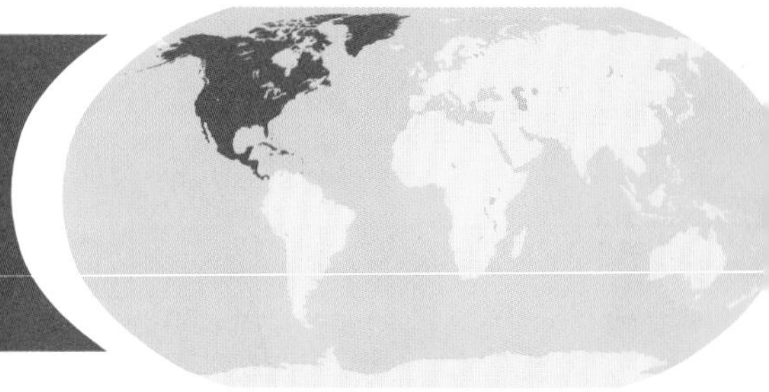

Mt. McKinley, Alaska, United States

North America is the third-largest continent. About 506,000,000 people live there.

It stretches 5,400 miles (8,700 kilometers) from northern Canada to the Panama-Colombia border.

Three countries—Canada, the United States, and Mexico—make up most of North America. The Caribbean island countries, the countries of Central America, and the island of Greenland make up the rest of the continent.

Central America is a region within North America. It is made up of the countries of Belize, Guatemala, Honduras, El Salvador, Nicaragua, Costa Rica, and Panama.

Central America is part of a larger region of North America called Middle America. This region consists of Central America, Mexico, and the Caribbean countries.

Generally, the people of North America have used its rich natural resources to great advantage. But not everyone has benefited. There are people throughout the continent who struggle with poverty, particularly in Central America and some Caribbean countries.

Parliament Hill, Ottawa, Ontario, Canada

San Francisco, California, United States

Pyramid of the Sun, Mexico

Did You Know?

Greenland, which is part of North America, is the largest island in the world.

A Historical Look At North America

About 20,000 years ago

First inhabitants of North America may have arrived from Asia across a land bridge that has since disappeared.

Corn (maize) is first cultivated in Middle America.

About 5000 B.C.

About 1200–1500 A.D.

Aztec civilization is dominant in Mexico.

Europeans explore North America.

About 1500

Urbanization in North America

In the late nineteenth century and early twentieth century, many new factories were built in the United States and Canada. People moved from farms to cities to take jobs in factories and offices. They were joined by immigrants from many countries. After World War II, many people in cities moved to suburbs, and urbanized areas began to grow together, especially along the East Coast between Boston and Washington, D.C. Now people in Mexico are moving to cities and to suburbs. Some of them cannot find steady jobs, and the cities have trouble providing water, sewers, and schools for the rapidly growing populations.

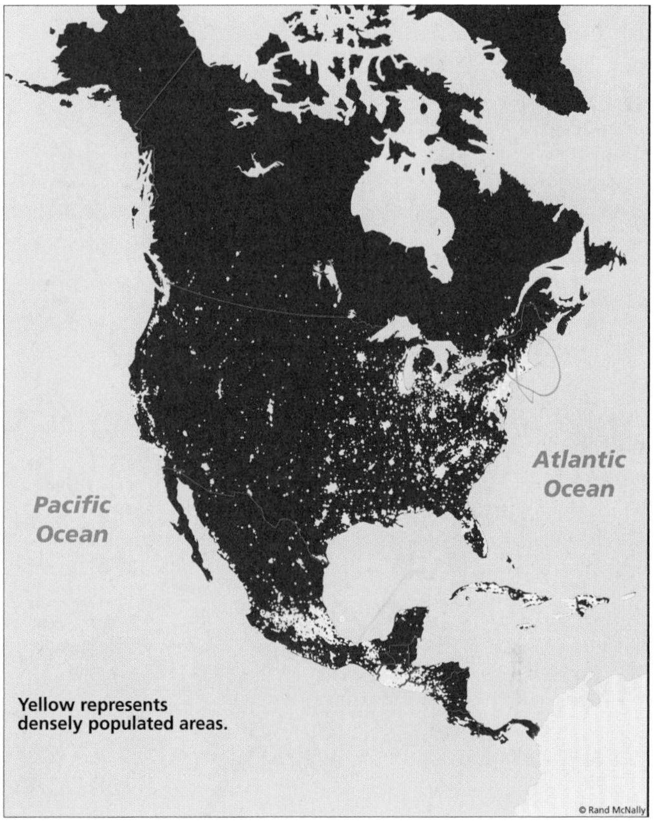
Pacific Ocean
Atlantic Ocean
Yellow represents densely populated areas.
© Rand McNally

Rising Urban Population
Urban population as a percentage of total population, 1900-2000

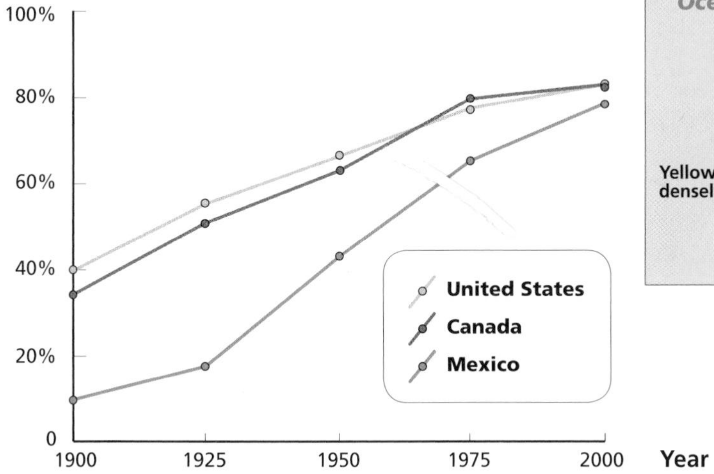

New York City, the largest city in the United States

An abandoned farm on the Great Plains

A village scene in Mexico

Suburban sprawl in Colorado

Toronto, the largest city in Canada

1776

The United States declares independence.

1820

Mexico becomes independent.

1867

Canada forms a confederation of four provinces.

1976

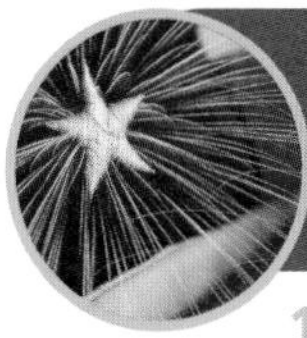

The United States celebrates its 200th birthday.

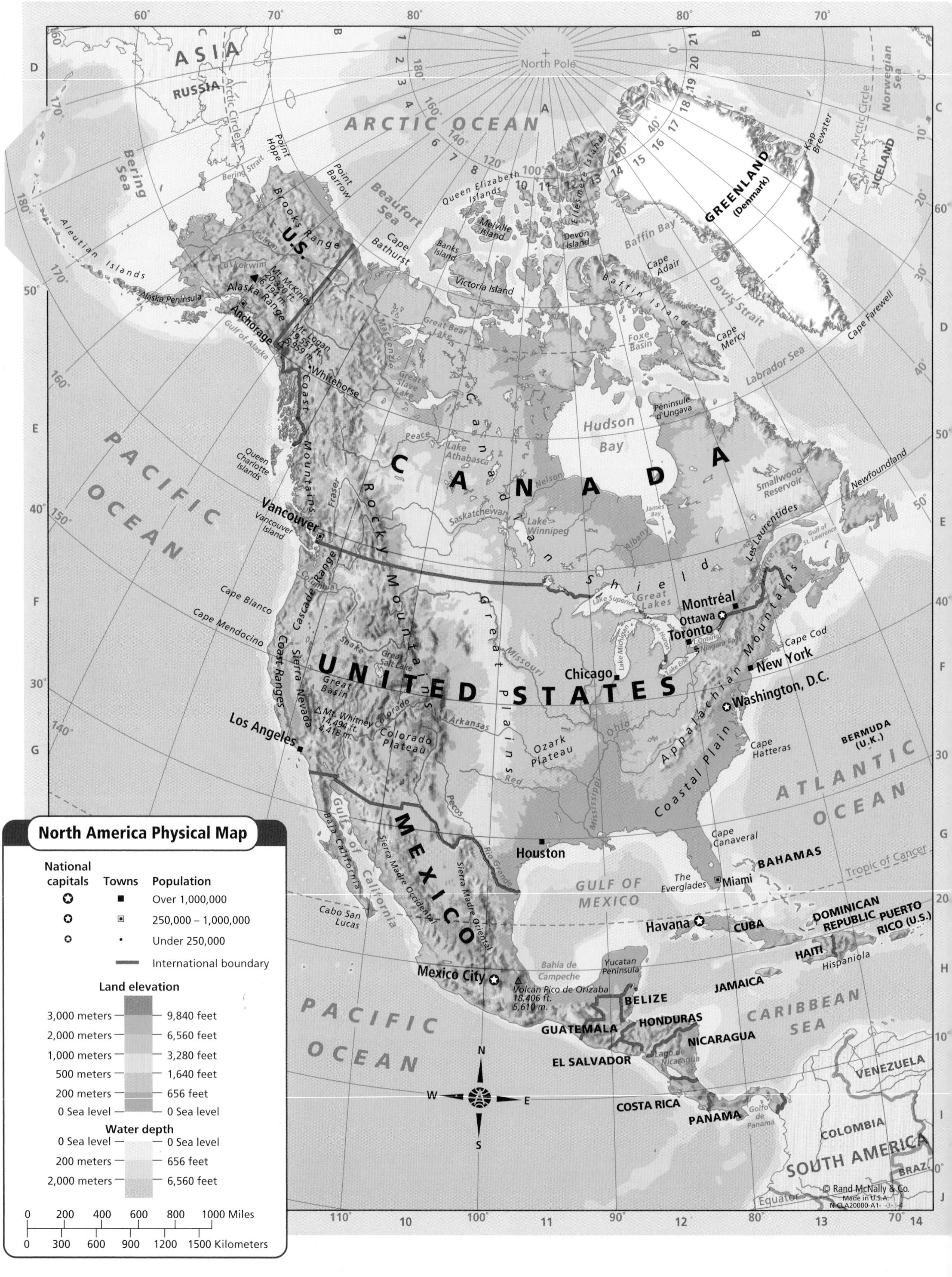

North America Physical Map
National capitals
Towns
Population
Over 1,000,000
250,000 – 1,000,000
Under 250,000
International boundary
Land elevation
3,000 meters
9,840 feet
2,000 meters
6,560 feet
1,000 meters
3,280 feet
500 meters
1,640 feet
200 meters
656 feet
0 Sea level
0 Sea level
Water depth
0 Sea level
0 Sea level
200 meters
656 feet
2,000 meters
6,560 feet
0 200 400 600 800 1000 Miles
0 300 600 900 1200 1500 Kilometers
ASIA
RUSSIA
Arctic Circle
North Pole
ARCTIC OCEAN
Bering Sea
Bering Strait
Point Hope
Point Barrow
Beaufort Sea
Aleutian Islands
Alaska Peninsula
Brooks Range
U.S.
Yukon
Kuskokwim
Mt. McKinley 20,320 ft. 6,194 m.
Alaska Range
Anchorage
Gulf of Alaska
Mt. Logan 19,551 ft. 5,959 m.
Whitehorse
Cape Bathurst
Queen Elizabeth Islands
Melville Island
Banks Island
Victoria Island
Ellesmere Island
Devon Island
Baffin Bay
Cape Adair
Baffin Island
Foxe Basin
Cape Mercy
Davis Strait
GREENLAND (Denmark)
Kap Brewster
ICELAND
Norwegian Sea
Cape Farewell
Labrador Sea
Great Bear Lake
Mackenzie
Great Slave Lake
Coast Mountains
Queen Charlotte Islands
Péninsule d'Ungava
Hudson Bay
CANADA
Canadian Shield
Peace
Lake Athabasca
Nelson
Saskatchewan
Lake Winnipeg
James Bay
Albany
Smallwood Reservoir
Newfoundland
Gulf of St. Lawrence
Les Laurentides
PACIFIC OCEAN
Vancouver
Vancouver Island
Fraser
Rocky Mountains
Columbia
Cascade Range
Cape Blanco
Cape Mendocino
Coast Ranges
Sierra Nevada
Snake
Great Salt Lake
Great Basin
Great Plains
Missouri
Lake Superior
Great Lakes
Lake Michigan
Lake Huron
Lake Ontario
Lake Erie
Niagara Falls
Montréal
Ottawa
Toronto
St. Lawrence
Cape Cod
New York
Chicago
UNITED STATES
Washington, D.C.
Appalachian Mountains
Mt. Whitney 14,494 ft. 4,418 m.
Colorado
Colorado Plateau
Los Angeles
Arkansas
Ozark Plateau
Ohio
Mississippi
Red
Pecos
Rio Grande
Coastal Plain
Cape Hatteras
BERMUDA (U.K.)
ATLANTIC OCEAN
Cape Canaveral
Houston
Baja California
Gulf of California
Sierra Madre Occidental
Sierra Madre Oriental
MEXICO
Cabo San Lucas
GULF OF MEXICO
The Everglades
Miami
BAHAMAS
Tropic of Cancer
Havana
CUBA
DOMINICAN REPUBLIC
PUERTO RICO (U.S.)
HAITI
Hispaniola
JAMAICA
Bahía de Campeche
Yucatan Peninsula
Mexico City
Volcán Pico de Orizaba 18,406 ft. 5,610 m.
BELIZE
GUATEMALA
HONDURAS
NICARAGUA
Lago de Nicaragua
EL SALVADOR
CARIBBEAN SEA
PACIFIC OCEAN
COSTA RICA
PANAMA
Golfo de Panamá
VENEZUELA
COLOMBIA
SOUTH AMERICA
BRAZ.
Equator
N
S
E
W
© Rand McNally & Co.
Made in U.S.A.

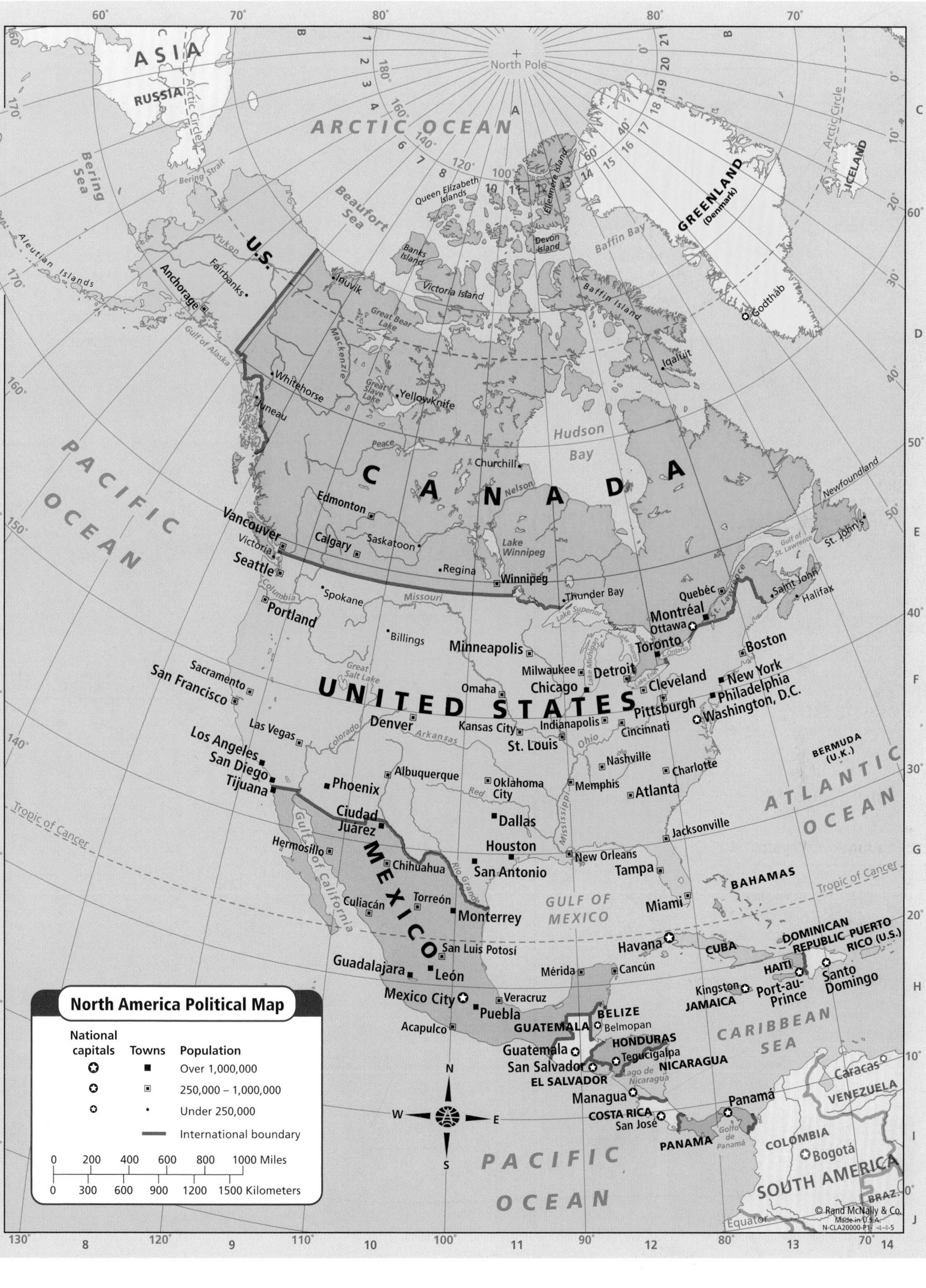
North America Political Map
ASIA
RUSSIA
Arctic Circle
ARCTIC OCEAN
North Pole
Bering Sea
Bering Strait
Beaufort Sea
Queen Elizabeth Islands
Ellesmere Island
Devon Island
Banks Island
Victoria Island
Baffin Island
Baffin Bay
GREENLAND (Denmark)
ICELAND
Godthåb
Iqaluit
Aleutian Islands
Yukon
U.S.
Fairbanks
Anchorage
Gulf of Alaska
Inuvik
Great Bear Lake
Mackenzie
Great Slave Lake
Yellowknife
Whitehorse
Juneau
Hudson Bay
Peace
Churchill
Nelson
CANADA
Edmonton
Vancouver
Victoria
Calgary
Saskatoon
Lake Winnipeg
Regina
Winnipeg
Thunder Bay
Lake Superior
Newfoundland
Gulf of St. Lawrence
St. John's
Saint John
Halifax
Québec
Montréal
Ottawa
St. Lawrence
PACIFIC OCEAN
Seattle
Columbia
Spokane
Missouri
Portland
Billings
Minneapolis
Lake Michigan
Lake Huron
Lake Ontario
Lake Erie
Toronto
Boston
Milwaukee
Detroit
Great Salt Lake
Sacramento
San Francisco
UNITED STATES
Omaha
Chicago
Cleveland
New York
Philadelphia
Pittsburgh
Washington, D.C.
Las Vegas
Colorado
Denver
Arkansas
Kansas City
Indianapolis
Cincinnati
Ohio
St. Louis
Los Angeles
San Diego
Tijuana
Nashville
Charlotte
BERMUDA (U.K.)
Albuquerque
Phoenix
Oklahoma City
Red
Memphis
Atlanta
ATLANTIC OCEAN
Tropic of Cancer
Ciudad Juárez
Dallas
Mississippi
Jacksonville
Gulf of California
Hermosillo
Houston
New Orleans
MEXICO
Chihuahua
Rio Grande
San Antonio
Tampa
BAHAMAS
Culiacán
Torreón
Monterrey
GULF OF MEXICO
Miami
San Luis Potosí
Havana
CUBA
DOMINICAN REPUBLIC
PUERTO RICO (U.S.)
Guadalajara
León
Mérida
Cancún
HAITI
Santo Domingo
Port-au-Prince
Kingston
JAMAICA
Mexico City
Veracruz
Puebla
BELIZE
Belmopan
GUATEMALA
CARIBBEAN SEA
Acapulco
HONDURAS
Guatemala
Tegucigalpa
San Salvador
NICARAGUA
EL SALVADOR
Lago de Nicaragua
Caracas
Managua
Panamá
VENEZUELA
COSTA RICA
San José
Golfo de Panamá
PANAMA
COLOMBIA
Bogotá
SOUTH AMERICA
BRAZ.
Equator
National capitals
Towns
Population
Over 1,000,000
250,000 – 1,000,000
Under 250,000
International boundary
0 200 400 600 800 1000 Miles
0 300 600 900 1200 1500 Kilometers
N
S
E
W
© Rand McNally & Co.
Made in U.S.A.
N-CLA20000-P1- -4-4-5

Climate

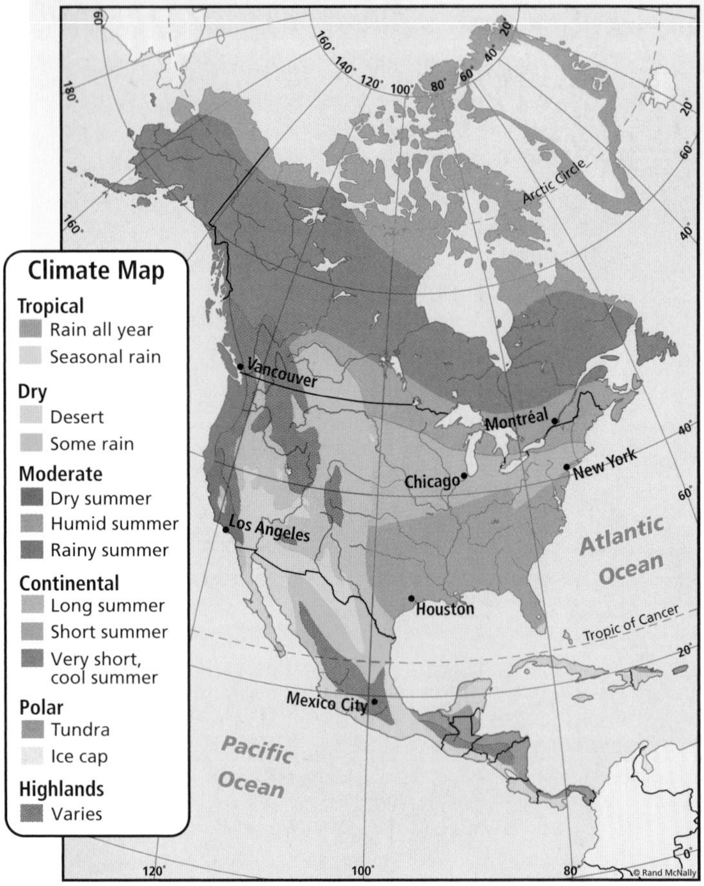

Environments

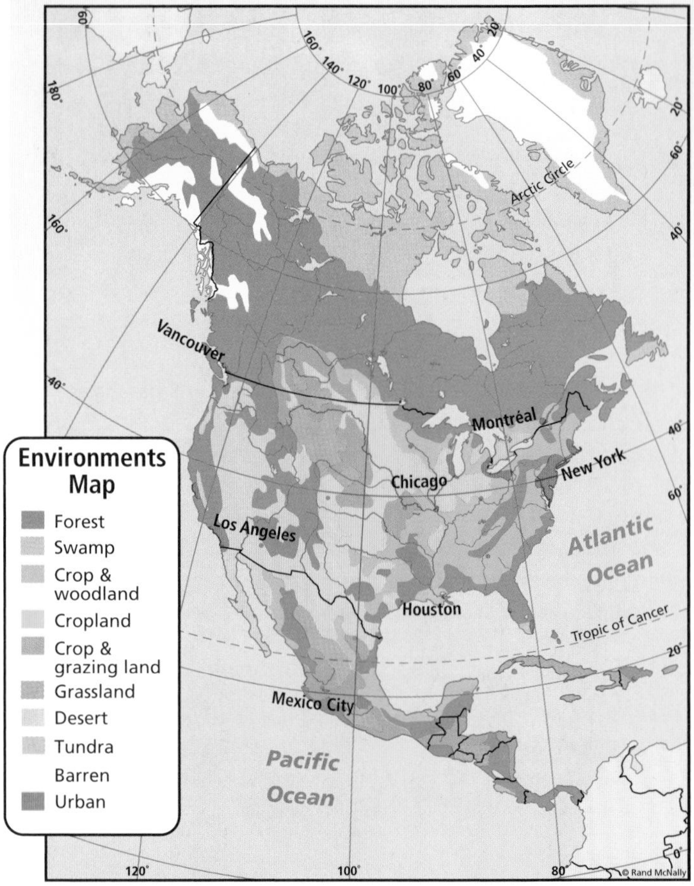

Population

More than one-half of North Americans live in the United States. Canada is the continent's largest country in area, but it is home to only six percent of the continent's population.

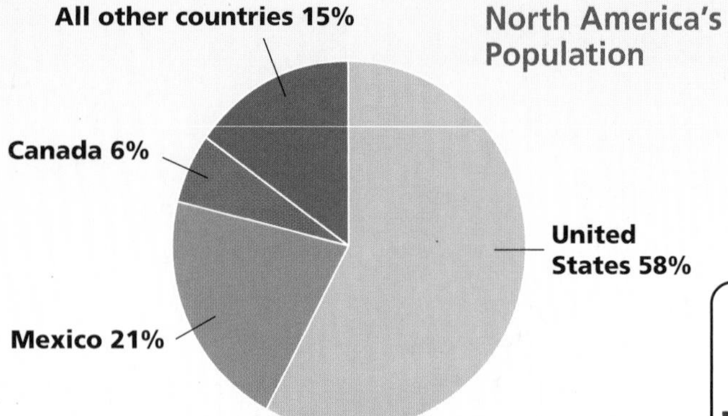

Vancouver, British Columbia, Canada

Street scene in Chicago, Illinois

Children in Havana, Cuba

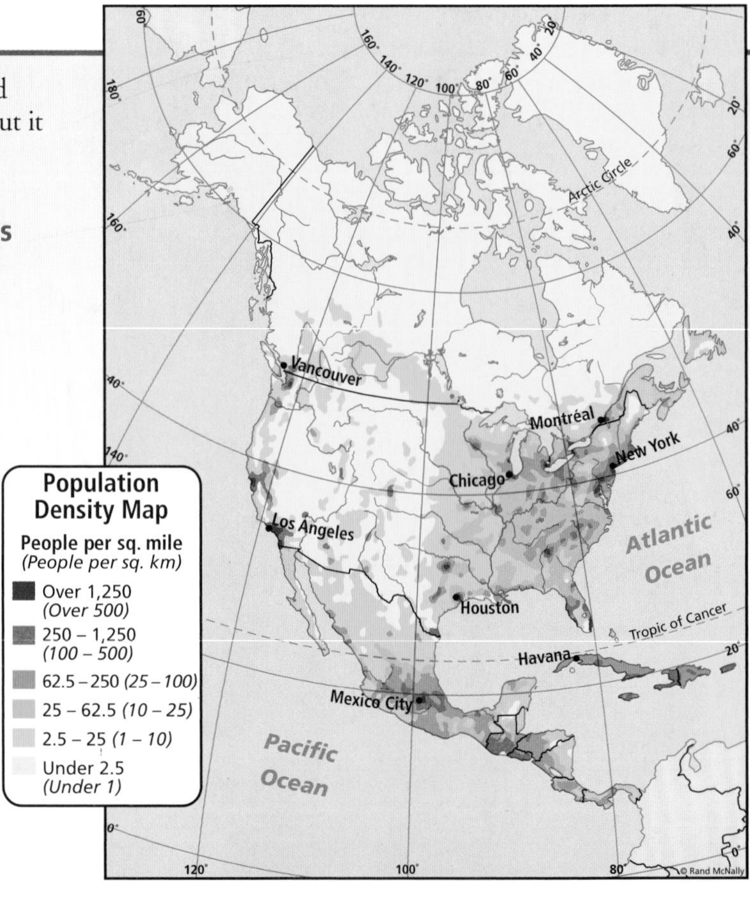

The Great Lakes

The Great Lakes lie along the border between the United States and Canada. Canals and rivers allow ocean-going ships to travel to the lakes and between them. Together, the lakes, canals, and rivers form a huge waterway that connects cities far inland with the ocean.

Size rank	Lake	Area sq. miles/ sq. kilometers	Greatest depth feet / meters
1	Superior	31,700 / 82,100	1,332 / 406
2	Huron	23,000 / 59,600	750 / 229
3	Michigan	22,300 / 57,800	925 / 282
4	Erie	9,910 / 25,700	210 / 64
5	Ontario	7,340 / 18,960	802 / 244

Lake Superior is the largest of the Great Lakes.

The Welland Canal in Ontario, Canada, connects Lake Erie and Lake Ontario.

Did You Know?

Lake Michigan gets its name from an Algonquin Indian word, *michigami,* which means "big lake."

Relative Depths of the Great Lakes

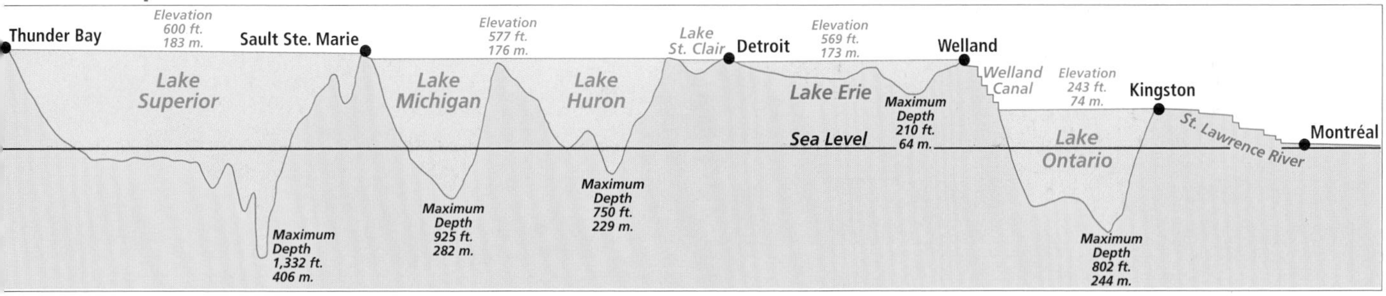

Economic Activities

The map at right shows that agriculture is the most important economic activity for a large part of North America. Much of the continent's manufacturing and commerce is concentrated in a wide band between Chicago and New York.

In 1994, Canada, the United States, and Mexico enacted the North American Free Trade Agreement (NAFTA) to remove all trade restrictions between the three countries.

Fishing trawlers in California

Grain elevators in Alberta, Canada

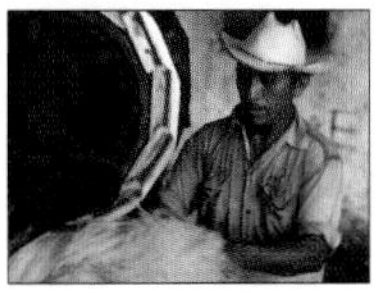

Factory worker in Mexico

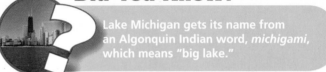

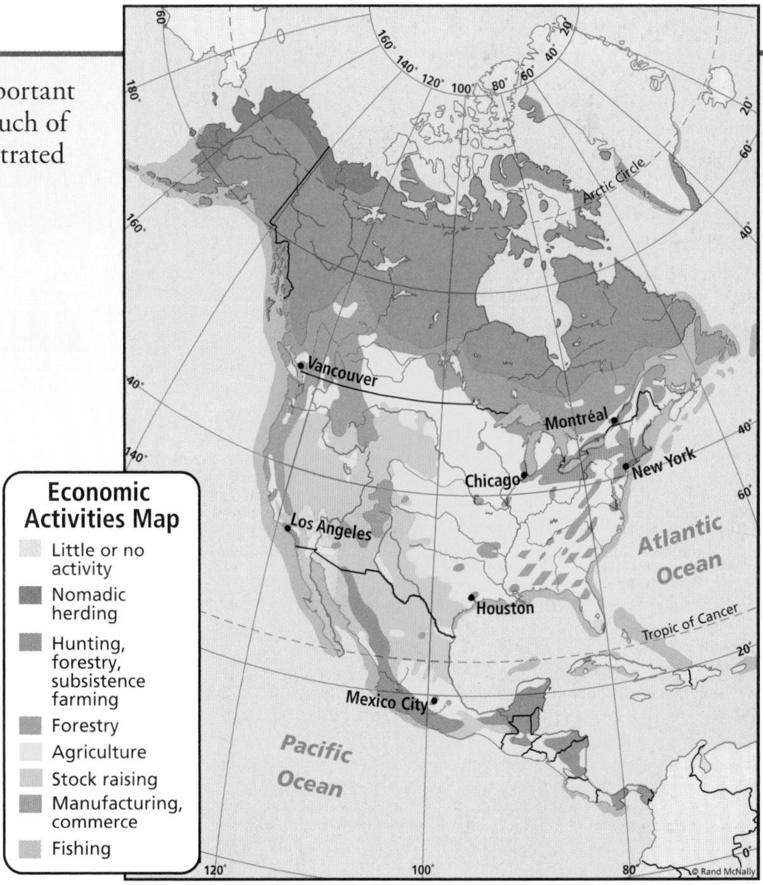
Economic Activities Map
Little or no activity
Nomadic herding
Hunting, forestry, subsistence farming
Forestry
Agriculture
Stock raising
Manufacturing, commerce
Fishing
Arctic Circle
Vancouver
Montréal
Chicago
New York
Los Angeles
Houston
Mexico City
Atlantic Ocean
Pacific Ocean
Tropic of Cancer
© Rand McNally

Natural Hazards

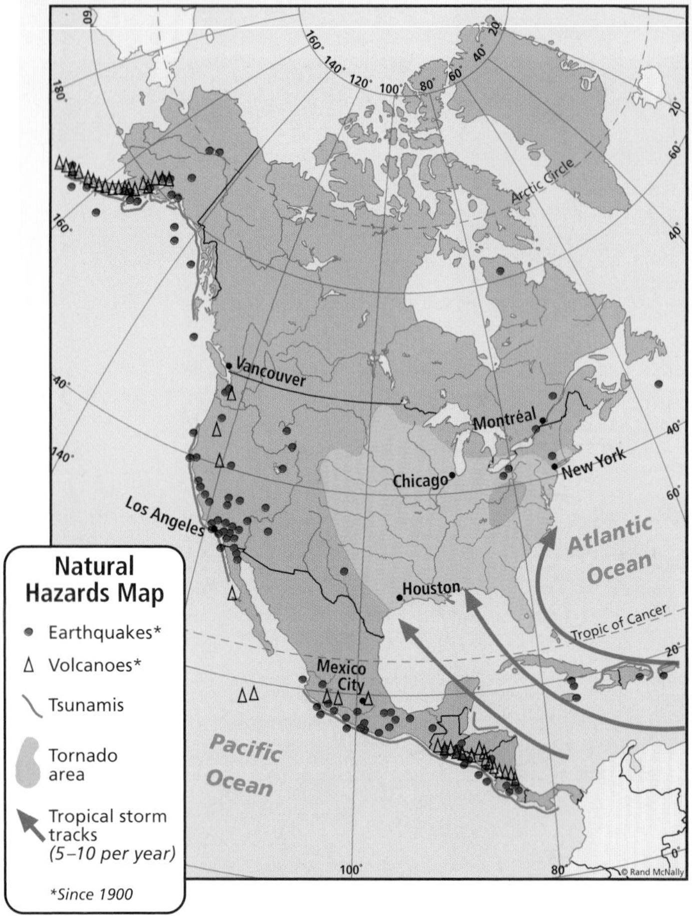

This satellite image shows a hurricane approaching the Atlantic coast of Florida.

Twister!

Tornadoes are rapidly rotating columns of air. They are usually funnel-shaped, and their winds may reach 200–500 miles per hour (320–800 kilometers per hour). They are usually less than one-quarter mile (400 meters) wide, but they can be extremely destructive. Texas has more tornadoes than any other state. Oklahoma ranks second in number of tornadoes, and Kansas ranks third.

What If?

Scientists track hurricanes by radar and satellites. What could happen if there were no way to warn people about these tropical storms?

Transportation

Automobiles in Mexico City add to the severe pollution problem there.

Automobiles per 1,000 people

More people in rich countries—especially those countries that do not offer much public transportation—own cars.

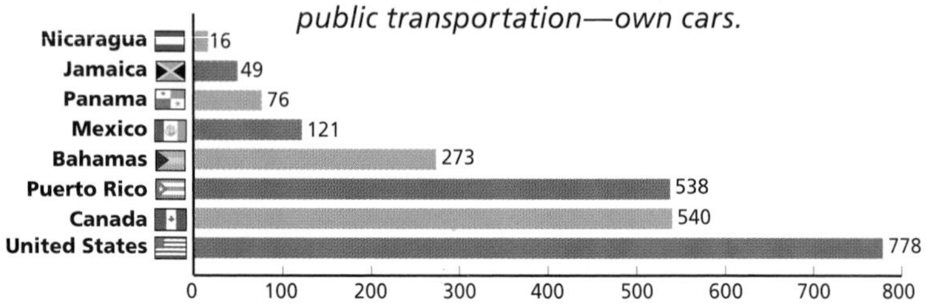

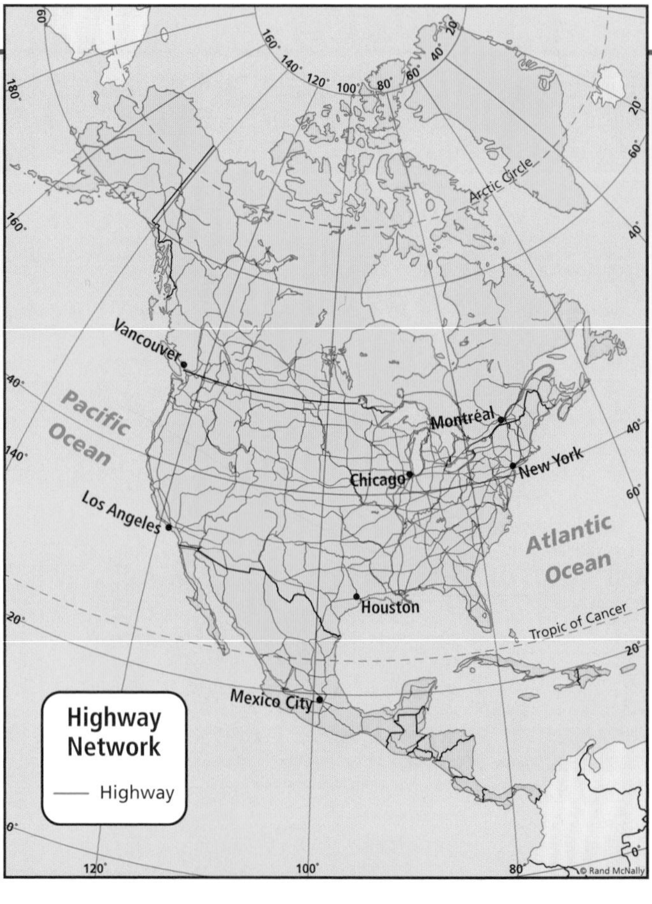

Energy

Most nuclear power plants in North America are in the eastern and central United States.

The Hoover Dam in Nevada provides hydroelectric power to three states.

Wind power is a promising alternative energy source.

Electricity Production by Type

More than two-thirds of North America's electricity is produced by power plants that burn coal, oil, and natural gas. This is called thermal energy. Most of the remaining electricity comes from nuclear plants and hydroelectric, or waterpower, plants. Less than one percent of the continent's electricity is produced by geothermal plants, which tap into the heat of the Earth's molten interior.

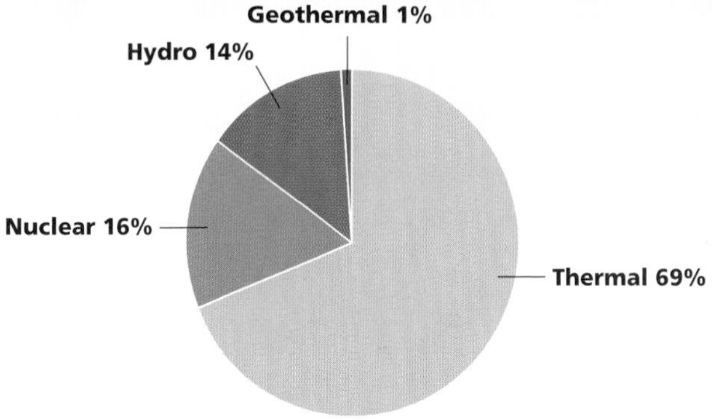

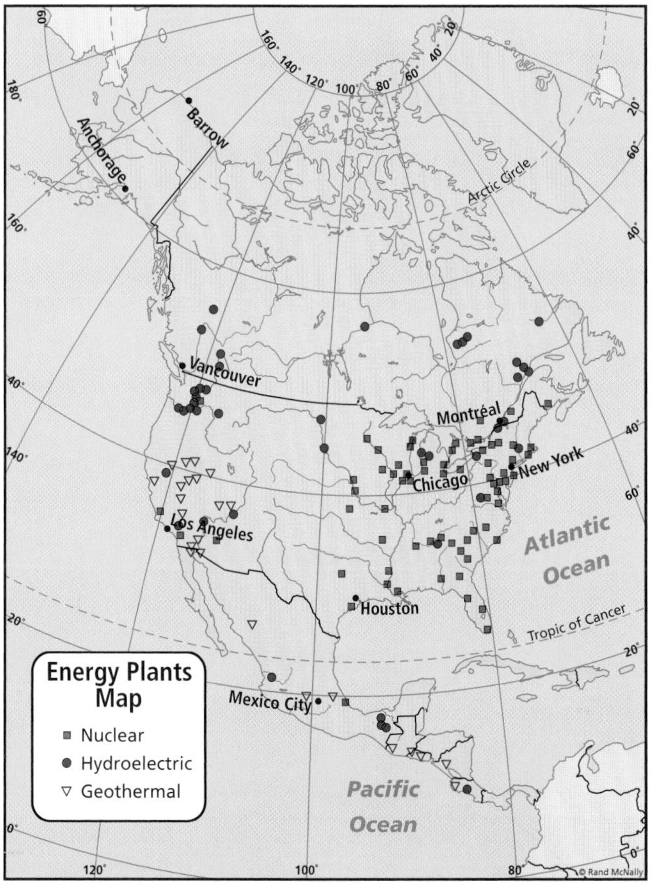

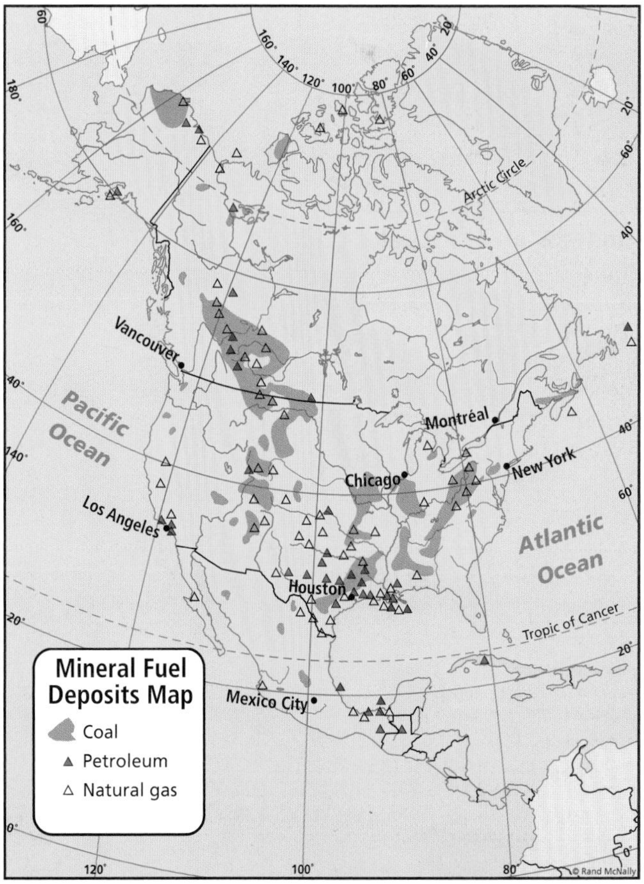

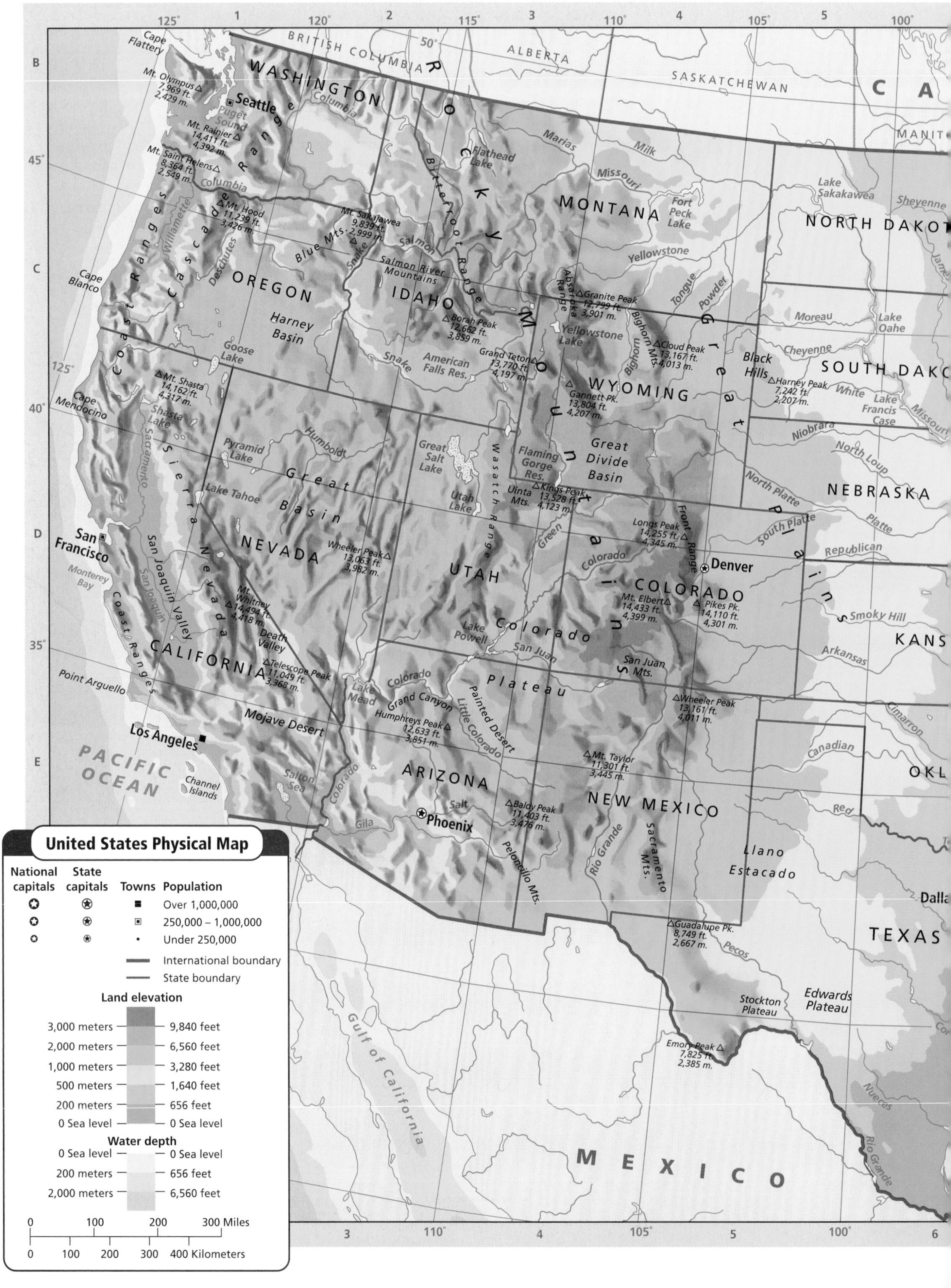

United States Physical Map

National capitals	State capitals	Towns	Population
✪	✪	■	Over 1,000,000
✪	✪	▣	250,000 – 1,000,000
✪	✪	•	Under 250,000
		▬▬	International boundary
		▬▬	State boundary

Land elevation

3,000 meters	9,840 feet
2,000 meters	6,560 feet
1,000 meters	3,280 feet
500 meters	1,640 feet
200 meters	656 feet
0 Sea level	0 Sea level

Water depth

0 Sea level	0 Sea level
200 meters	656 feet
2,000 meters	6,560 feet

0	100	200	300 Miles	
0	100	200	300	400 Kilometers

BRITISH COLUMBIA ALBERTA SASKATCHEWAN MANIT CA

WASHINGTON
Cape Flattery
Mt. Olympus 7,969 ft. 2,429 m.
Seattle
Puget Sound
Mt. Rainier 14,411 ft. 4,392 m.
Mt. Saint Helens 8,364 ft. 2,549 m.
Columbia
Mt. Hood 11,239 ft. 3,426 m.

OREGON
Cape Blanco
Coast Ranges
Cascade R.
Willamette
Deschutes
Harney Basin
Blue Mts.
Mt. Sacajawea 9,839 ft. 2,999 m.
Snake
Salmon
Salmon River Mountains
American Falls Res.

IDAHO
Bitterroot Range
Borah Peak 12,662 ft. 3,859 m.
Grand Teton 13,770 ft. 4,197 m.

MONTANA
Flathead Lake
Marias
Milk
Missouri
Yellowstone
Fort Peck Lake
Tongue
Powder
Bighorn Mts.

WYOMING
Absaroka Range
Granite Peak 12,799 ft. 3,901 m.
Yellowstone Lake
Cloud Peak 13,167 ft. 4,013 m.
Gannett Pk. 13,804 ft. 4,207 m.
Great Divide Basin
Flaming Gorge Res.
Kings Peak 13,528 ft. 4,123 m.
Uinta Mts.

NORTH DAKO
Lake Sakakawea
Sheyenne
Moreau
Lake Oahe
SOUTH DAKO
Cheyenne
Black Hills
Harney Peak 7,242 ft. 2,207 m.
White
Lake Francis Case
Missouri
Niobrara
North Loup
North Platte
NEBRASKA
South Platte
Platte
Republican

Cape Mendocino
Mt. Shasta 14,162 ft. 4,317 m.
Shasta Lake
Pyramid Lake
Goose Lake
Humboldt
Great Basin
Great Salt Lake
Utah Lake
Wasatch Range
Colorado
Green

NEVADA
Sierra Nevada
Lake Tahoe
Sacramento
Wheeler Peak 13,063 ft. 3,982 m.

San Francisco
Monterey Bay
San Joaquin Valley
San Joaquin
Coast Ranges
Mt. Whitney 14,494 ft. 4,418 m.
Death Valley

UTAH
Lake Powell
San Juan
Colorado Plateau

CALIFORNIA
Point Arguello
Telescope Peak 11,049 ft. 3,368 m.
Los Angeles
Channel Islands
PACIFIC OCEAN
Mojave Desert
Salton Sea
Colorado
Gila
Lake Mead
Grand Canyon
Little Colorado
Humphreys Peak 12,633 ft. 3,851 m.
Painted Desert

COLORADO
Longs Peak 14,255 ft. 4,345 m.
Denver
Front Range
Mt. Elbert 14,433 ft. 4,399 m.
Pikes Pk. 14,110 ft. 4,301 m.
San Juan Mts.
Wheeler Peak 13,161 ft. 4,011 m.
Smoky Hill
KANS
Arkansas
Great Plains

ARIZONA
Phoenix
Salt
Baldy Peak 11,403 ft. 3,476 m.
Pecos

NEW MEXICO
Mt. Taylor 11,301 ft. 3,445 m.
Rio Grande
Sacramento Mts.
Llano Estacado
Canadian
Red
OKL
Cimarron
Dallas
TEXAS
Guadalupe Pk. 8,749 ft. 2,667 m.
Pelancillo Mts.
Stockton Plateau
Edwards Plateau
Emory Peak 7,825 ft. 2,385 m.

Gulf of California
MEXICO
Rio Grande
Nueces

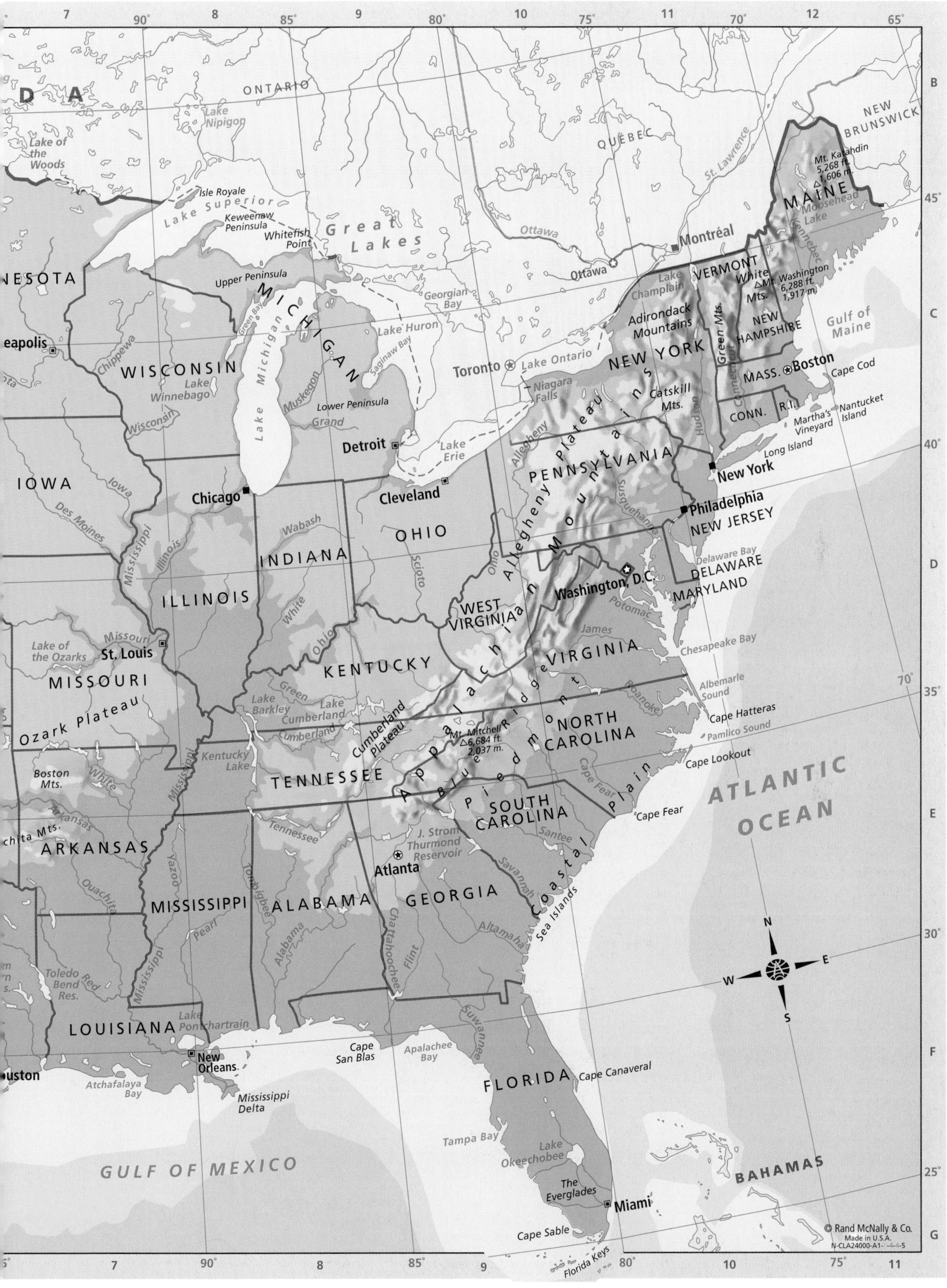
ONTARIO
QUÉBEC
NEW BRUNSWICK
Lake Nipigon
Lake of the Woods
Isle Royale
Lake Superior
Keweenaw Peninsula
Whitefish Point
Great Lakes
Upper Peninsula
MICHIGAN
Green Bay
Lake Michigan
Georgian Bay
Lake Huron
Saginaw Bay
Lower Peninsula
Muskegon
Grand
Detroit
Lake Erie
Lake Ontario
Toronto
Niagara Falls
Ottawa
Montréal
St. Lawrence
Mt. Katahdin 5,268 ft. 1,606 m.
MAINE
Moosehead Lake
Kennebec
VERMONT
White Mts.
Mt. Washington 6,288 ft. 1,917 m.
Lake Champlain
Adirondack Mountains
Green Mts.
NEW HAMPSHIRE
Gulf of Maine
NEW YORK
MASS.
Boston
Cape Cod
Catskill Mts.
Hudson
Connecticut
CONN.
R.I.
Martha's Vineyard
Nantucket Island
Long Island
New York
PENNSYLVANIA
Allegheny Plateau
Allegheny
Susquehanna
Philadelphia
NEW JERSEY
Delaware Bay
DELAWARE
MARYLAND
Washington, D.C.
Potomac
Chesapeake Bay
WEST VIRGINIA
Allegheny Mountains
Appalachian Mountains
James
VIRGINIA
Albemarle Sound
Roanoke
Cape Hatteras
Pamlico Sound
NORTH CAROLINA
Cape Lookout
Blue Ridge
Piedmont
Mt. Mitchell 6,684 ft. 2,037 m.
Cape Fear
SOUTH CAROLINA
Santee
Coastal Plain
J. Strom Thurmond Reservoir
Savannah
Sea Islands
Cape Fear
ATLANTIC OCEAN
NESOTA
eapolis
Chippewa
WISCONSIN
Lake Winnebago
Wisconsin
IOWA
Iowa
Des Moines
Chicago
Illinois
Mississippi
ILLINOIS
Wabash
INDIANA
White
Cleveland
OHIO
Scioto
Ohio
KENTUCKY
Green
Lake Barkley
Lake Cumberland
Cumberland
Cumberland Plateau
Missouri
St. Louis
Lake of the Ozarks
MISSOURI
Ozark Plateau
Boston Mts.
White
Kentucky Lake
TENNESSEE
Arkansas
ARKANSAS
chita Mts.
Ouachita
Tennessee
Yazoo
Tombigbee
MISSISSIPPI
ALABAMA
Atlanta
GEORGIA
Altamaha
Pearl
Alabama
Chattahoochee
Flint
Toledo Bend Res.
Red
LOUISIANA
Lake Pontchartrain
New Orleans
uston
Atchafalaya Bay
Mississippi Delta
Cape San Blas
Apalachee Bay
Suwannee
FLORIDA
Cape Canaveral
Tampa Bay
Lake Okeechobee
The Everglades
Miami
Cape Sable
Florida Keys
GULF OF MEXICO
BAHAMAS
N
E
S
W
© Rand McNally & Co.
Made in U.S.A.

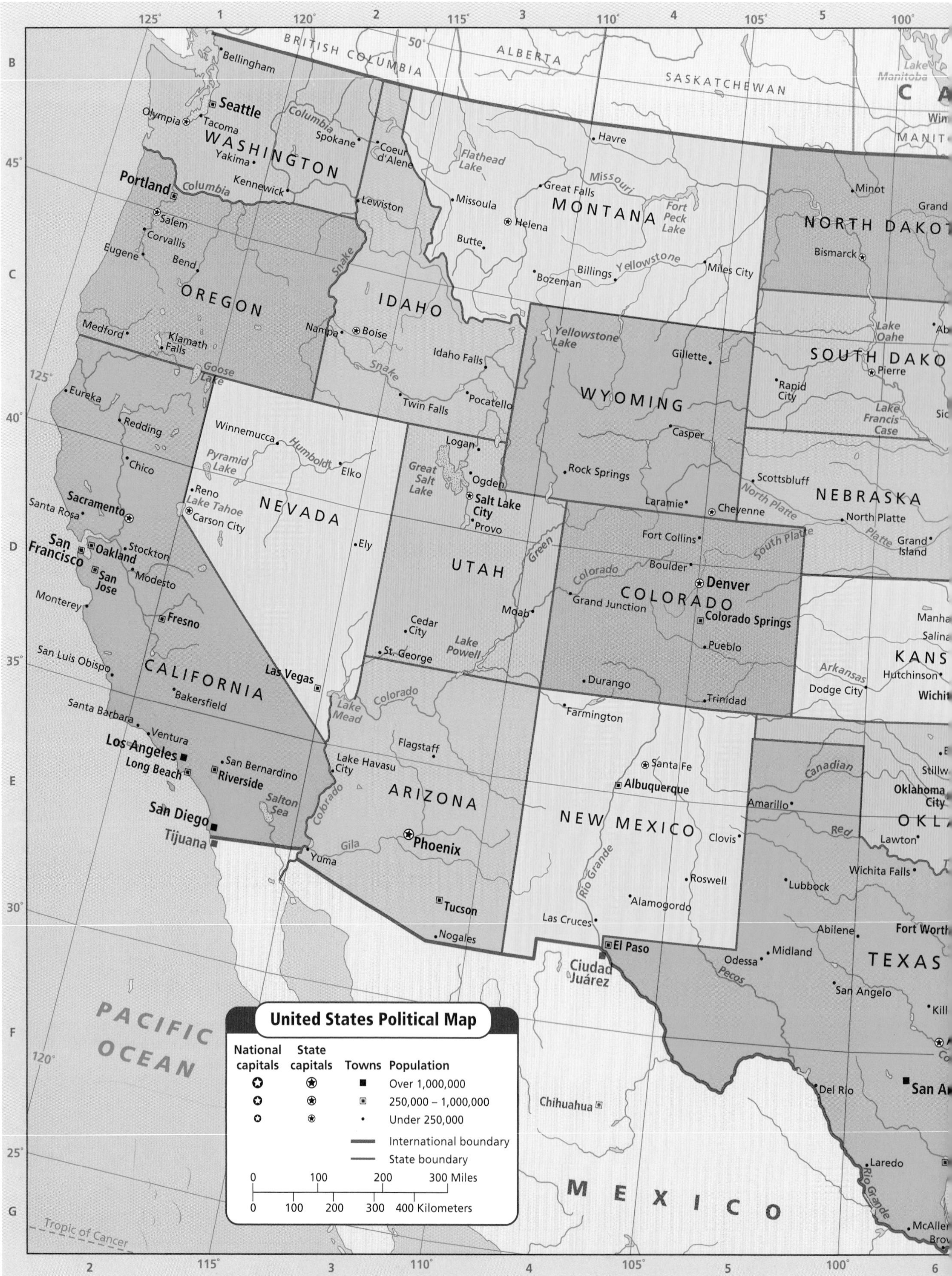

United States Political Map
National capitals
State capitals
Towns
Population
Over 1,000,000
250,000 – 1,000,000
Under 250,000
International boundary
State boundary
0 100 200 300 Miles
0 100 200 300 400 Kilometers
BRITISH COLUMBIA
ALBERTA
SASKATCHEWAN
Lake Manitoba
MANIT
WASHINGTON
OREGON
CALIFORNIA
NEVADA
IDAHO
MONTANA
WYOMING
UTAH
COLORADO
ARIZONA
NEW MEXICO
NORTH DAKO
SOUTH DAKO
NEBRASKA
KANS
OKL
TEXAS
MEXICO
PACIFIC OCEAN
Tropic of Cancer
Bellingham
Seattle
Olympia
Tacoma
Spokane
Coeur d'Alene
Yakima
Kennewick
Columbia
Portland
Salem
Corvallis
Eugene
Bend
Medford
Klamath Falls
Goose Lake
Lewiston
Snake
Nampa
Boise
Idaho Falls
Twin Falls
Pocatello
Missoula
Flathead Lake
Great Falls
Havre
Missouri
Fort Peck Lake
Helena
Butte
Billings
Yellowstone
Bozeman
Miles City
Minot
Bismarck
Grand
Lake Oahe
Pierre
Rapid City
Lake Francis Case
Yellowstone Lake
Gillette
Casper
Rock Springs
Laramie
Cheyenne
Scottsbluff
North Platte
South Platte
Grand Island
Eureka
Redding
Chico
Sacramento
Santa Rosa
San Francisco
Oakland
San Jose
Stockton
Modesto
Monterey
Fresno
San Luis Obispo
Bakersfield
Santa Barbara
Ventura
Los Angeles
Long Beach
San Bernardino
Riverside
Salton Sea
San Diego
Tijuana
Winnemucca
Humboldt
Pyramid Lake
Elko
Reno
Lake Tahoe
Carson City
Ely
Las Vegas
Lake Mead
Logan
Great Salt Lake
Ogden
Salt Lake City
Provo
Green
Cedar City
St. George
Lake Powell
Moab
Grand Junction
Colorado
Fort Collins
Boulder
Denver
Colorado Springs
Pueblo
Durango
Trinidad
Arkansas
Dodge City
Hutchinson
Salina
Wichit
Flagstaff
Lake Havasu City
Gila
Yuma
Phoenix
Tucson
Nogales
Farmington
Santa Fe
Albuquerque
Rio Grande
Clovis
Roswell
Alamogordo
Las Cruces
El Paso
Ciudad Juárez
Chihuahua
Amarillo
Canadian
Red
Lawton
Oklahoma City
Wichita Falls
Lubbock
Abilene
Fort Worth
Odessa
Midland
Pecos
San Angelo
Del Rio
San A
Laredo
McAller

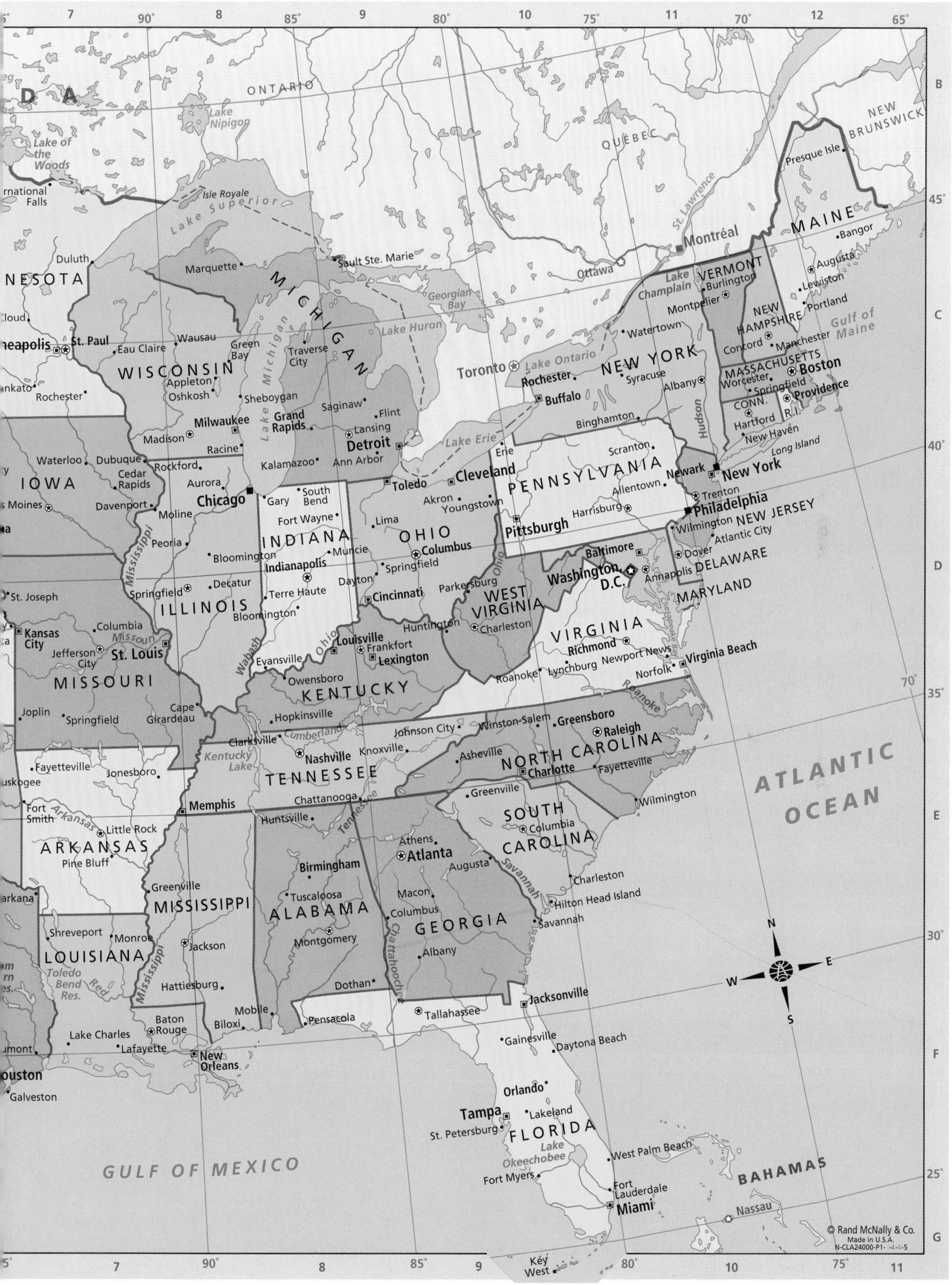
ONTARIO
QUEBEC
NEW BRUNSWICK
Lake Nipigon
Lake of the Woods
International Falls
Isle Royale
Lake Superior
Duluth
Marquette
Sault Ste. Marie
MICHIGAN
Georgian Bay
Lake Huron
Lake Michigan
St. Lawrence
Montréal
Ottawa
Lake Champlain
VERMONT
Burlington
Montpelier
MAINE
Presque Isle
Bangor
Augusta
Lewiston
Portland
NEW HAMPSHIRE
Concord
Manchester
Gulf of Maine
MASSACHUSETTS
Boston
Worcester
Springfield
Providence
R.I.
CONN.
Hartford
New Haven
Long Island
New York
Newark
Trenton
Philadelphia
NEW JERSEY
Wilmington
Atlantic City
Dover
DELAWARE
Annapolis
Baltimore
Washington, D.C.
MARYLAND
Chesapeake Bay
NEW YORK
Watertown
Syracuse
Albany
Hudson
Rochester
Buffalo
Toronto
Lake Ontario
Binghamton
Scranton
PENNSYLVANIA
Allentown
Harrisburg
Pittsburgh
Erie
Lake Erie
Cleveland
Toledo
Akron
Youngstown
OHIO
Lima
Columbus
Springfield
Dayton
Cincinnati
Ohio
Parkersburg
WEST VIRGINIA
Charleston
Huntington
VIRGINIA
Richmond
Lynchburg
Roanoke
Newport News
Norfolk
Virginia Beach
Roanoke
Detroit
Ann Arbor
Lansing
Flint
Saginaw
Grand Rapids
Kalamazoo
Traverse City
Green Bay
Wausau
WISCONSIN
Appleton
Oshkosh
Sheboygan
Milwaukee
Madison
Racine
Eau Claire
St. Paul
Minneapolis
St. Cloud
MINNESOTA
Mankato
Rochester
IOWA
Waterloo
Dubuque
Cedar Rapids
Davenport
Des Moines
Rockford
Aurora
Chicago
Moline
Peoria
Bloomington
ILLINOIS
Springfield
Decatur
Mississippi
Gary
South Bend
Fort Wayne
INDIANA
Muncie
Indianapolis
Terre Haute
Bloomington
Wabash
Evansville
Owensboro
Louisville
Frankfort
Lexington
KENTUCKY
Hopkinsville
Cumberland
St. Joseph
Kansas City
Columbia
Missouri
Jefferson City
St. Louis
MISSOURI
Cape Girardeau
Joplin
Springfield
Clarksville
Nashville
Kentucky Lake
Knoxville
Johnson City
TENNESSEE
Chattanooga
Memphis
Tennessee
Winston-Salem
Greensboro
Raleigh
NORTH CAROLINA
Asheville
Charlotte
Fayetteville
Wilmington
Greenville
SOUTH CAROLINA
Columbia
Charleston
Hilton Head Island
Savannah
Augusta
Athens
Atlanta
Macon
Columbus
GEORGIA
Albany
Chattahoochee
Huntsville
Birmingham
Tuscaloosa
ALABAMA
Montgomery
Dothan
Mobile
Fayetteville
Jonesboro
Muskogee
Fort Smith
Arkansas
Little Rock
ARKANSAS
Pine Bluff
Texarkana
Greenville
MISSISSIPPI
Jackson
Hattiesburg
Biloxi
Shreveport
Monroe
LOUISIANA
Toledo Bend Res.
Red
Baton Rouge
Lake Charles
Lafayette
New Orleans
Beaumont
Houston
Galveston
Pensacola
Tallahassee
Jacksonville
Gainesville
Daytona Beach
Orlando
Tampa
Lakeland
St. Petersburg
FLORIDA
Lake Okeechobee
West Palm Beach
Fort Myers
Fort Lauderdale
Miami
Key West
GULF OF MEXICO
ATLANTIC OCEAN
BAHAMAS
Nassau
N
E
S
W
© Rand McNally & Co.
Made in U.S.A.

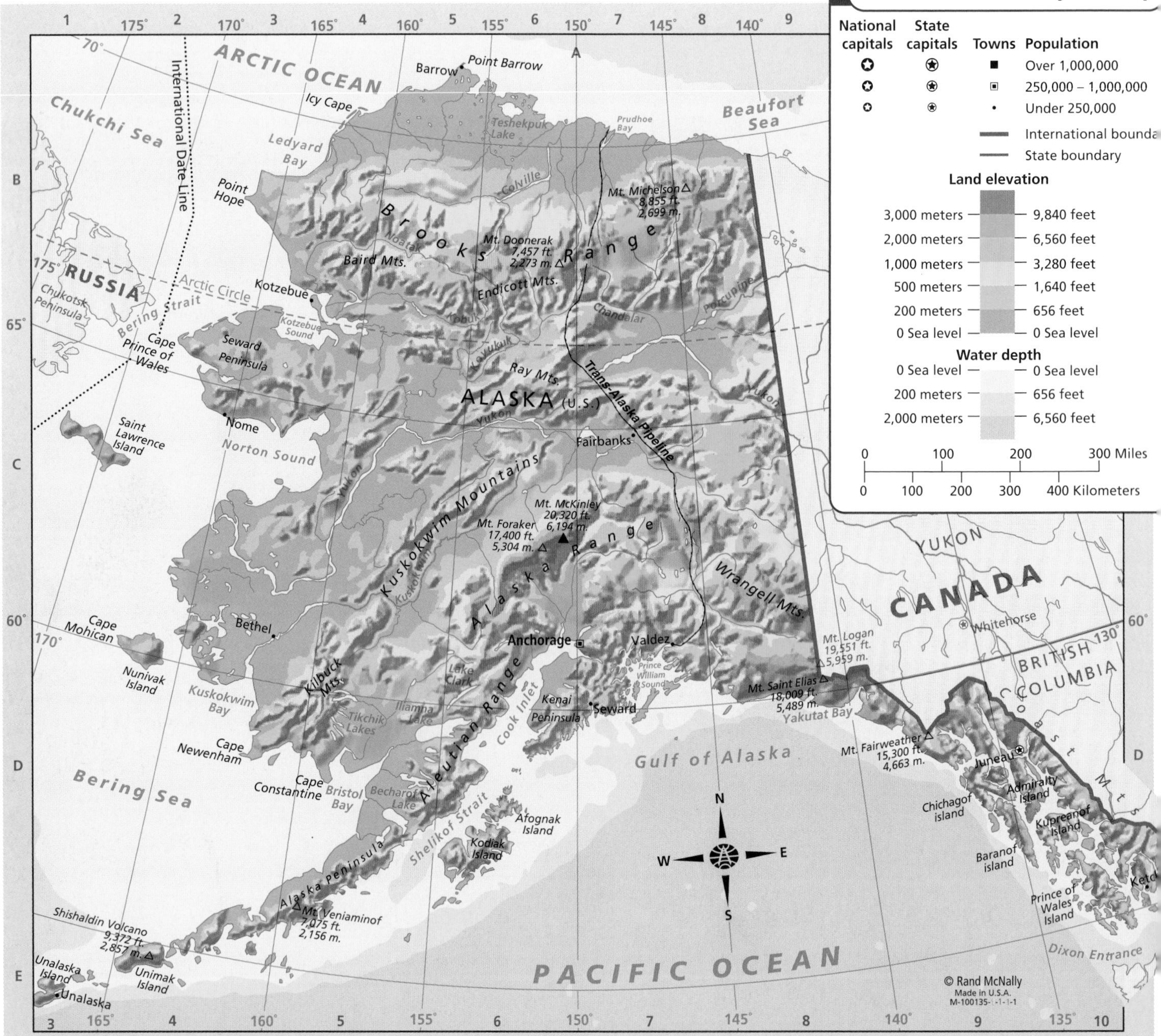

Alaska and Hawaii Physical Map

	National capitals	State capitals	Towns	Population
	⊛	⊛	■	Over 1,000,000
	⊕	⊛	▫	250,000 – 1,000,000
	⊙	⊛	•	Under 250,000

International boundary
State boundary

Land elevation

3,000 meters	9,840 feet
2,000 meters	6,560 feet
1,000 meters	3,280 feet
500 meters	1,640 feet
200 meters	656 feet
0 Sea level	0 Sea level

Water depth

0 Sea level	0 Sea level
200 meters	656 feet
2,000 meters	6,560 feet

0 100 200 300 Miles
0 100 200 300 400 Kilometers

ARCTIC OCEAN
Chukchi Sea
Beaufort Sea
Barrow · Point Barrow
Icy Cape
Prudhoe Bay
Teshekpuk Lake
Ledyard Bay
International Date Line
Point Hope
Mt. Michelson △ 8,855 ft. 2,699 m.
Brooks Range
Baird Mts.
Mt. Doonerak 7,457 ft. 2,273 m. △
Endicott Mts.
Colville
RUSSIA
175°
Arctic Circle
Kotzebue
Chukotsk Peninsula
Kotzebue Sound
Bering Strait
Cape Prince of Wales
Seward Peninsula
65°
Chandalar
Porcupine
Ray Mts.
Yukon
ALASKA (U.S.)
Trans-Alaska Pipeline
Norton Sound
Nome
Saint Lawrence Island
Fairbanks ·
170°
Cape Mohican
Bethel ·
Kuskokwim Mountains
Mt. McKinley 20,320 ft. 6,194 m.
Mt. Foraker 17,400 ft. 5,304 m. △
Alaska Range
Wrangell Mts.
CANADA
YUKON
Whitehorse ⊛
60°
Nunivak Island
Kuskokwim Bay
Kilbuck Mts.
Lake Clark
Illamna
Tikchik Lakes
Anchorage ▫
Valdez ·
Prince William Sound
Kenai Peninsula
Seward ·
Mt. Logan 19,551 ft. 5,959 m.
Mt. Saint Elias △ 18,009 ft. 5,489 m.
Yakutat Bay
BRITISH COLUMBIA 130°
Cape Newenham
Cape Constantine
Bristol Bay
Becharof Lake
Cook Inlet
Gulf of Alaska
Mt. Fairweather △ 15,300 ft. 4,663 m.
Chichagof Island
Admiralty Island
Juneau ⊛
Kupreanof Island
Bering Sea
Aleutian Range
Alaska Peninsula
Shelikof Strait
Afognak Island
Kodiak Island
N
W E
S
Baranof Island
Prince of Wales Island
Coast Mts
Ketc
Dixon Entrance
Shishaldin Volcano 9,372 ft. 2,857 m. △
Mt. Veniaminof 7,075 ft. 2,156 m. △
Unalaska Island
Unimak Island
· Unalaska
PACIFIC OCEAN
© Rand McNally
Made in U.S.A.
M-100135- ·1· ·1·1

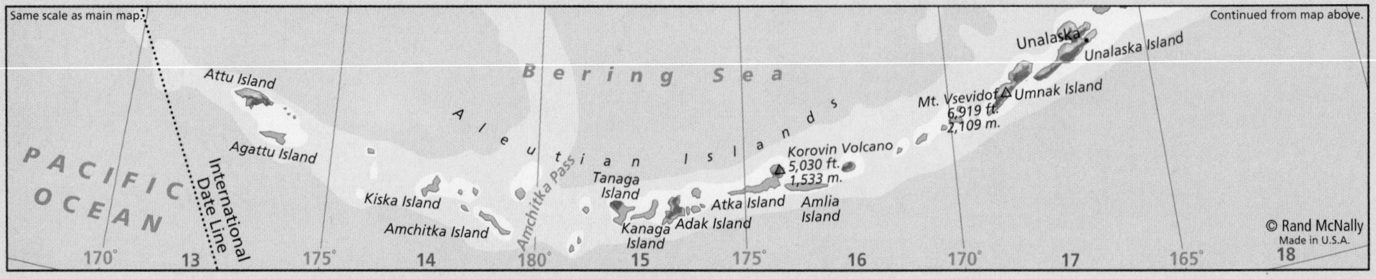

Same scale as main map.
Continued from map above.
Attu Island
Bering Sea
Unalaska ·
Unalaska Island
PACIFIC OCEAN
International Date Line
Agattu Island
Aleutian Islands
Mt. Vsevidof 6,919 ft. 2,109 m. △
Umnak Island
Kiska Island
Amchitka Pass
Tanaga Island
Atka Island
Korovin Volcano 5,030 ft. 1,533 m. △
Amlia Island
Amchitka Island
Kanaga Island
Adak Island
© Rand McNally
Made in U.S.A.

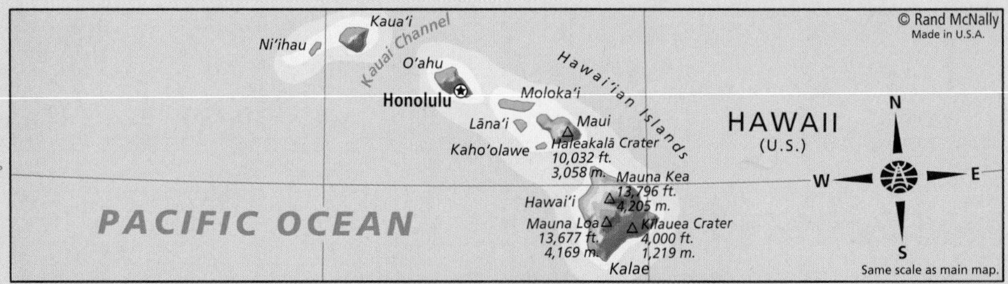

Kaua'i
Kauai Channel
O'ahu
Hawaiian Islands
© Rand McNally
Made in U.S.A.
Ni'ihau
Honolulu ⊛
Moloka'i
Lāna'i
Maui
Haleakalā Crater 10,032 ft. 3,058 m.
HAWAII (U.S.)
N
W E
S
Kaho'olawe
Mauna Kea 13,796 ft. 4,205 m.
Hawai'i
Mauna Loa 13,677 ft. 4,169 m.
Kilauea Crater 4,000 ft. 1,219 m.
Kalae
PACIFIC OCEAN
Same scale as main map.

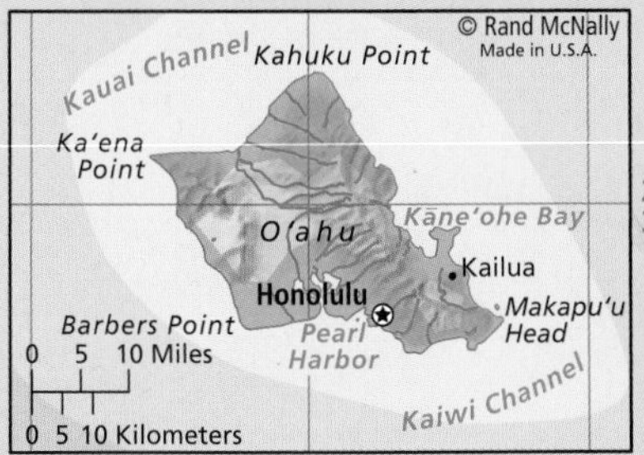

© Rand McNally
Made in U.S.A.
Kauai Channel
Kahuku Point
Ka'ena Point
O'ahu
Kāne'ohe Bay
21° 30'
Kailua
Honolulu ⊛
Makapu'u Head
Barbers Point
Pearl Harbor
0 5 10 Miles
0 5 10 Kilometers
Kaiwi Channel

Location of Alaska and Hawaii

The states of Alaska and Hawaii are separated from the 48 conterminous states. Canada lies between Alaska and the other states. Hawaii is a chain of islands in the middle of the Pacific Ocean.

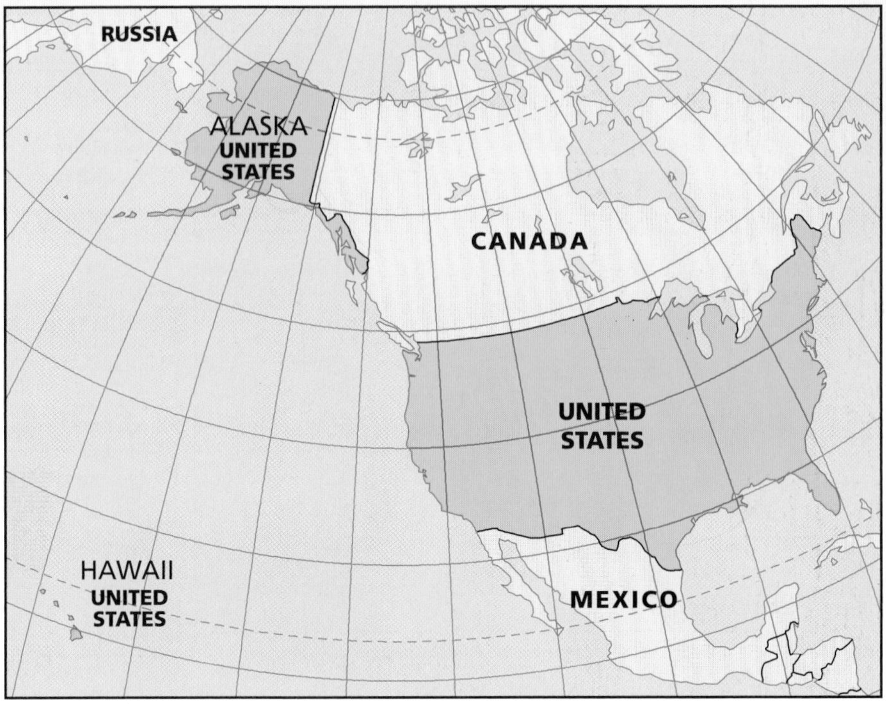

The United States annexed Hawaii in 1898. It became the 50th state in 1959. This photo shows the coast of Maui, the second-largest of the Hawai'ian islands.

The United States purchased the vast territory of Alaska from Russia in 1867. When Alaska became the 49th U.S. state in 1959, it increased the size of the country by nearly one-fifth.

Indian Reservations of the Conterminous United States

About two million Native Americans, or American Indians, live in the United States. Half of them live on or near reservations.

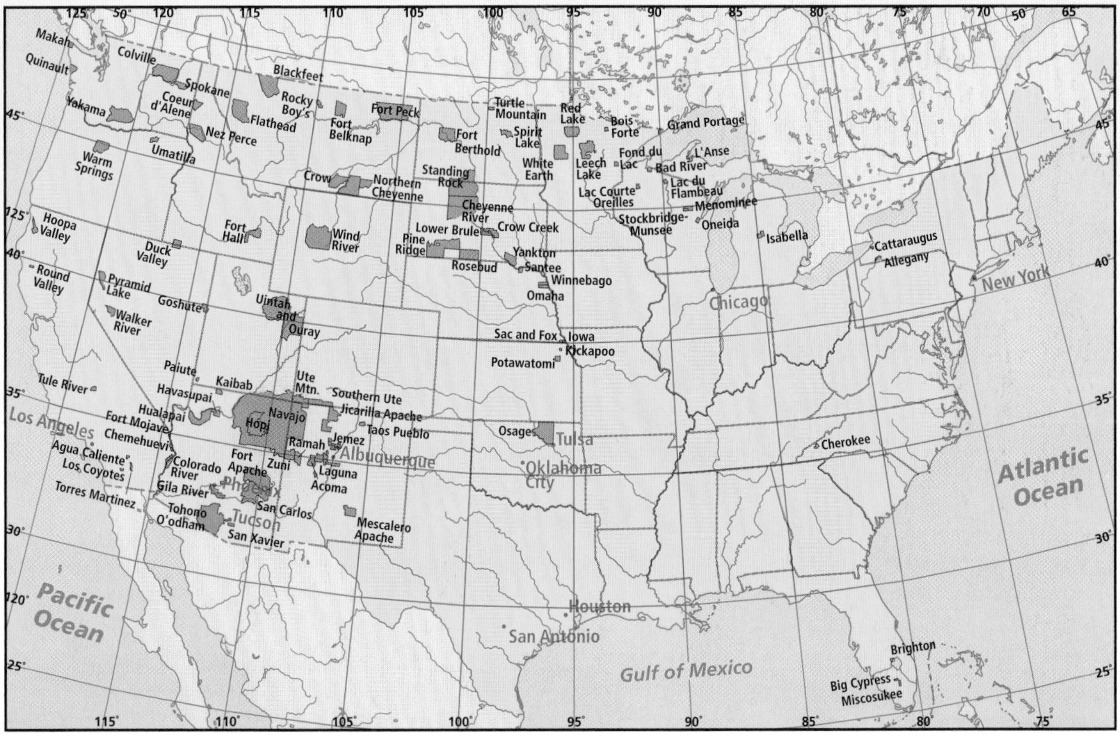

Pueblo Indian ruins in New Mexico reflect an ancient culture.

The Flathead Indian Reservation in Montana.

A Sioux powwow dancer in full costume.

Climate

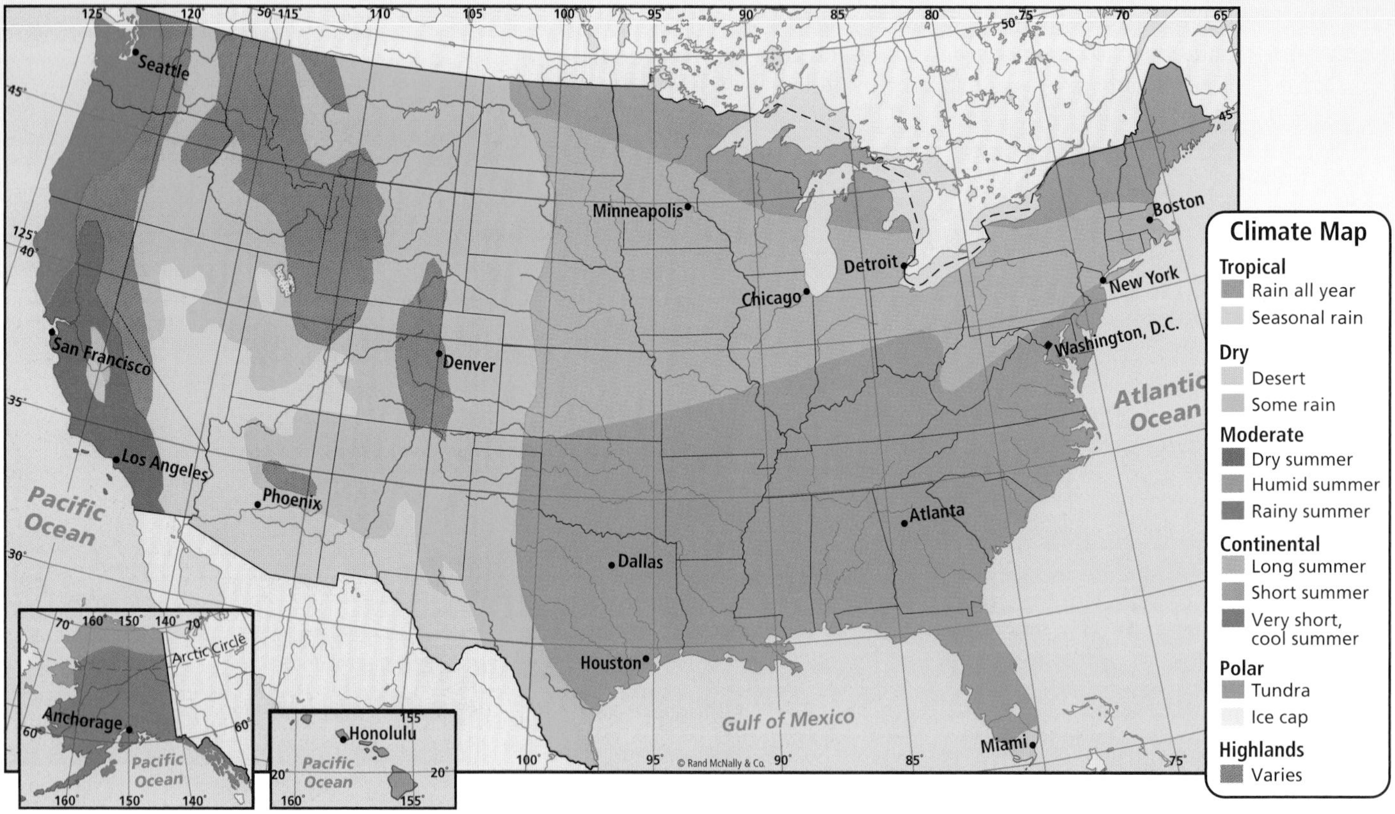
Seattle
Minneapolis
Boston
Detroit
Chicago
New York
San Francisco
Denver
Washington, D.C.
Atlantic Ocean
Los Angeles
Phoenix
Pacific Ocean
Atlanta
Dallas
Houston
Arctic Circle
Anchorage
Pacific Ocean
Honolulu
Pacific Ocean
Gulf of Mexico
Miami
© Rand McNally & Co.
Climate Map
Tropical
Rain all year
Seasonal rain
Dry
Desert
Some rain
Moderate
Dry summer
Humid summer
Rainy summer
Continental
Long summer
Short summer
Very short, cool summer
Polar
Tundra
Ice cap
Highlands
Varies

Economic Activities

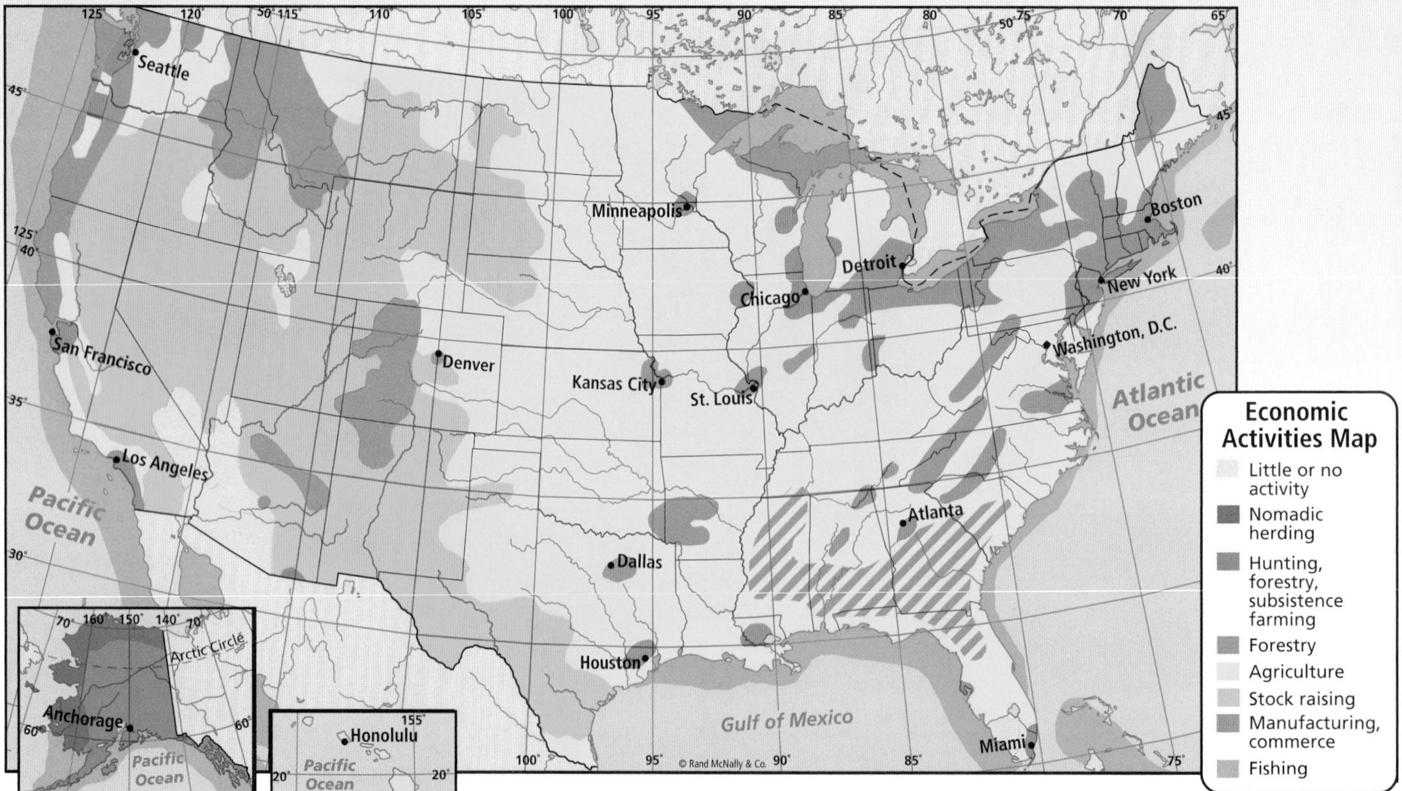
Seattle
Minneapolis
Boston
Detroit
Chicago
New York
San Francisco
Denver
Kansas City
St. Louis
Washington, D.C.
Atlantic Ocean
Los Angeles
Pacific Ocean
Atlanta
Dallas
Houston
Arctic Circle
Anchorage
Pacific Ocean
Honolulu
Pacific Ocean
Gulf of Mexico
Miami
© Rand McNally & Co.
Economic Activities Map
Little or no activity
Nomadic herding
Hunting, forestry, subsistence farming
Forestry
Agriculture
Stock raising
Manufacturing, commerce
Fishing

Population

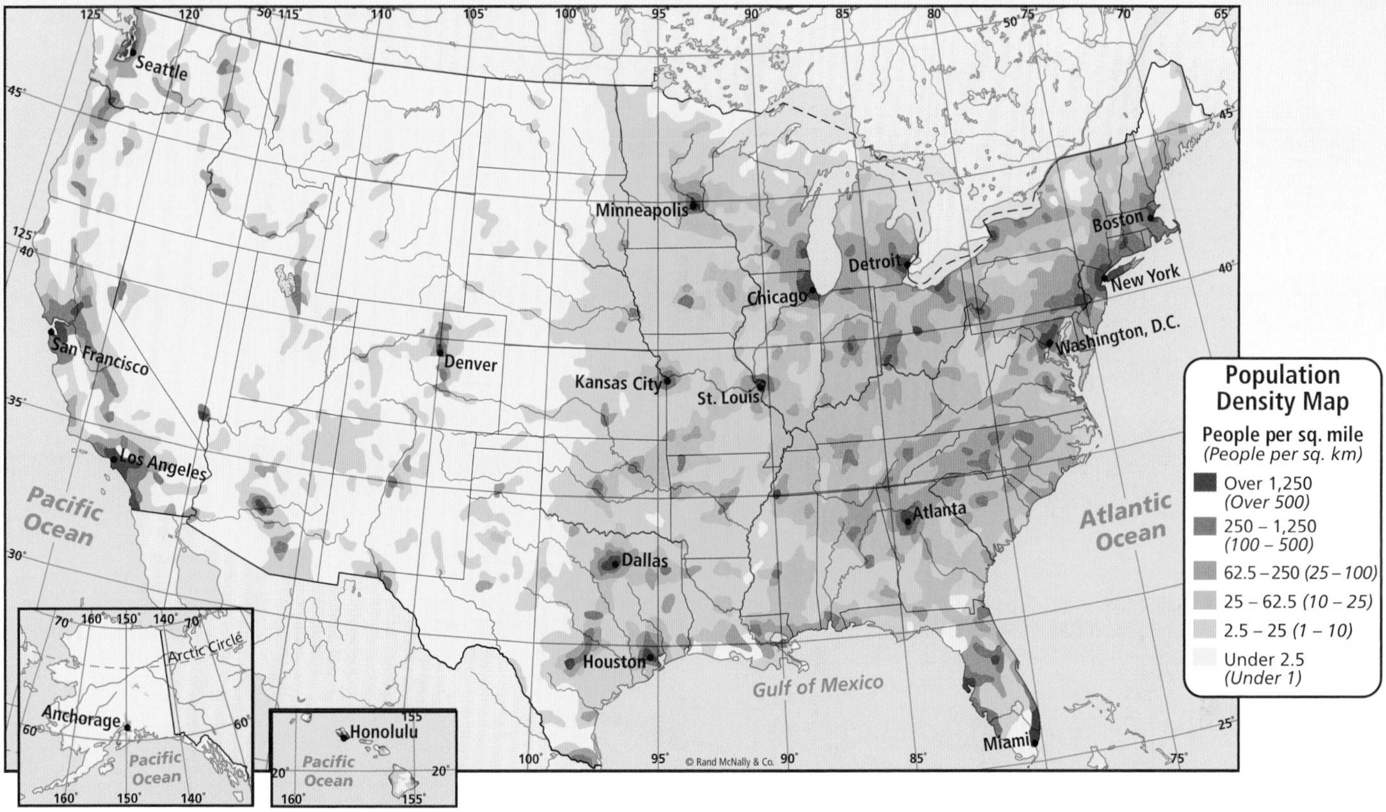

The United States has always been a nation of immigrants. It is one of the most culturally diverse countries in the world.

More than three-fourths of all Americans live in cities and towns.

Urban and Rural Population in the United States

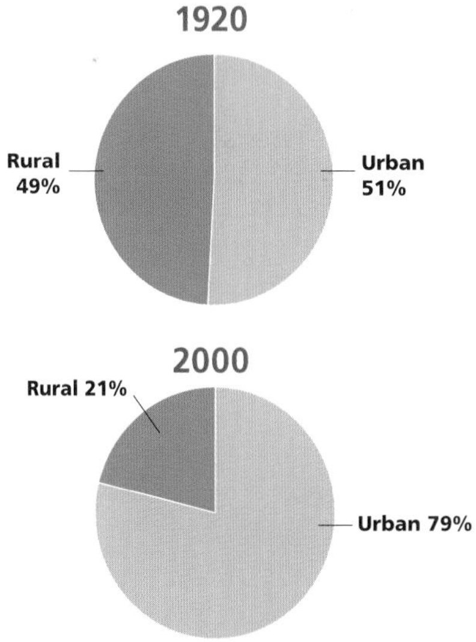

City Landmarks

Many cities have famous landmarks, such as buildings, bridges, and monuments. How many of these landmarks, and their cities, can you name? The answers are at the bottom of the page.

1

2

3

4

5

6

Answers: 1. The Gateway Arch in St. Louis, Missouri 2. The Space Needle in Seattle, Washington 3. The Alamo in San Antonio, Texas 4. The Golden Gate Bridge in San Francisco, California 5. The Empire State Building in New York, New York. 6. The Corn Palace in Mitchell, South Dakota

Environments

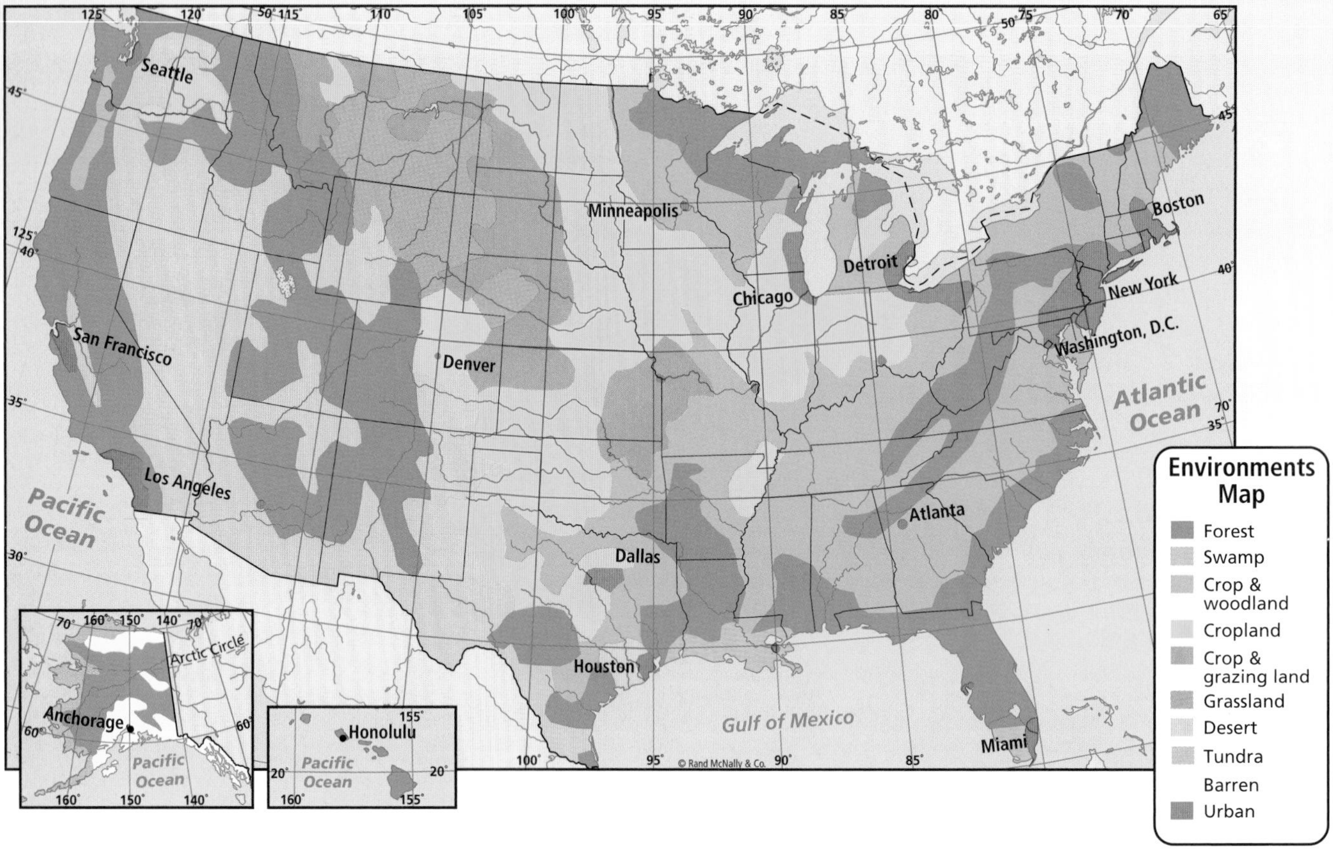

Transportation

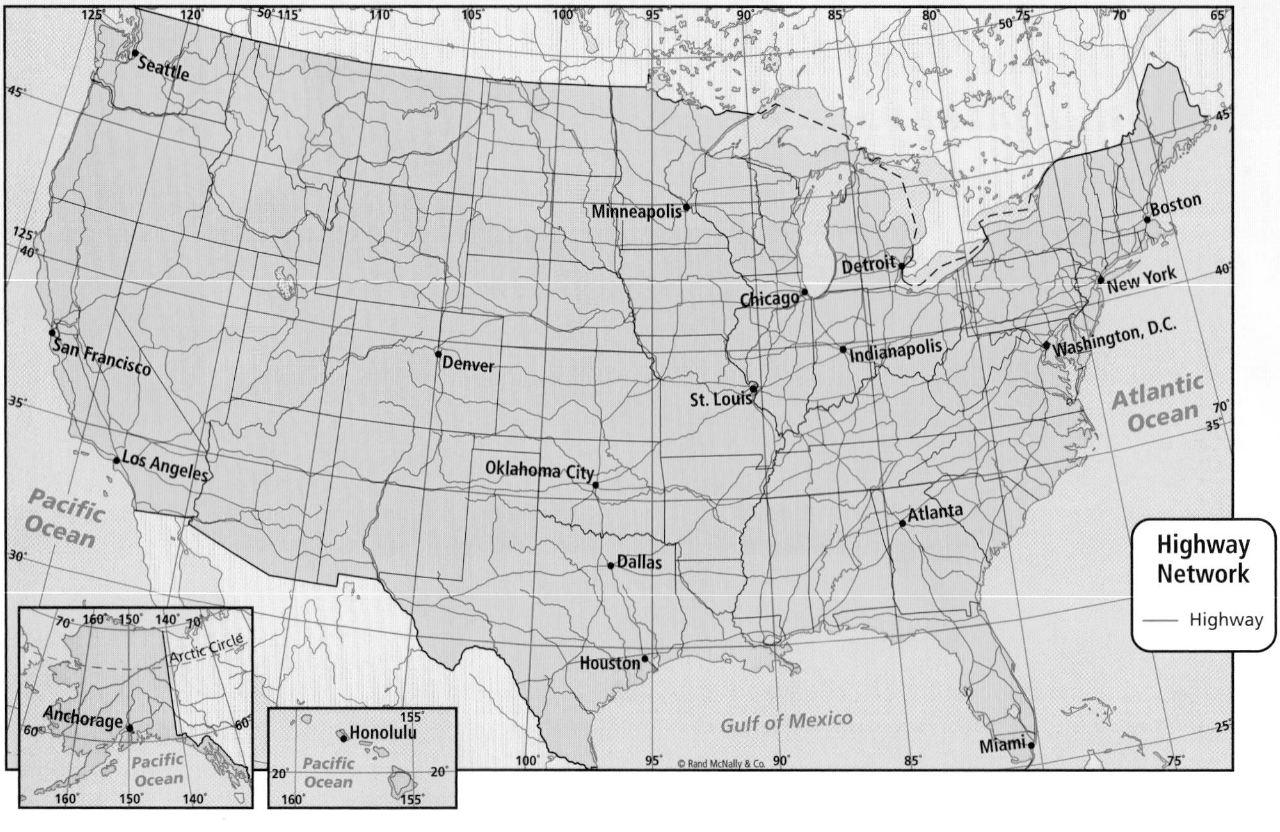

United States Regions

The United States can be divided into regions in many different ways. The maps on this page show two different ways of grouping the states.

There are many opinions about what to call the different regions. There are also many opinions about where the boundary lines between regions belong. What do you call the region where you live? Why?

The pages that follow show information about the regions shown on Map 2.

The Northeast Region

The Northeast Region was settled by people from Western Europe. In fact, the six states east of New York are known as New England. The Northeast was the site of five of the original 13 American colonies. Because much of the land is not suitable for farming, manufacturing has always been important in this region.

Vermont is known for its brilliant fall colors and its abundant dairy farms.

Every state in the Northeast Region except Vermont borders the Atlantic Ocean. This lighthouse is in Maine.

States of the Northeast Region

State	Land Area (square miles)	Population	Capital
Connecticut	4,845	3,510,297	Hartford
Maine	30,862	1,321,505	Augusta
Massachusetts	7,840	6,398,743	Boston
New Hampshire	8,968	1,309,940	Concord
New York	47,214	19,254,630	Albany
Rhode Island	1,045	1,076,189	Providence
Vermont	9,250	623,050	Montpelier

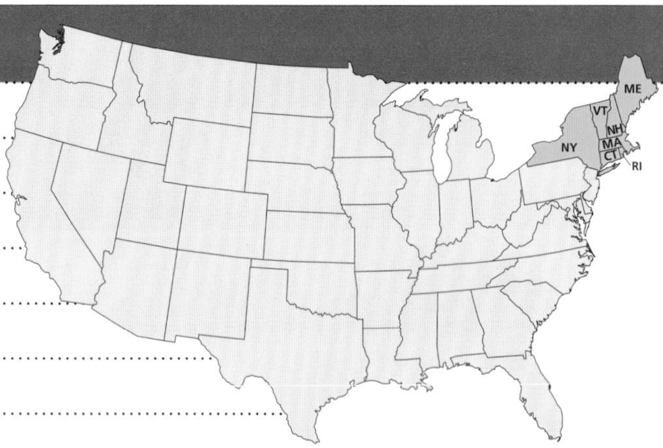

New York, New York, is the most populous city in the Northeast and in the United States.

The original Mayflower *ship brought 102 passengers from England to Massachusetts in 1620. Today, visitors can tour this replica in Plymouth, Massachusetts.*

Niagara Falls, in New York and Canada, provide hydroelectric power to the Northeast.

The Mid-Atlantic Region

The Mid-Atlantic Region is small in size but large in population. Oil, steel, and coal from this region fueled America's industry and power for many decades. Washington, D.C., the national capital, is not part of any state. The letters "D.C." stand for District of Columbia, a federal district sandwiched between Maryland and Virginia.

Philadelphia, Pennsylvania, is the most populous city in the Mid-Atlantic region.

The Senate and House of Representatives meet in the U.S. Capitol Building in Washington, D.C.

States of the Mid-Atlantic Region

State	Land Area (square miles)	Population	Capital
Delaware	1,954	843,254	Dover
Maryland	9,774	5,600,388	Annapolis
New Jersey	7,417	8,717,925	Trenton
Pennsylvania	44,817	12,429,616	Harrisburg
Virginia	39,594	7,567,465	Richmond
West Virginia	24,078	1,816,856	Charleston
Washington, D.C.*	61	550,521	——

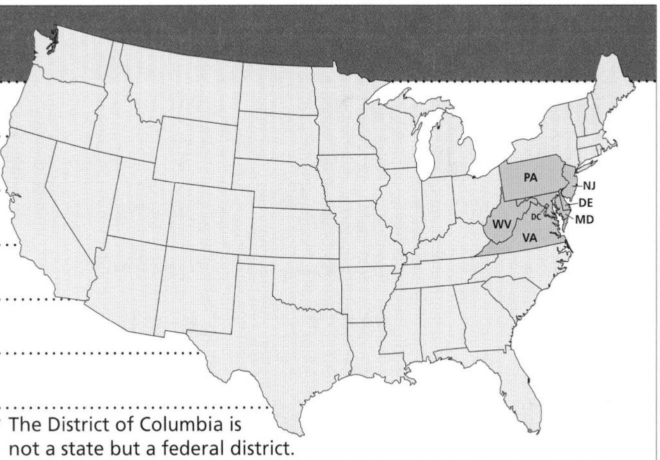

* The District of Columbia is not a state but a federal district.

Much of the land in the Mid-Atlantic Region is used for agriculture. This dairy farm is in Virginia.

Atlantic City, Cape May, and other resort cities draw millions of visitors to the New Jersey shore each year.

West Virginia is the most rural state in the Mid-Atlantic region. This quaint scene is in Babcock State Park.

The Southeast Region

This region stretches from the Atlantic Ocean in the east to the Mississippi River in the west. Its warm, humid climate is ideal for growing many crops, including cotton, sugarcane, and oranges. Manufacturing and tourism are also important to the region's economy.

The Great Smoky Mountains in Tennessee and North Carolina are part of the Appalachian mountain chain.

The space shuttle is launched at Cape Canaveral, Florida.

States of the Southeast Region

State	Land Area (square miles)	Population	Capital
Alabama	50,744	4,557,808	Montgomery
Florida	53,927	17,789,864	Tallahassee
Georgia	57,906	9,072,576	Atlanta
Mississippi	46,907	2,921,088	Jackson
North Carolina	48,711	8,683,242	Raleigh
South Carolina	30,109	4,255,083	Columbia
Tennessee	41,217	5,962,959	Nashville

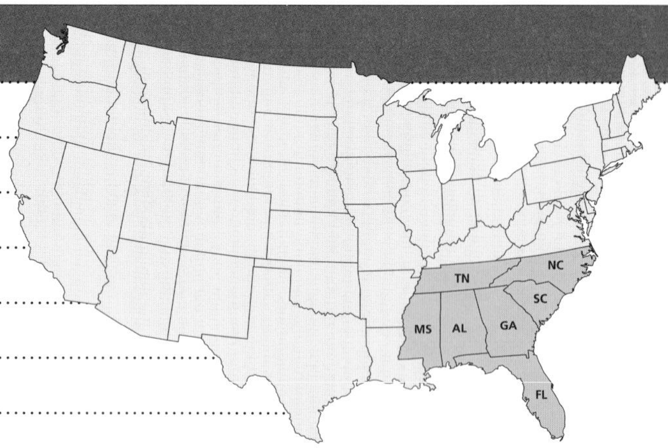

Located near the southern tip of Florida, Miami Beach is a popular vacation spot.

Charleston, South Carolina, is noted for its historic homes and buildings.

Nashville, the capital of Tennessee, is known as Music City, U.S.A.

The Mississippi River is one of the nation's most important waterways.

The Midwest Region

With some of the best farmland in the world, the Midwest is an important agricultural region. Manufacturing also plays a big role in the region's economy. Large cities such as Chicago, Milwaukee, and Cleveland grew up as manufacturing centers along the shores of the Great Lakes.

Wisconsin is a leading producer of dairy products such as cheese and milk.

Chicago, Illinois, is the most populous city in the Midwest Region and the third most populous in the United States.

States of the Midwest Region

State	Land Area (square miles)	Population	Capital
Illinois	55,584	12,763,371	Springfield
Indiana	35,867	6,271,973	Indianapolis
Kentucky	39,728	4,173,405	Frankfort
Michigan	56,804	10,120,860	Lansing
Ohio	40,948	11,464,042	Columbus
Wisconsin	54,310	5,536,201	Madison

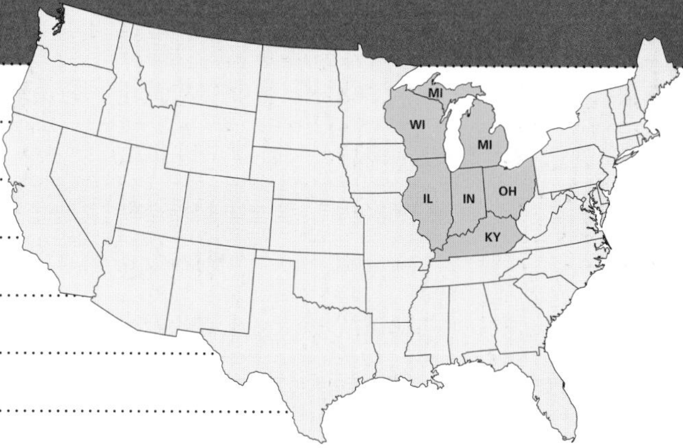

The northernmost part of this region is blanketed by forest and dotted with lakes. This photo shows Lake of the Clouds in northwestern Michigan.

The Ohio River is a major transportation artery. In this photo, a tugboat pushes barges past Cincinnati, Ohio.

Soybeans and corn are two of the most important crops grown in the Midwest Region. This soybean field is in northern Indiana.

The North Central Region

The land in the North Central Region is mostly flat or gently rolling, but it rises steadily from east to west. The climate changes across the region, too: it gradually becomes drier from east to west. Most of the land in the region is used for growing crops and for raising cattle.

The Mississippi River flows past downtown St. Louis and the graceful Gateway Arch.

Sunflowers grow on fertile prairie land in southeastern Minnesota.

States of the North Central Region

State	Land Area (square miles)	Population	Capital
Iowa	55,869	2,966,334	Des Moines
Kansas	81,815	2,744,687	Topeka
Minnesota	79,610	5,132,799	St. Paul
Missouri	68,886	5,800,310	Jefferson City
Nebraska	76,872	1,758,787	Lincoln
North Dakota	68,976	636,677	Bismarck
South Dakota	75,885	775,933	Pierre

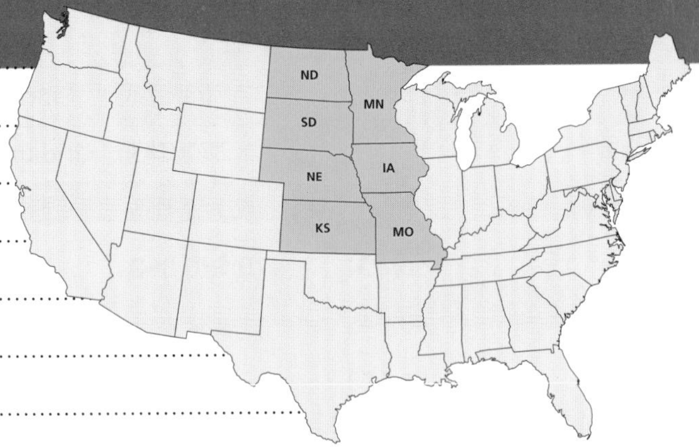

Roughly nine-tenths of the land in Iowa is used for farming.

Abandoned farms are a common sight in the western half of this region. Some areas have been losing population for decades.

In the drier western half of this region, farmers make use of center-pivot irrigation systems, which tap into underground water.

In the Badlands of South Dakota, wind and water have sculpted the land into fantastic shapes.

The South Central Region

The South Central Region is similar to the North Central Region in many ways. From east to west, the land rises and the climate becomes drier. Farmers in this region grow crops such as wheat, cotton, and rice, and they raise cattle and sheep. Oil production is an important part of the economy.

The Dallas-Fort Worth area is the fourth-largest metropolitan area in the United States.

Swamps and bayous cover much of southern Louisiana.

States of the South Central Region

State	Land Area (square miles)	Population	Capital
Arkansas	52,068	2,779,154	Little Rock
Louisiana	43,562	4,523,628	Baton Rouge
Oklahoma	68,667	3,547,884	Oklahoma City
Texas	261,797	22,859,968	Austin

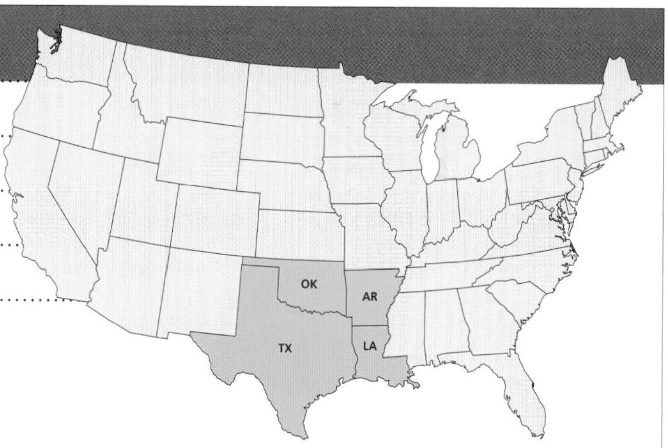

Raising livestock is an important economic activity in Texas and Oklahoma.

Canoeing, hiking, and other types of outdoor recreation are popular in the mountains of northwestern Arkansas.

The western half of this region is far more rugged than the eastern half. This photo is from Big Bend National Park in western Texas.

The Southwest Region

This region stretches from the Great Plains in the east to the Pacific Ocean in the west. In between are high mountains, rugged canyonlands, barren deserts, and areas of rich farmland. In recent decades, the population has boomed in many parts of the region. However, because of the dry climate, lack of water is a growing problem.

San Francisco, California, is located on one of the world's finest natural harbors.

Rock formations called "hoodoos" rise majestically in Utah's Bryce Canyon National Park.

States of the Southwest Region

State	Land Area (square miles)	Population	Capital
Arizona	113,635	5,939,292	Phoenix
California	155,959	36,132,147	Sacramento
Colorado	103,718	4,665,177	Denver
Nevada	109,826	2,414,807	Carson City
New Mexico	121,356	1,928,384	Santa Fe
Utah	82,144	2,469,585	Salt Lake City

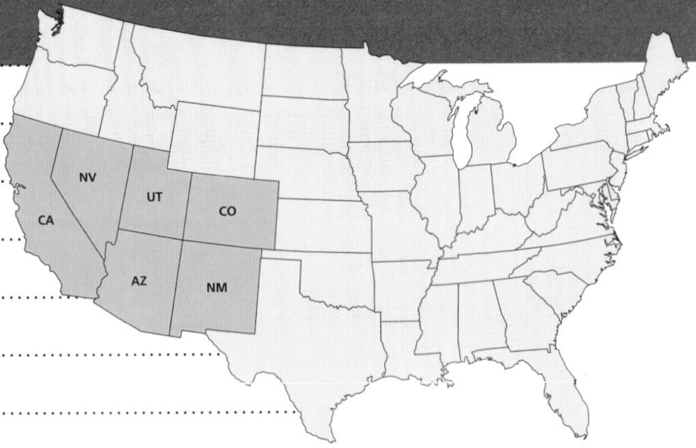

Las Vegas is Nevada's economic center and largest city.

The Cliff Palace in Mesa Verde National Park, Colorado, was built by Native Americans more than 700 years ago.

The Grand Canyon in Arizona was carved by the Colorado River over the course of millions of years.

The Northwest Region

The Northwest Region, like the Southwest Region, extends from the Great Plains in the east to the Pacific Ocean in the west. Much of the land is mountainous and thinly populated. Many of the region's people live near its western edge, between the Pacific Ocean and the Cascade Range.

The jagged peaks of the Teton Range in western Wyoming were sculpted by glaciers.

Seattle, Washington, is a technology center and an important trading partner with nations across the Pacific Ocean.

States of the Northwest Region

State	Land Area (square miles)	Population	Capital
Idaho	82,747	1,429,096	Boise
Montana	145,552	935,670	Helena
Oregon	95,997	3,641,056	Salem
Washington	66,544	6,287,759	Olympia
Wyoming	97,100	509,294	Cheyenne

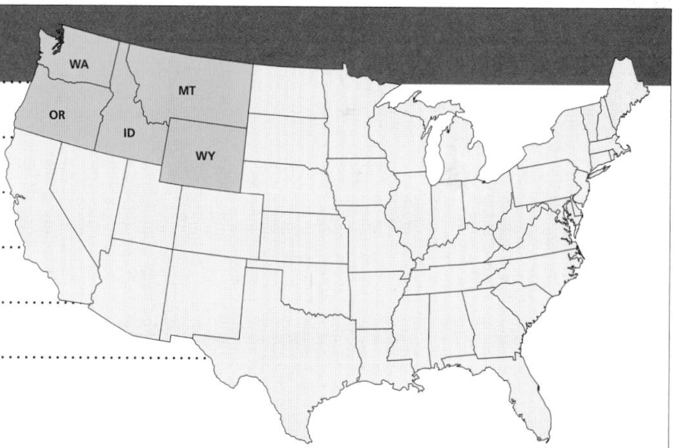

ce-chiseled peaks soar skyward in Montana's Glacier National Park.

Some of the richest agricultural land in the United States is found along the Snake River in Idaho. This photo shows rows of potato plants.

Oregon's Crater Lake lies in the crater of a dormant volcano.

Alaska

Alaska lies hundreds of miles northwest of the "lower 48" states. It is by far the largest of the 50 states. However, because of its cold climate, it has a smaller population than all but three other states. Most Alaskans live in the southern part of the state. Alaska's landforms include broad plains, vast plateaus, and long mountain ranges.

Soaring to 20,320 feet, Alaska's Mount McKinley is the highest peak in North America.

Much of Alaska is pristine wilderness.

Mountains provide a dramatic backdrop for Anchorage, Alaska's most populous city.

Alaska has more than 40 active volcanoes. This photo shows the volcano that forms Augustine Island in the Cook Inlet.

North of the Brooks Range lies a coastal lowland that is home to enormous herds of caribou. This photo shows a caribou bull.

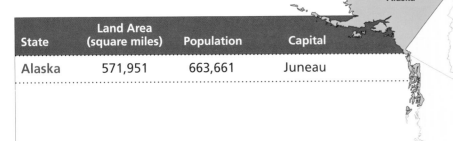

State	Land Area (square miles)	Population	Capital
Alaska	571,951	663,661	Juneau

Hawaii

The islands that make up the state of Hawaii are located in the middle of the Pacific Ocean. The islands are actually the tops of volcanic mountains that rise from the ocean floor. Some of the volcanoes are still active. Because of Hawaii's warm, sunny climate, its beaches, and its spectacular scenery, the state is a popular destination for tourists from other states and from all over the world.

Honolulu is Hawaii's capital, most populous city, and main port. It stretches for about 10 miles along the coast of O'ahu.

Kilauea, located on the "Big Island" of Hawai'i, is one of the most active volcanoes in the world.

Hawaii's pleasant climate is a result of its location in the tropics, the fact that it is surrounded by ocean, and the moderating effect of trade winds.

Rugged cliffs rise thousands of feet above the Pacific Ocean along the Na Pali Coast on the island of Kaua'i.

Fertile volcanic soils and a tropical climate make Hawaii ideal for agriculture. This photo shows a taro field on the island of Kaua'i.

State	Land Area (square miles)	Population	Capital
Hawaii	6,423	1,275,194	Honolulu

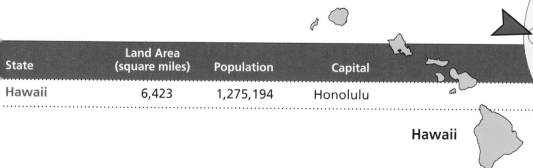

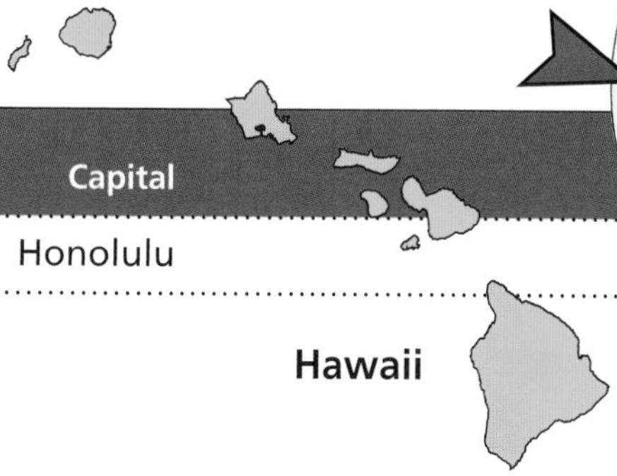

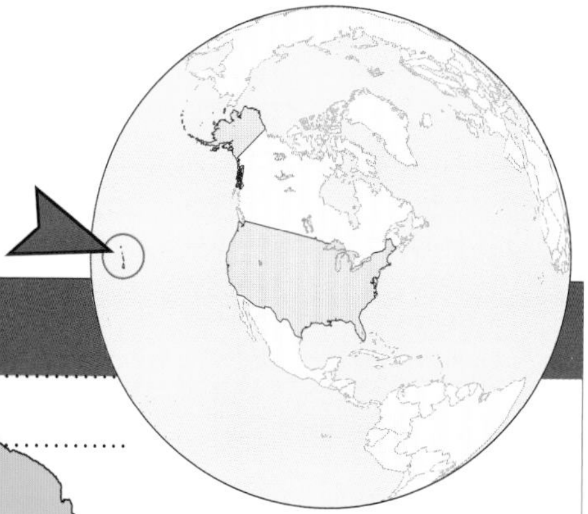

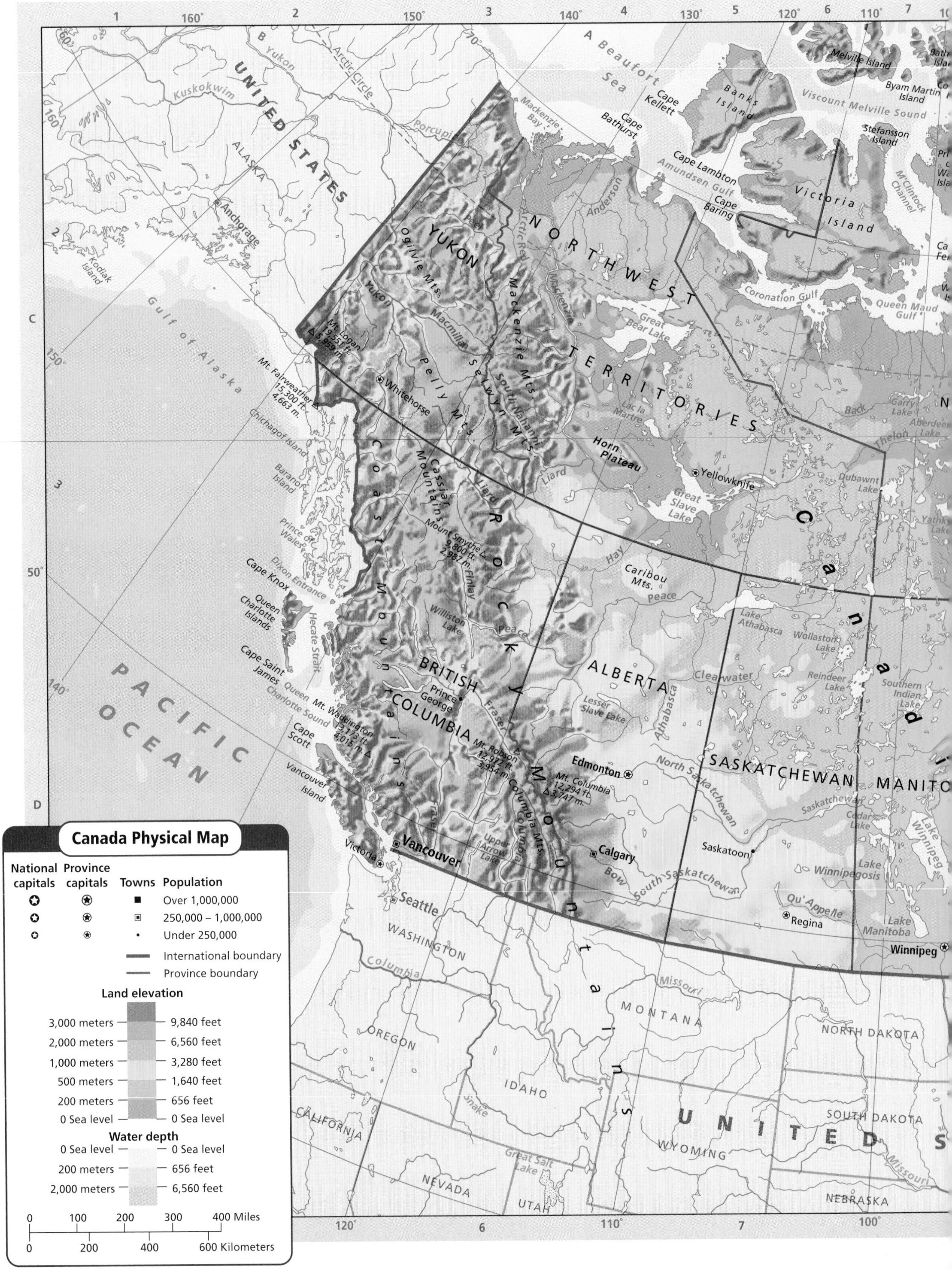
Canada Physical Map
National capitals
Province capitals
Towns
Population
Over 1,000,000
250,000 – 1,000,000
Under 250,000
International boundary
Province boundary
Land elevation
3,000 meters — 9,840 feet
2,000 meters — 6,560 feet
1,000 meters — 3,280 feet
500 meters — 1,640 feet
200 meters — 656 feet
0 Sea level — 0 Sea level
Water depth
0 Sea level — 0 Sea level
200 meters — 656 feet
2,000 meters — 6,560 feet
0 100 200 300 400 Miles
0 200 400 600 Kilometers
PACIFIC OCEAN
UNITED STATES
ALASKA
Anchorage
Kodiak Island
Gulf of Alaska
Kuskokwim
Yukon
Arctic Circle
Porcupine
Beaufort Sea
Mackenzie Bay
Cape Kellett
Cape Bathurst
Banks Island
Melville Island
Byam Martin Island
Viscount Melville Sound
Stefansson Island
Cape Lambton
Amundsen Gulf
Cape Baring
Victoria Island
M'Clintock Channel
Coronation Gulf
Queen Maud Gulf
YUKON
NORTHWEST TERRITORIES
Anderson
Peel
Arctic Red
Mackenzie
Ogilvie Mts.
Macmillan
Mackenzie Mts.
Great Bear Lake
Mt. Logan 19,551 ft. 5,959 m.
Mt. Fairweather 15,300 ft. 4,663 m.
Whitehorse
Pelly Mts.
Selwyn Mts.
South Nahanni
Lac la Martre
Horn Plateau
Yellowknife
Great Slave Lake
Liard
Back
Garry Lake
Aberdeen Lake
Thelon
Dubawnt Lake
Chichagof Island
Baranof Island
Prince of Wales Island
Dixon Entrance
Cape Knox
Queen Charlotte Islands
Hecate Strait
Cape Saint James
Queen Charlotte Sound
Cape Scott
Vancouver Island
Victoria
Vancouver
Seattle
Coast Mountains
Cassiar Mountains
Mount Smythe 9,800 ft. 2,987 m.
Finlay
Williston Lake
Peace
ROCKY MOUNTAINS
BRITISH COLUMBIA
Prince George
Mt. Waddington 13,173 ft. 4,015 m.
Fraser
Mt. Robson 12,972 ft. 3,954 m.
Columbia
Columbia Mts.
Upper Arrow Lake
Mt. Columbia 12,294 ft. 3,747 m.
Hay
Caribou Mts.
ALBERTA
Lesser Slave Lake
Athabasca
Clearwater
Edmonton
Calgary
Bow
North Saskatchewan
South Saskatchewan
Lake Athabasca
Wollaston Lake
Reindeer Lake
Southern Indian Lake
SASKATCHEWAN
MANITOBA
Saskatoon
Saskatchewan
Cedar Lake
Lake Winnipegosis
Lake Winnipeg
Qu'Appelle
Regina
Lake Manitoba
Winnipeg
Canada
WASHINGTON
OREGON
IDAHO
MONTANA
NORTH DAKOTA
SOUTH DAKOTA
WYOMING
NEBRASKA
CALIFORNIA
NEVADA
UTAH
Great Salt Lake
Snake
Missouri
UNITED STATES
160° 150° 140° 130° 120° 110° 100°
70° 60° 50°
1 2 3 4 5 6 7
A B C D

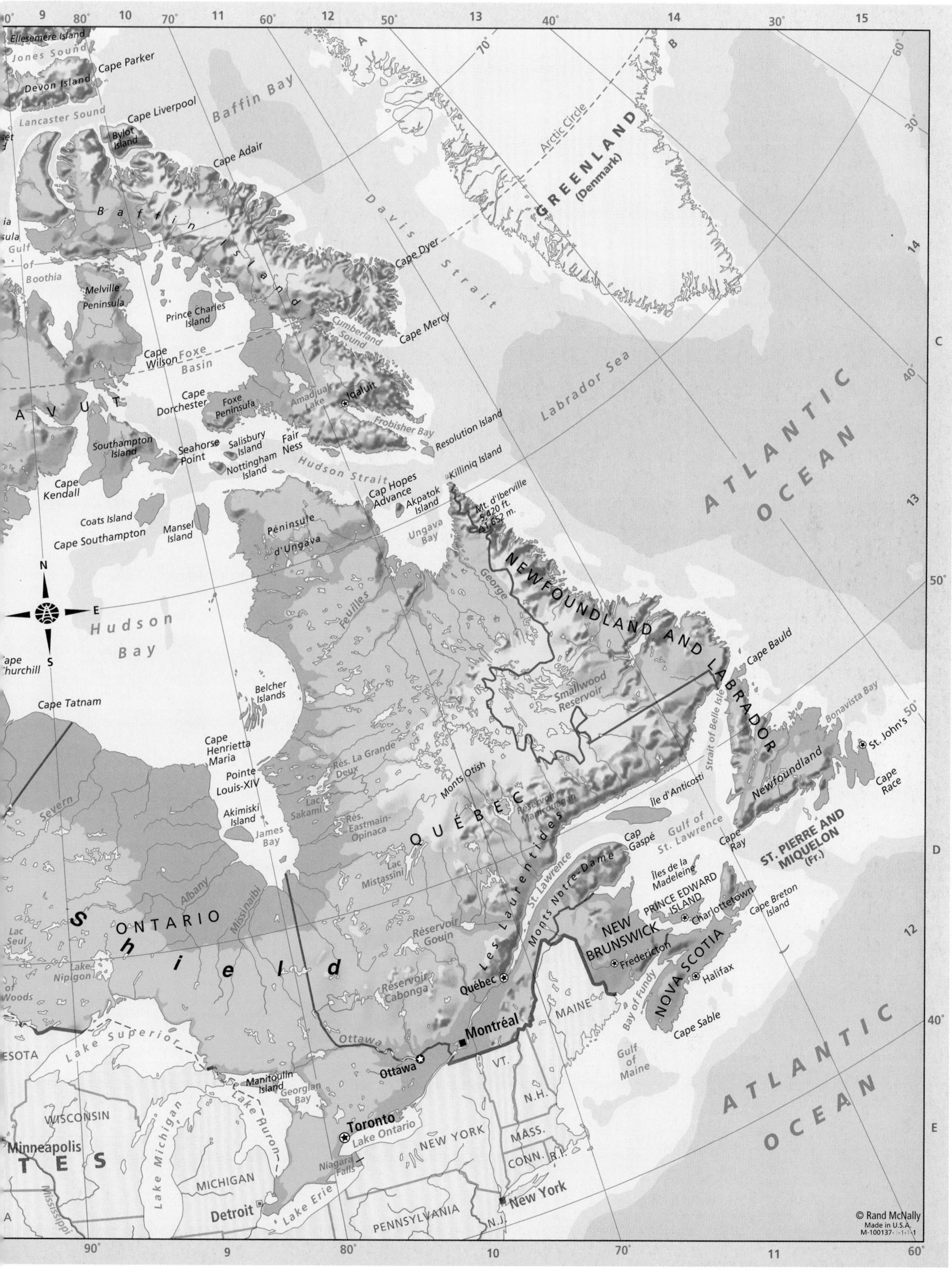
Ellesmere Island
Jones Sound
Cape Parker
Devon Island
Lancaster Sound
Cape Liverpool
Baffin Bay
Bylot Island
Cape Adair
Baffin Island
Gulf of Boothia
Melville Peninsula
Prince Charles Island
Cape Dyer
Davis Strait
Cumberland Sound
Cape Mercy
Cape Wilson
Foxe Basin
Cape Dorchester
Foxe Peninsula
Amadjuak Lake
Iqaluit
Frobisher Bay
Resolution Island
Southampton Island
Seahorse Point
Salisbury Island
Nottingham Island
Fair Ness
Hudson Strait
Killiniq Island
Cape Kendall
Cap Hopes Advance
Akpatok Island
Mt. d'Iberville 5,420 ft. 1,652 m.
Coats Island
Cape Southampton
Mansel Island
Péninsule d'Ungava
Ungava Bay
George
Feuilles
N
E
S
Hudson Bay
Cape Churchill
Cape Tatnam
Belcher Islands
Cape Henrietta Maria
Pointe Louis-XIV
Akimiski Island
James Bay
Severn
Rés. La Grande Deux
Lac Sakami
Rés. Eastmain-Opinaca
Lac Mistassini
Monts Otish
Réservoir Manicouagan
QUÉBEC
Smallwood Reservoir
NEWFOUNDLAND AND LABRADOR
Cape Bauld
Strait of Belle Isle
Bonavista Bay
St. John's
Newfoundland
Cape Race
Île d'Anticosti
Gulf of St. Lawrence
Cape Ray
Cap Gaspé
ST. PIERRE AND MIQUELON (Fr.)
Îles de la Madeleine
PRINCE EDWARD ISLAND
Charlottetown
Cape Breton Island
Monts Notre-Dame
St. Lawrence
Les Laurentides
NEW BRUNSWICK
Fredericton
NOVA SCOTIA
Halifax
Bay of Fundy
Cape Sable
Gulf of Maine
ONTARIO
Shield
Albany
Missinaibi
Lac Seul
Lake Nipigon
Réservoir Gouin
Réservoir Cabonga
Québec
Montréal
Ottawa
MAINE
VT.
N.H.
MASS.
CONN.
R.I.
NEW YORK
New York
N.J.
PENNSYLVANIA
Lake Superior
Manitoulin Island
Georgian Bay
Lake Huron
Lake Michigan
WISCONSIN
MICHIGAN
Minneapolis
Toronto
Lake Ontario
Niagara Falls
Lake Erie
Detroit
Mississippi
GREENLAND (Denmark)
Arctic Circle
Labrador Sea
ATLANTIC OCEAN
ATLANTIC OCEAN
© Rand McNally
Made in U.S.A.

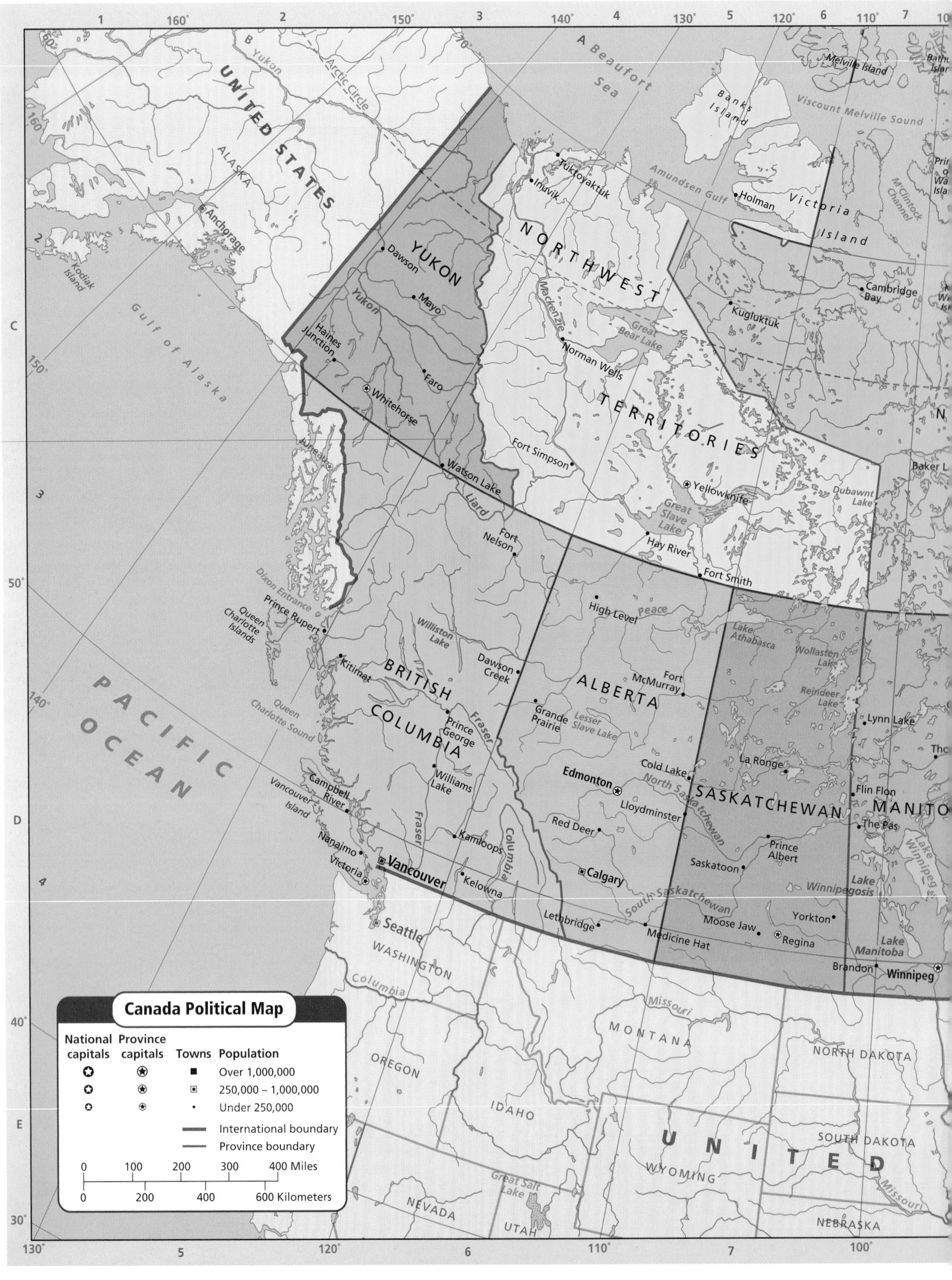
Canada Political Map
National capitals
Province capitals
Towns
Population
Over 1,000,000
250,000 – 1,000,000
Under 250,000
International boundary
Province boundary
0
100
200
300
400 Miles
0
200
400
600 Kilometers
UNITED STATES
ALASKA
Anchorage
Kodiak Island
Gulf of Alaska
Yukon
Arctic Circle
Beaufort Sea
Banks Island
Viscount Melville Sound
Melville Island
Amundsen Gulf
Victoria Island
M'Clintock Channel
Tuktoyaktuk
Inuvik
Holman
Cambridge Bay
Kugluktuk
YUKON
Dawson
Mayo
Haines Junction
Faro
Whitehorse
Watson Lake
Liard
NORTHWEST TERRITORIES
Mackenzie
Great Bear Lake
Norman Wells
Fort Simpson
Yellowknife
Great Slave Lake
Hay River
Fort Smith
Dubawnt Lake
Baker L
Juneau
Fort Nelson
Dixon Entrance
Prince Rupert
Queen Charlotte Islands
Williston Lake
Kitimat
BRITISH COLUMBIA
Dawson Creek
Fraser
Prince George
Williams Lake
Queen Charlotte Sound
PACIFIC OCEAN
Vancouver Island
Campbell River
Nanaimo
Victoria
Vancouver
Kamloops
Kelowna
Columbia
High Level
Peace
ALBERTA
Fort McMurray
Grande Prairie
Lesser Slave Lake
Edmonton
Cold Lake
North Saskatchewan
Lloydminster
Red Deer
Calgary
South Saskatchewan
Lethbridge
Medicine Hat
Lake Athabasca
Wollaston Lake
Reindeer Lake
SASKATCHEWAN
La Ronge
Prince Albert
Saskatoon
Moose Jaw
Regina
Yorkton
Lynn Lake
Flin Flon
The Pas
MANITO
Lake Winnipegosis
Lake Winnipeg
Lake Manitoba
Brandon
Winnipeg
Seattle
WASHINGTON
Columbia
Missouri
MONTANA
NORTH DAKOTA
OREGON
IDAHO
WYOMING
SOUTH DAKOTA
Great Salt Lake
NEVADA
UTAH
NEBRASKA
UNITED
160°
150°
140°
130°
120°
110°
100°
70°
50°
40°
30°
1
2
3
4
5
6
7
C
D
E

GREENLAND (Denmark)
Ellesmere Island
Devon Island
Lancaster Sound
Baffin Bay
Pond Inlet
Baffin Island
Gulf of Boothia
Igloolik
Davis Strait
Arctic Circle
Godthåb
Pangnirtung
Cumberland Sound
Foxe Basin
Repulse Bay
Iqaluit
Labrador Sea
Southampton Island
Hudson Strait
ATLANTIC OCEAN
Salluit
Rankin Inlet
Coats Island
Mansel Island
Ungava Bay
NEWFOUNDLAND AND LABRADOR
Kuujjuaq
Feuilles
Cartwright
Hudson Bay
Inukjuak
Happy Valley-Goose Bay
St. Anthony
Belcher Islands
Strait of Belle Isle
Gander
St. John's
Grand Falls-Windsor
Newfoundland
Labrador City
Corner Brook
Île d'Anticosti
Chisasibi
QUÉBEC
Réservoir Manicouagan
Severn
James Bay
Sept-Îles
Gulf of St. Lawrence
ST. PIERRE AND MIQUELON (Fr.)
Waskaganish
Lac Mistassini
Gaspé
Îles de la Madeleine
Sydney
Albany
Moosonee
Baie-Comeau
St. Lawrence
Cape Breton Island
Chibougamau
Rimouski
PRINCE EDWARD ISLAND
Charlottetown
ONTARIO
Réservoir Gouin
Saguenay
Edmundston
NEW BRUNSWICK
Moncton
Kapuskasing
Lake Nipigon
Rouyn-Noranda
Saint John
NOVA SCOTIA
Halifax
Québec
Fredericton
Timmins
Drummondville
Trois-Rivières
Sherbrooke
MAINE
Yarmouth
Thunder Bay
Lake Superior
Sudbury
North Bay
Montréal
Sault Sainte Marie
Ottawa
VT.
Gulf of Maine
Georgian Bay
Kingston
N.H.
Peterborough
WISCONSIN
Barrie
Toronto
Lake Ontario
Minneapolis
NEW YORK
MASS.
Lake Huron
Lake Michigan
Kitchener
Hamilton
CONN.
R.I.
MICHIGAN
London
Sarnia
Windsor
Detroit
Lake Erie
New York
PENNSYLVANIA
N.J.
Mississippi
© Rand McNally
Made in U.S.A.

Population

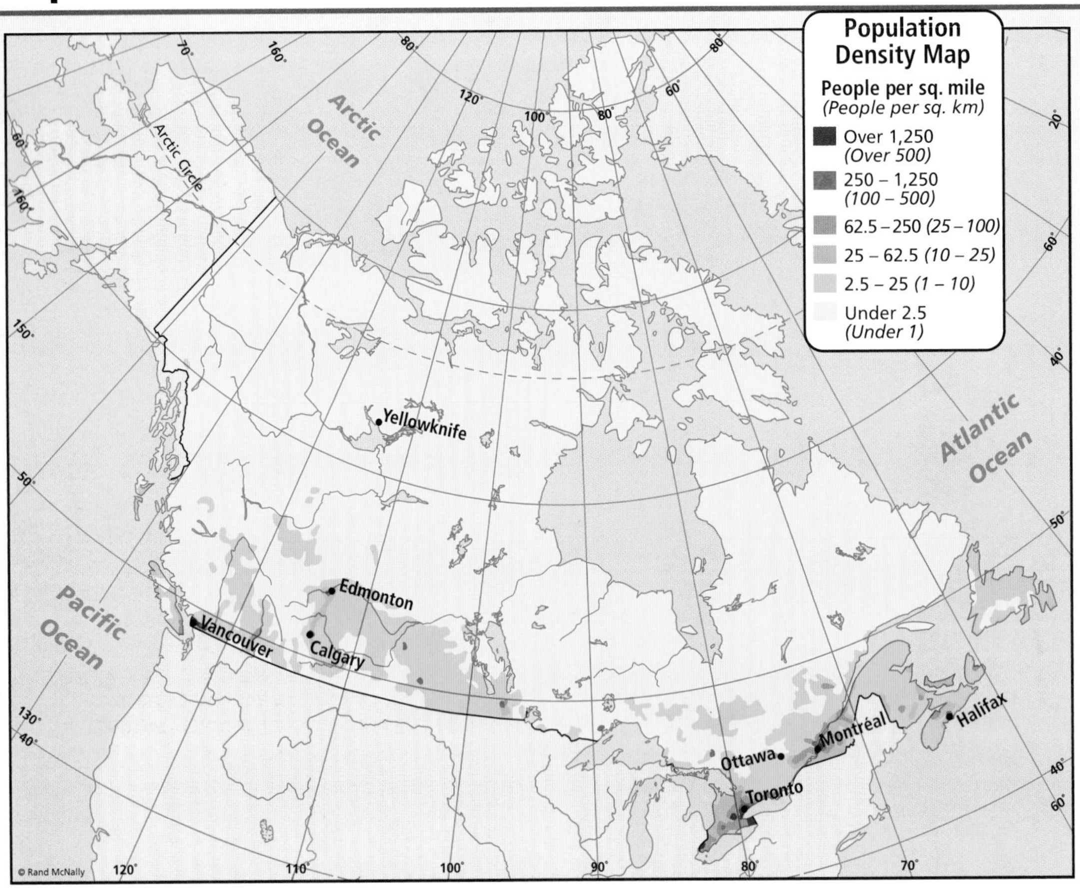

Approximately 90% of Canada's population lives within 100 miles of the United States border.

Canada's Population Growth since 1851

Canada's population grew rapidly in the twentieth century when many immigrants arrived from other countries.

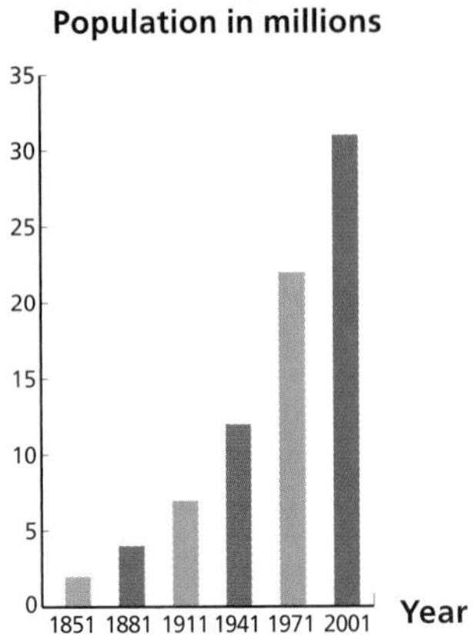

Environments

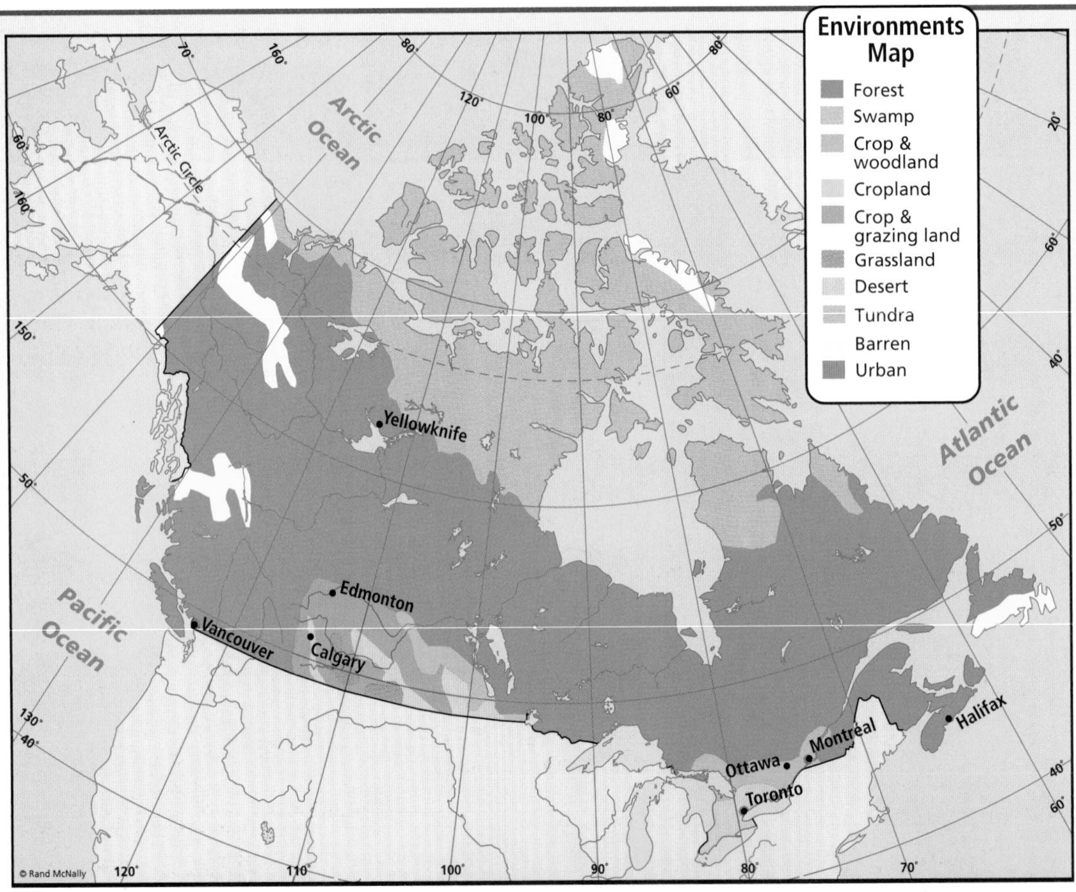

The Canadian Rocky Mountains extend through Alberta, British Columbia, and the Yukon territory.

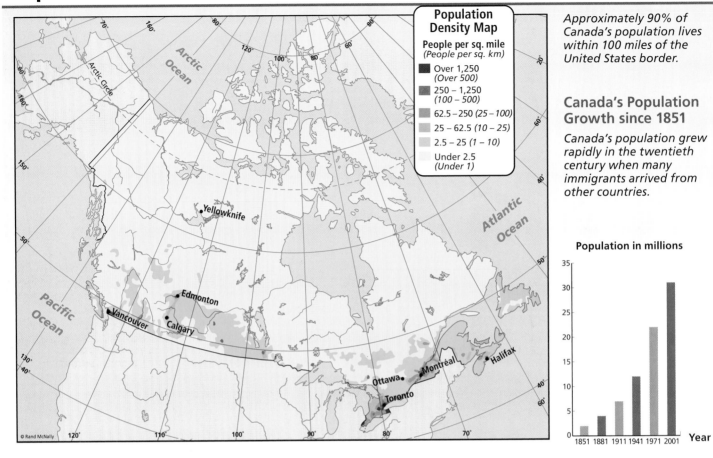

The rocky plateau known as the Canadian Shield ends as headlands at the water's edge. Lighthouses help to guide ships away from the danger.

Transportation

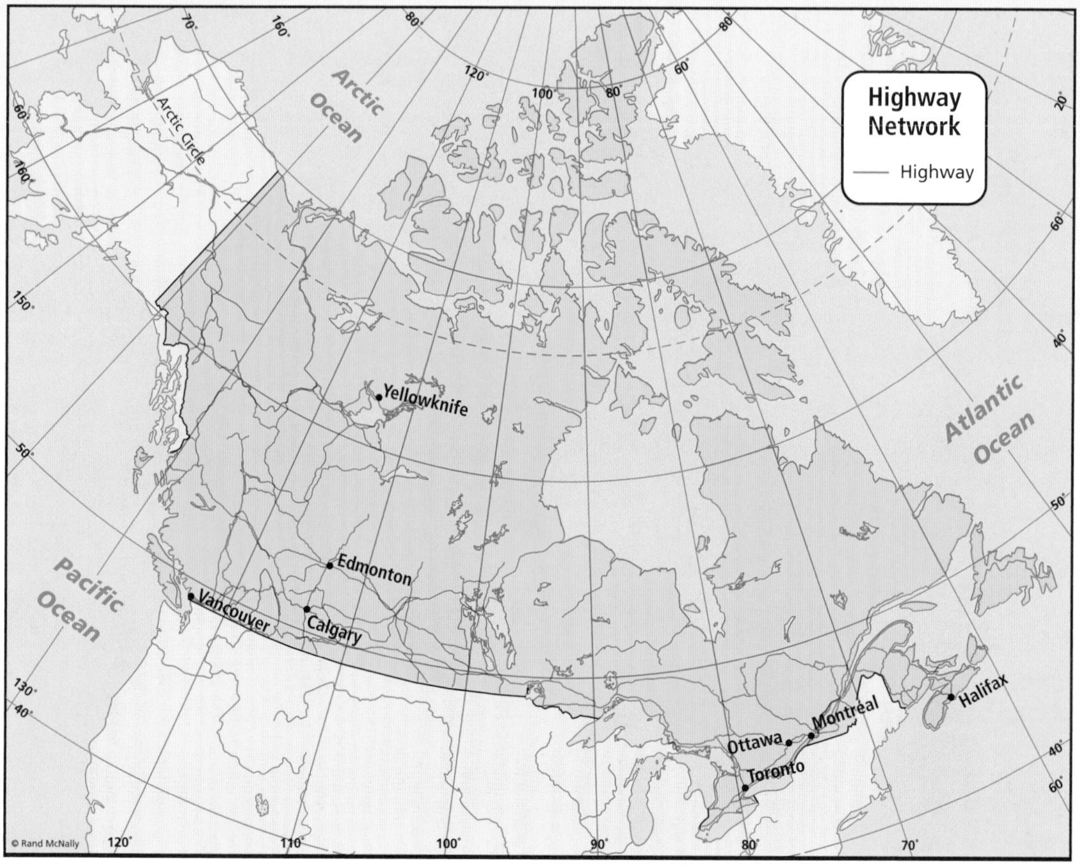

Scenic roads wind along the coasts of Canada's Maritime Provinces.

Canada's highways help to connect widely separated clusters of people across the country's vast expanse.

Economic Activities

Most of Canada's grain is grown in the "prairie provinces" of Alberta, Saskatchewan, and Manitoba.

Atlantic coast fishing is important to Canada's economy.

Toronto is Canada's financial center and the headquarters for many of the country's largest companies.

Canada's Economy

Services—such as banking, transportation, and government—account for more than two-thirds of Canada's economic output.

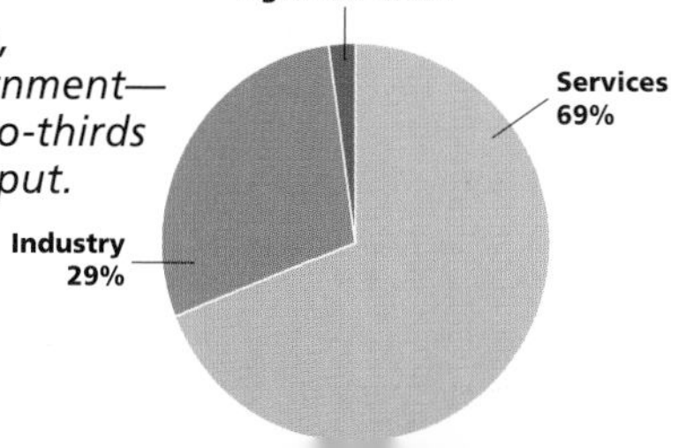
Agriculture 2%
Services 69%
Industry 29%

World Lumber Exports

Canada, with its vast forestlands, accounts for nearly one-third of the world's lumber exports.

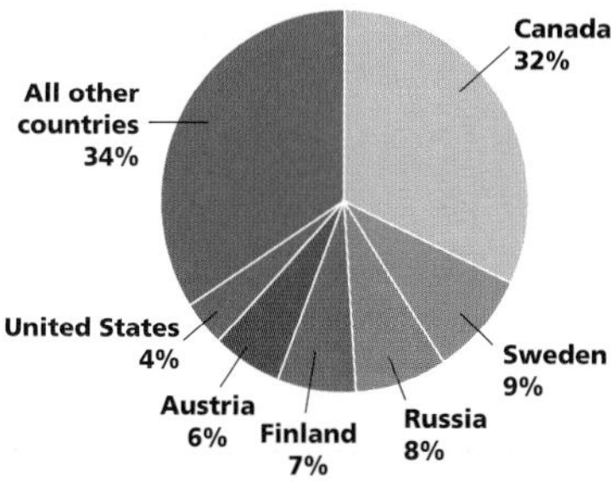
Canada 32%
All other countries 34%
United States 4%
Austria 6%
Finland 7%
Russia 8%
Sweden 9%

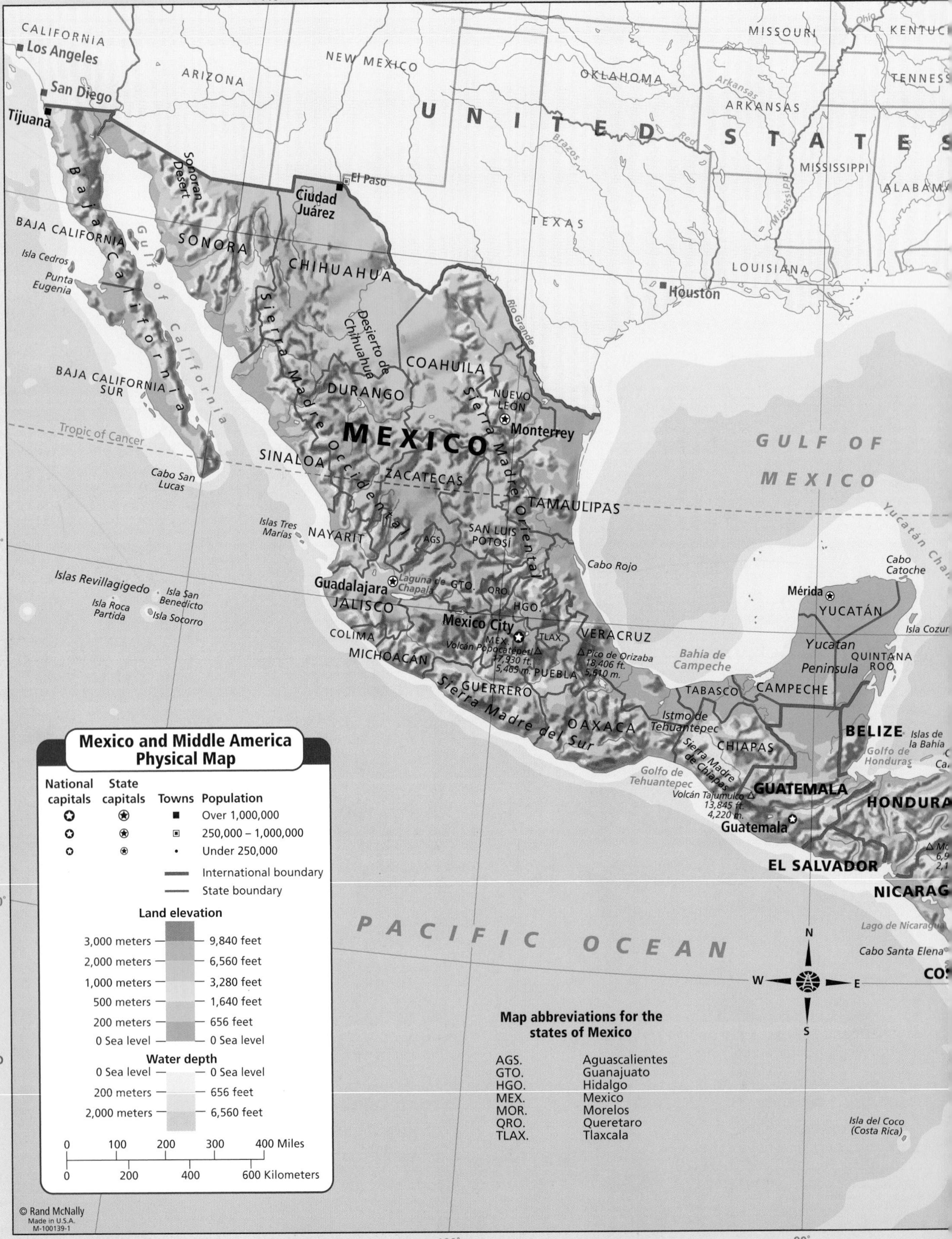
Mexico and Middle America
Physical Map
National capitals
State capitals
Towns
Population
Over 1,000,000
250,000 – 1,000,000
Under 250,000
International boundary
State boundary
Land elevation
3,000 meters — 9,840 feet
2,000 meters — 6,560 feet
1,000 meters — 3,280 feet
500 meters — 1,640 feet
200 meters — 656 feet
0 Sea level — 0 Sea level
Water depth
0 Sea level — 0 Sea level
200 meters — 656 feet
2,000 meters — 6,560 feet
0 100 200 300 400 Miles
0 200 400 600 Kilometers
Map abbreviations for the states of Mexico
AGS. Aguascalientes
GTO. Guanajuato
HGO. Hidalgo
MEX. Mexico
MOR. Morelos
QRO. Queretaro
TLAX. Tlaxcala
1
2
3
110°
100°
90°
A
B
C
D
30°
20°
10°
CALIFORNIA
Los Angeles
San Diego
Tijuana
ARIZONA
NEW MEXICO
OKLAHOMA
MISSOURI
KENTUC
TENNESS
ARKANSAS
MISSISSIPPI
ALABAMA
TEXAS
LOUISIANA
Houston
UNITED STATES
Ohio
Arkansas
Red
Brazos
Mississippi
El Paso
Ciudad Juárez
Sonoran Desert
Baja California
BAJA CALIFORNIA
Isla Cedros
Punta Eugenia
Gulf of California
SONORA
CHIHUAHUA
Desierto de Chihuahua
Sierra Madre Occidental
COAHUILA
Rio Grande
BAJA CALIFORNIA SUR
DURANGO
NUEVO LEON
Monterrey
Sierra Madre Oriental
MEXICO
Tropic of Cancer
SINALOA
ZACATECAS
Cabo San Lucas
TAMAULIPAS
Islas Tres Marias
NAYARIT
AGS.
SAN LUIS POTOSÍ
Cabo Rojo
Islas Revillagigedo
Isla San Benedicto
Isla Roca Partida
Isla Socorro
Guadalajara
Laguna de Chapala
GTO.
QRO.
JALISCO
HGO.
Mexico City
MEX.
TLAX.
VERACRUZ
COLIMA
MICHOACÁN
Volcán Popocatépetl 17,930 ft. 5,465 m.
Pico de Orizaba 18,406 ft. 5,610 m.
PUEBLA
GUERRERO
Sierra Madre del Sur
OAXACA
Bahía de Campeche
TABASCO
CAMPECHE
Istmo de Tehuantepec
CHIAPAS
Sierra Madre de Chiapas
Golfo de Tehuantepec
Volcán Tajumulco 13,845 ft. 4,220 m.
GULF OF MEXICO
Yucatán Channel
Cabo Catoche
Mérida
YUCATÁN
Isla Cozumel
Yucatan Peninsula
QUINTANA ROO
BELIZE
Islas de la Bahia
Golfo de Honduras
GUATEMALA
Guatemala
HONDURA
EL SALVADOR
NICARAG
Lago de Nicaragua
Cabo Santa Elena
PACIFIC OCEAN
N
S
E
W
Isla del Coco (Costa Rica)
© Rand McNally
Made in U.S.A.
M-100139-1

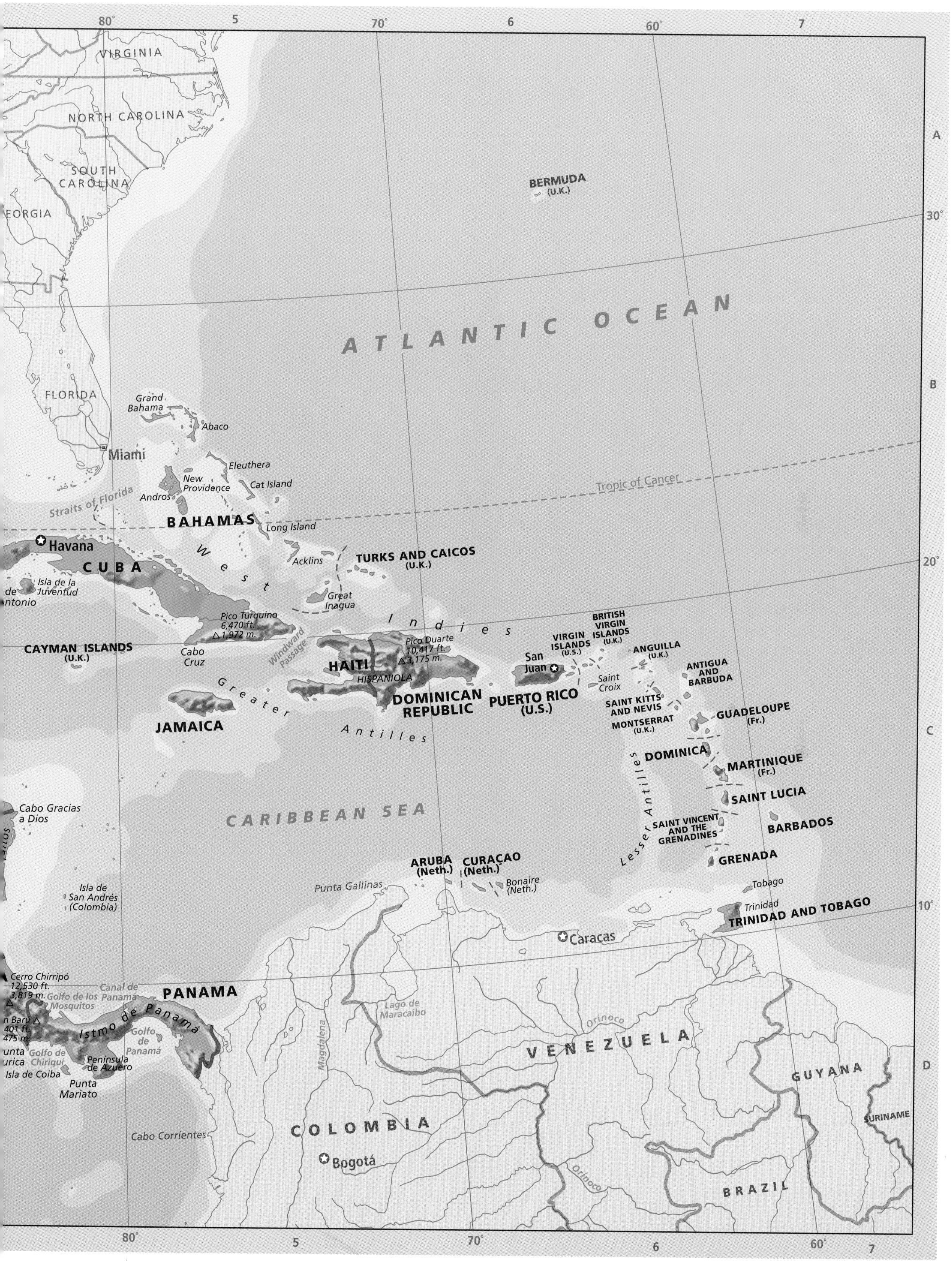
80°
5
70°
6
60°
7
A
B
C
D
30°
20°
10°
VIRGINIA
NORTH CAROLINA
SOUTH CAROLINA
GEORGIA
FLORIDA
BERMUDA (U.K.)
ATLANTIC OCEAN
Grand Bahama
Abaco
Miami
Eleuthera
New Providence
Cat Island
Andros
Straits of Florida
Tropic of Cancer
BAHAMAS
Long Island
Havana
CUBA
Acklins
TURKS AND CAICOS (U.K.)
West Indies
Isla de la Juventud
Great Inagua
Pico Turquino 6,470 ft. 1,972 m.
CAYMAN ISLANDS (U.K.)
Cabo Cruz
Windward Passage
HAITI
Pico Duarte 10,417 ft. 3,175 m.
HISPANIOLA
BRITISH VIRGIN ISLANDS (U.K.)
VIRGIN ISLANDS (U.S.)
San Juan
ANGUILLA (U.K.)
ANTIGUA AND BARBUDA
Saint Croix
Greater Antilles
JAMAICA
DOMINICAN REPUBLIC
PUERTO RICO (U.S.)
SAINT KITTS AND NEVIS
MONTSERRAT (U.K.)
GUADELOUPE (Fr.)
DOMINICA
MARTINIQUE (Fr.)
SAINT LUCIA
SAINT VINCENT AND THE GRENADINES
BARBADOS
GRENADA
Lesser Antilles
Cabo Gracias a Dios
CARIBBEAN SEA
ARUBA (Neth.)
CURAÇAO (Neth.)
Bonaire (Neth.)
Punta Gallinas
Tobago
Trinidad
TRINIDAD AND TOBAGO
Isla de San Andrés (Colombia)
Caracas
Cerro Chirripó 12,530 ft. 3,819 m.
Golfo de los Mosquitos
Canal de Panamá
PANAMA
Istmo de Panamá
Golfo de Panamá
Golfo de Chiriquí
Península de Azuero
Isla de Coiba
Punta Mariato
Lago de Maracaibo
Orinoco
VENEZUELA
Magdalena
GUYANA
SURINAME
COLOMBIA
Cabo Corrientes
Bogotá
BRAZIL

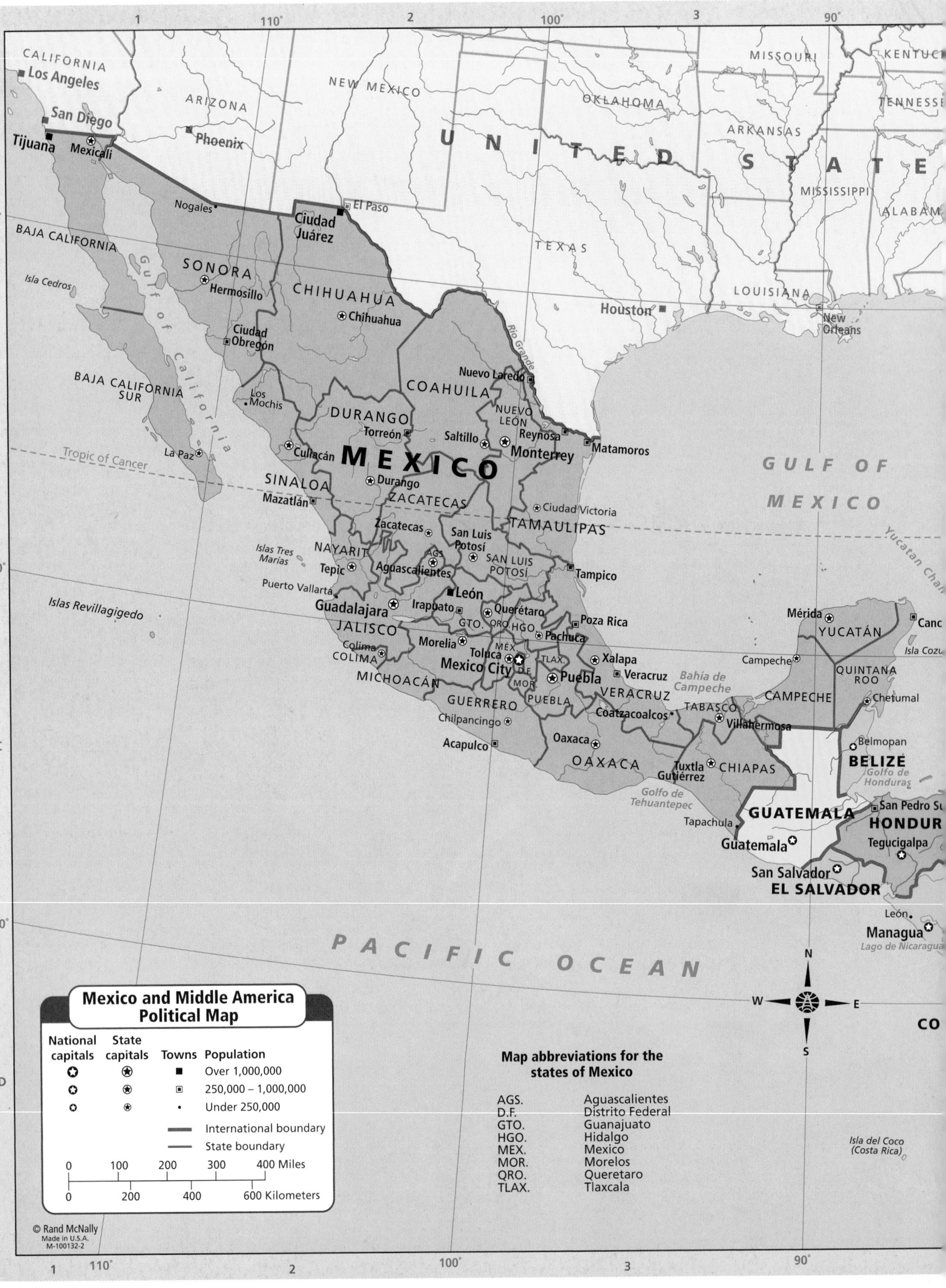
Mexico and Middle America Political Map
National capitals
State capitals
Towns
Population
Over 1,000,000
250,000 – 1,000,000
Under 250,000
International boundary
State boundary
0 100 200 300 400 Miles
0 200 400 600 Kilometers
Map abbreviations for the states of Mexico
AGS. Aguascalientes
D.F. Distrito Federal
GTO. Guanajuato
HGO. Hidalgo
MEX. Mexico
MOR. Morelos
QRO. Queretaro
TLAX. Tlaxcala
MEXICO
UNITED STATES
GULF OF MEXICO
PACIFIC OCEAN
Gulf of California
Tropic of Cancer
Yucatan Channel
CALIFORNIA
Los Angeles
San Diego
Tijuana
Mexicali
ARIZONA
Phoenix
NEW MEXICO
OKLAHOMA
TEXAS
El Paso
Houston
ARKANSAS
LOUISIANA
New Orleans
MISSOURI
MISSISSIPPI
ALABAMA
TENNESSEE
KENTUCKY
Nogales
Ciudad Juárez
BAJA CALIFORNIA
Isla Cedros
SONORA
Hermosillo
Ciudad Obregón
CHIHUAHUA
Chihuahua
Rio Grande
BAJA CALIFORNIA SUR
La Paz
Los Mochis
COAHUILA
Nuevo Laredo
NUEVO LEÓN
DURANGO
Torreón
Saltillo
Reynosa
Monterrey
Matamoros
Culiacán
SINALOA
Durango
Mazatlán
ZACATECAS
Ciudad Victoria
TAMAULIPAS
Zacatecas
San Luis Potosí
SAN LUIS POTOSÍ
NAYARIT
Islas Tres Marías
Tepic
AGS.
Aguascalientes
Tampico
Puerto Vallarta
León
Islas Revillagigedo
Guadalajara
Irapuato
Querétaro
GTO.
QRO.
HGO.
Poza Rica
JALISCO
Pachuca
Colima
COLIMA
Morelia
MEX.
Toluca
Mexico City
D.F.
TLAX.
Xalapa
Puebla
Veracruz
Bahía de Campeche
MICHOACÁN
MOR.
PUEBLA
VERACRUZ
GUERRERO
Chilpancingo
Coatzacoalcos
TABASCO
Villahermosa
Acapulco
Oaxaca
OAXACA
Tuxtla Gutiérrez
CHIAPAS
Golfo de Tehuantepec
Tapachula
Mérida
YUCATÁN
Cancún
Isla Cozumel
Campeche
CAMPECHE
QUINTANA ROO
Chetumal
Belmopan
BELIZE
Golfo de Honduras
GUATEMALA
Guatemala
San Pedro Sula
HONDURAS
Tegucigalpa
San Salvador
EL SALVADOR
León
Managua
Lago de Nicaragua
Isla del Coco (Costa Rica)
CO
N
S
E
W
© Rand McNally
Made in U.S.A.
M-100132-2

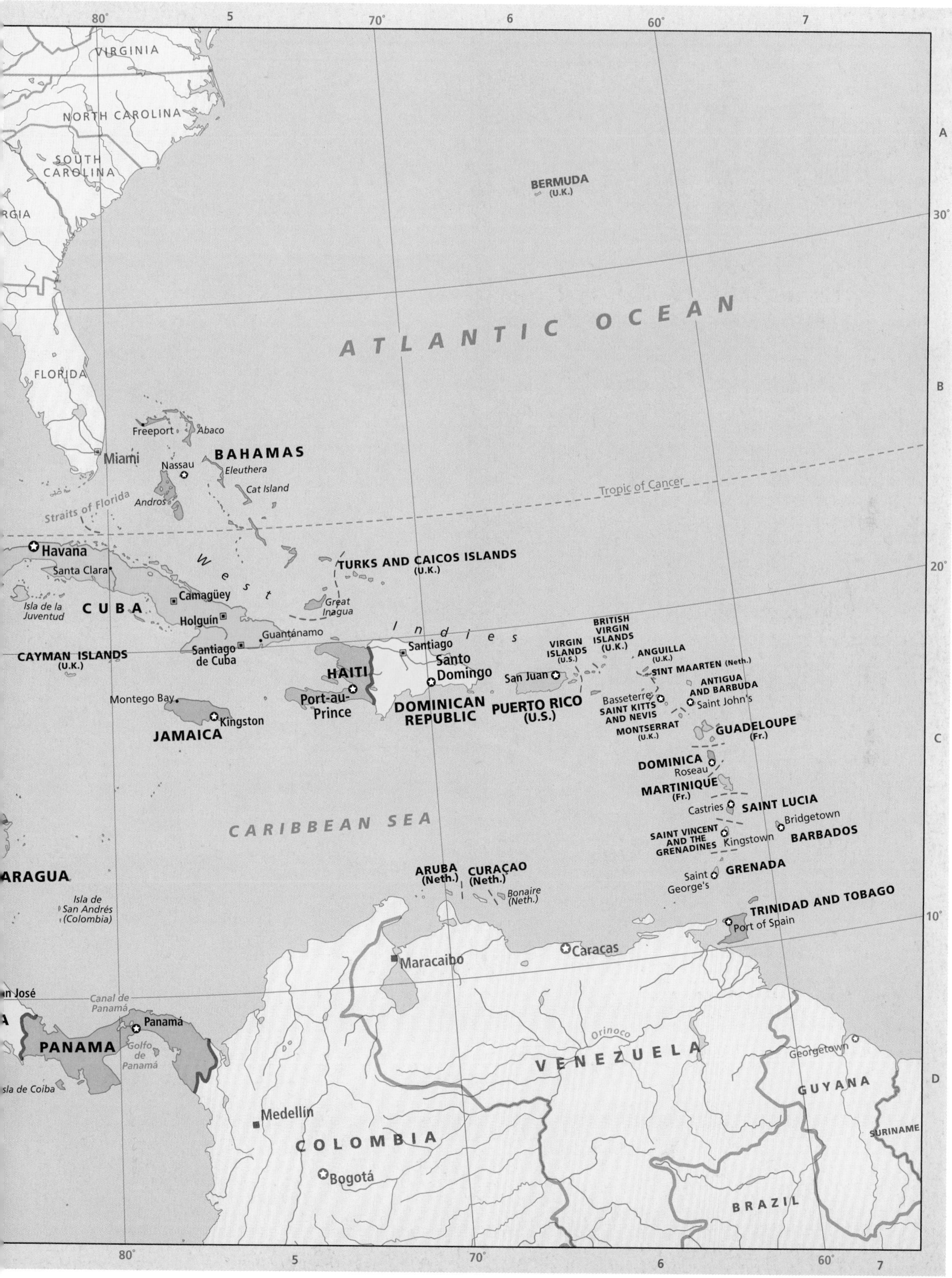
VIRGINIA
NORTH CAROLINA
SOUTH CAROLINA
FLORIDA
BERMUDA (U.K.)
ATLANTIC OCEAN
Freeport
Abaco
Miami
BAHAMAS
Nassau
Eleuthera
Cat Island
Andros
Straits of Florida
Tropic of Cancer
Havana
Santa Clara
West Indies
TURKS AND CAICOS ISLANDS (U.K.)
Camagüey
Isla de la Juventud
CUBA
Great Inagua
Holguín
Guantánamo
Santiago de Cuba
CAYMAN ISLANDS (U.K.)
HAITI
Santiago
Santo Domingo
BRITISH VIRGIN ISLANDS (U.K.)
VIRGIN ISLANDS (U.S.)
ANGUILLA (U.K.)
SINT MAARTEN (Neth.)
San Juan
ANTIGUA AND BARBUDA
Saint John's
Basseterre
SAINT KITTS AND NEVIS
Montego Bay
Port-au-Prince
DOMINICAN REPUBLIC
PUERTO RICO (U.S.)
Kingston
JAMAICA
MONTSERRAT (U.K.)
GUADELOUPE (Fr.)
DOMINICA
Roseau
MARTINIQUE (Fr.)
Castries
SAINT LUCIA
CARIBBEAN SEA
Bridgetown
SAINT VINCENT AND THE GRENADINES
Kingstown
BARBADOS
ARAGUA
ARUBA (Neth.)
CURAÇAO (Neth.)
Bonaire (Neth.)
Saint George's
GRENADA
Isla de San Andrés (Colombia)
TRINIDAD AND TOBAGO
Port of Spain
Caracas
Maracaibo
an José
Canal de Panamá
Panamá
PANAMA
Golfo de Panamá
Orinoco
VENEZUELA
Georgetown
sla de Coiba
GUYANA
Medellín
SURINAME
COLOMBIA
Bogotá
BRAZIL
80°
70°
60°
30°
20°
10°
A
B
C
D

Population

Population Density Map

People per sq. mile
(People per sq. km)

■	Over 1,250 *(Over 500)*
■	250 – 1,250 *(100 – 500)*
■	62.5 – 250 *(25 – 100)*
■	25 – 62.5 *(10 – 25)*
■	2.5 – 25 *(1 – 10)*
□	Under 2.5 *(Under 1)*

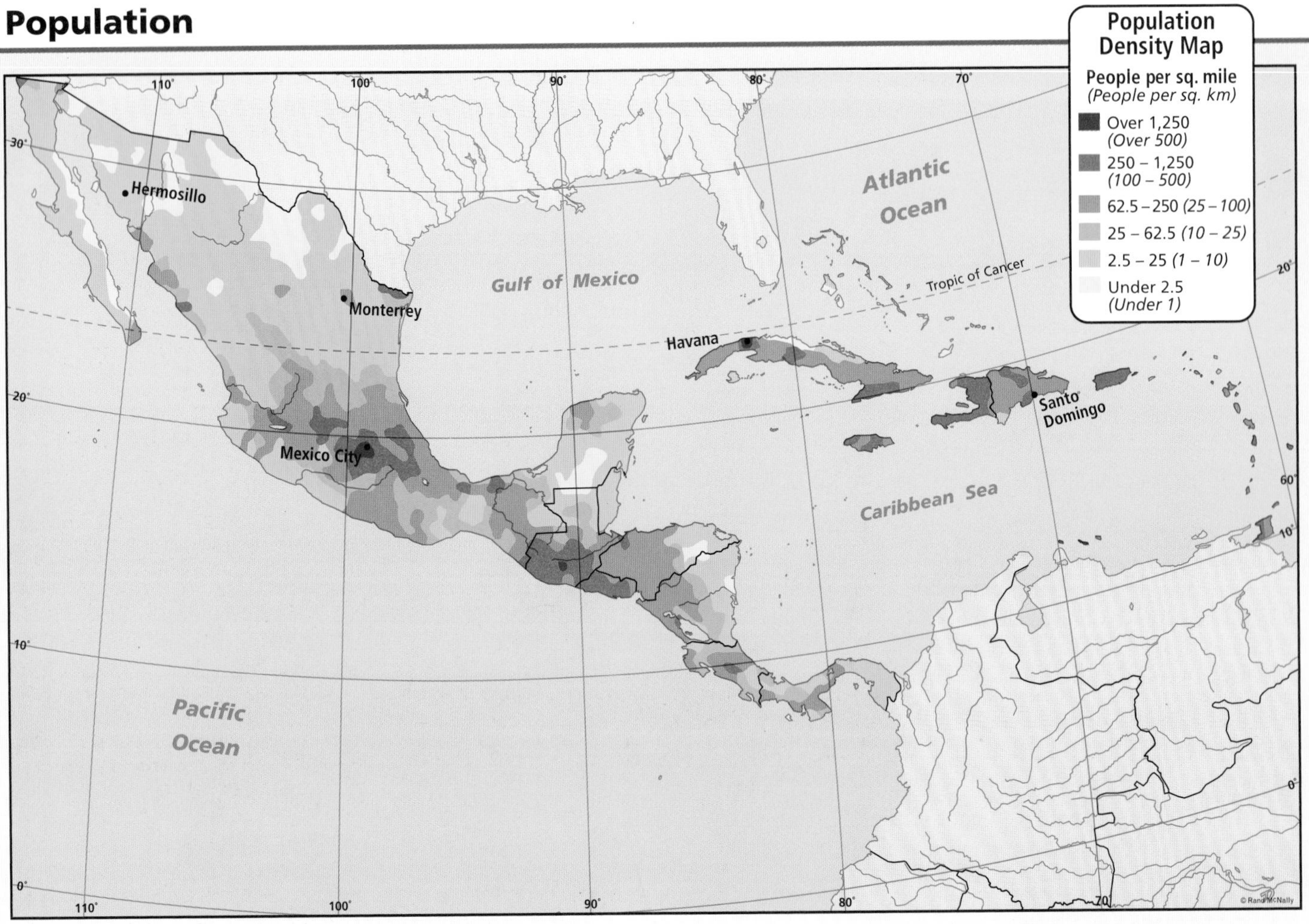

Comparing Urban and Rural Population

Rural 60% — **Urban 40%**
Guatemala

Rural 64% — **Urban 36%**
Haiti

Rural 25% — **Urban 75%**
Mexico

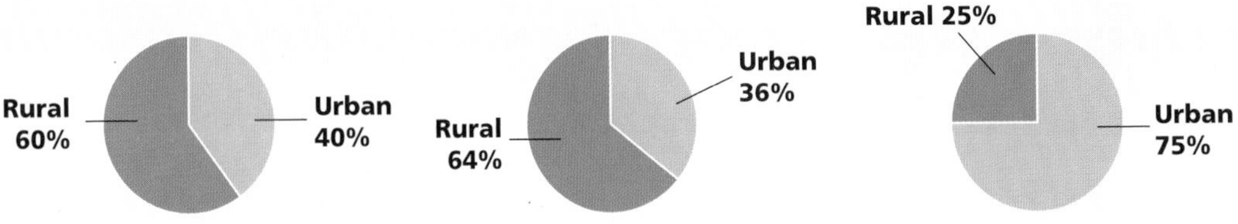

Mexico City is home to nearly one-fifth of Mexico's people.

A Timeline of Mexico City, Mexico

1500 B.C.
Native Americans settle in farm villages along the shores of Lake Texcoco.

1325 A.D.
Aztecs build the city of Tenochtitlán on an island in Lake Texcoco.

1521
Spaniards capture and destroy Tenochtitlán. They drain the lake, fill it with land, and build a new city they call Mexico City.

1961
Mexico City's population reaches 5 million.

1985
An earthquake does extensive damage, partly because Mexico City is built on soft, spongy soil.

2000
Mexico City's population reaches 17 million.

Economies

Per capita income is one way of measuring the relative wealth of countries. This graph compares the per capita income of six countries in Middle America. It shows how greatly wealth varies across the region, from relatively rich countries like Aruba to poor countries like Haiti.

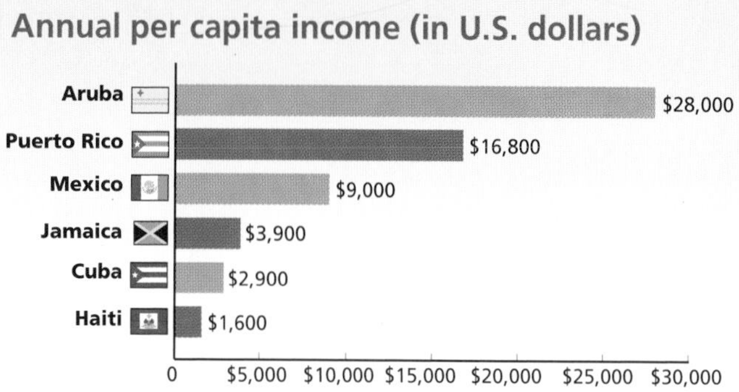
Annual per capita income (in U.S. dollars)
Aruba
$28,000
Puerto Rico
$16,800
Mexico
$9,000
Jamaica
$3,900
Cuba
$2,900
Haiti
$1,600
0
$5,000
$10,000
$15,000
$20,000
$25,000
$30,000

Environments

Cactuses grow in the hot, dry climate of Baja California, Mexico.

Tropical rain forest covers much of Central America.

Palm trees flourish in the warm climate of the Caribbean Sea.

Transportation

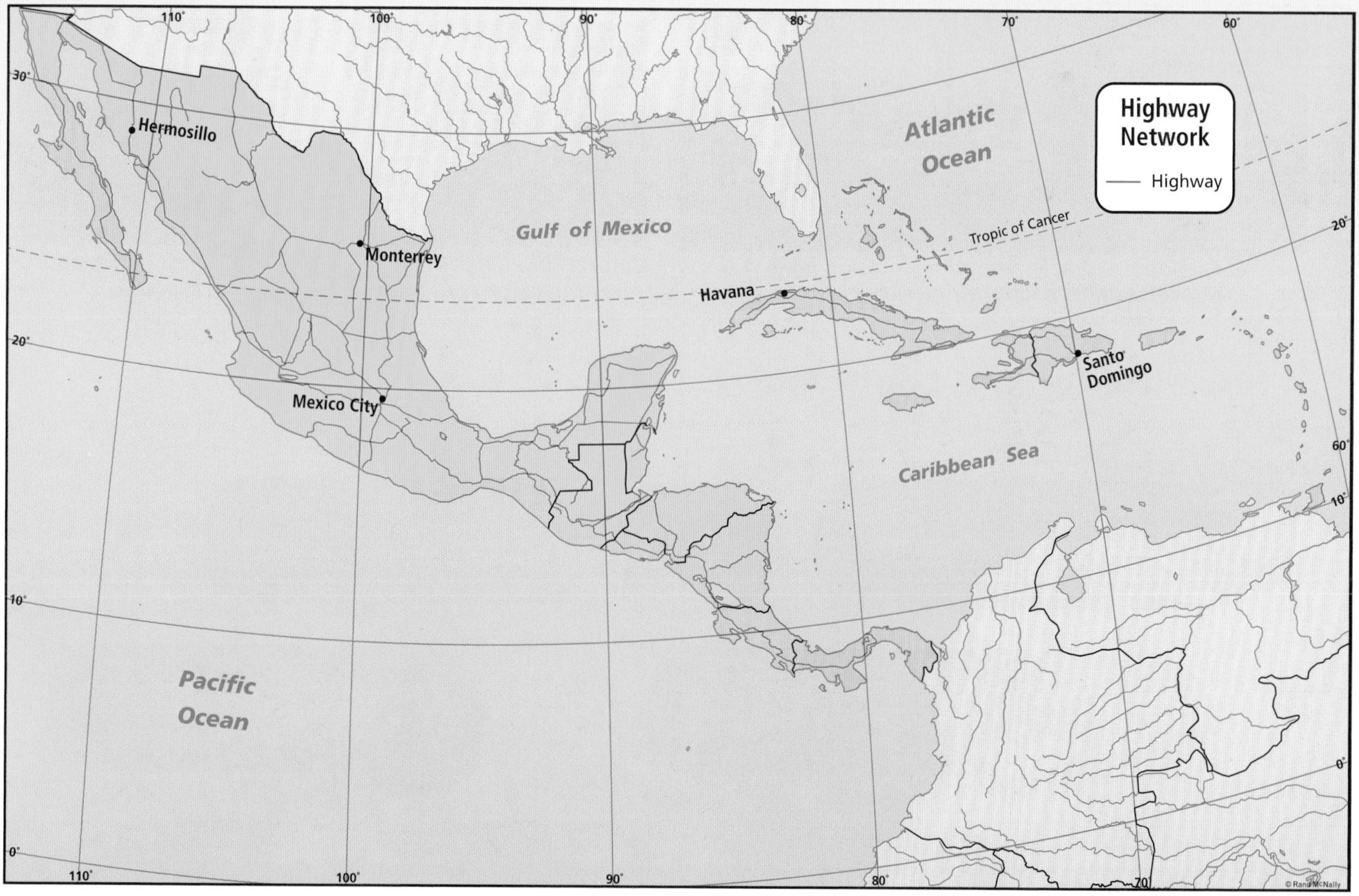

South America

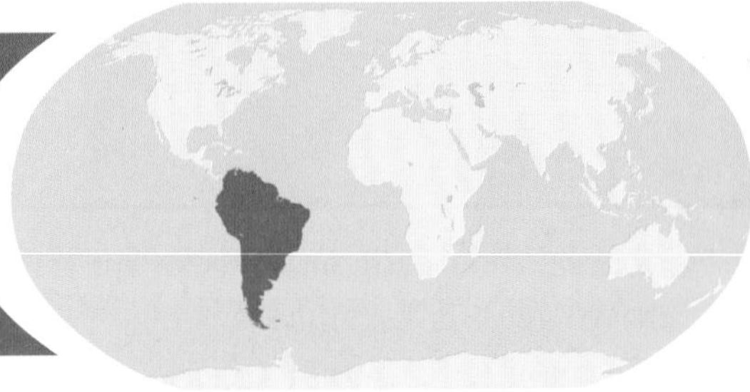

Iguassu Falls on the Brazil-Argentina border is among the most spectacular sights in South America.

South America is a continent of extremes. The Andes Mountains stretch 4,500 miles (7,200 kilometers) from north to south. They form the longest mountain chain in the world. Lake Titicaca, on the Peru-Bolivia border, is the highest lake in the world used for transportation. Arica, Chile, experienced the longest dry period ever recorded: No rain fell there for more than 14 years!

The Amazon River has the greatest volume of water of any river in the world. The Amazon discharges so much water into the Atlantic that it changes the color of the ocean's water for more than 100 miles (160 kilometers) off the shore.

Most South Americans live in cities that are major ports or are near major ports. São Paulo and Rio de Janeiro, Brazil, and Buenos Aires, Argentina, are among the world's largest cities. Altogether, almost 367 million people live in South America.

Colorful buildings in Buenos Aires, Argentina

Giant tortoises on Ecuador's Galapagos Islands

A Historical Look At South America

Circa A.D. 600

Tiahuanaco civilization prospers along the shore of Lake Titicaca.

1438–1535

The Incan Empire controls the Andes and the Pacific Coast.

1498

Christopher Columbus reaches the Orinoco River.

1530s

The Portuguese establish sugar plantations in Brazil.

Rain Forests

A rain forest is a dense forest that receives at least 100 inches (250 centimeters) of rain a year. The Amazon rain forest is rich in plant and animal life, and new species are discovered almost daily. Scientists have learned that many of the plants can be used to produce life-saving drugs.

However, the rain forest is disappearing. It once covered more than 2.7 million square miles (7 million square kilometers). Through a process called deforestation, more than 12% of the rain forest has been cleared for farming, mining, and grazing.

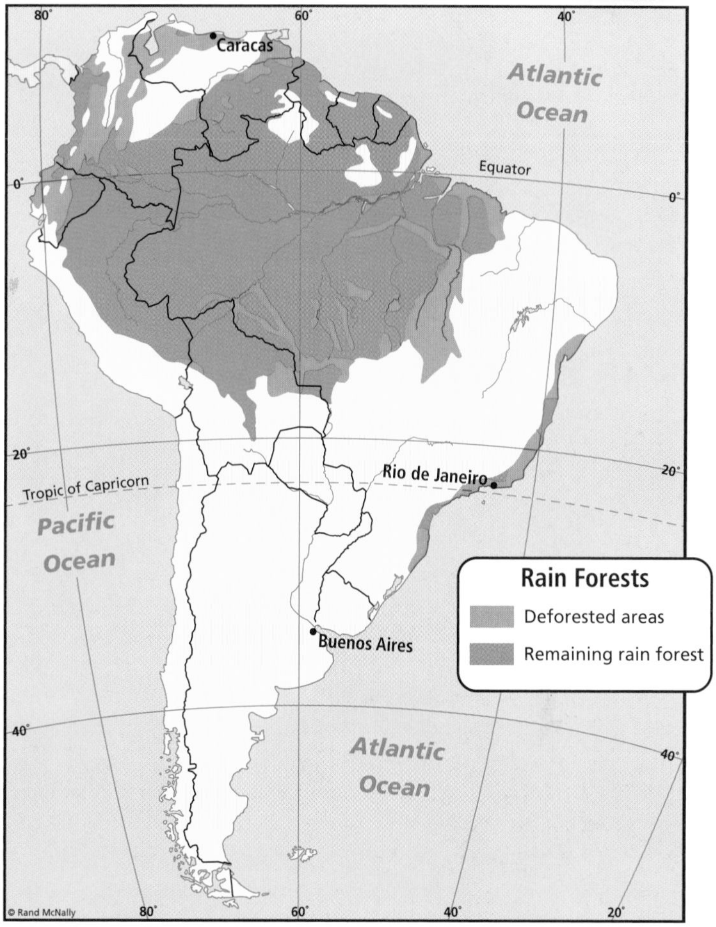
Caracas
Atlantic Ocean
Equator
Rio de Janeiro
Tropic of Capricorn
Pacific Ocean
Buenos Aires
Atlantic Ocean
80°
60°
40°
20°
0°
Rain Forests
Deforested areas
Remaining rain forest
© Rand McNally

Did You Know?

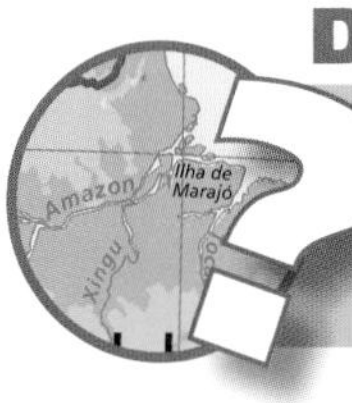

The Amazon River in South America is longer than any other river in the world except the Nile River in Africa.

Sights of the Andes Mountains

More than 40 peaks in the Andes rise 20,000 feet (6,000 meters) or higher. Mining is important in the Andes, and tourism is a growing industry.

The ancient Incan city of Machu Picchu, Peru

Lake Titicaca on the Peru-Bolivia border

A jagged peak along the Argentina-Chile border

The South American llama, a relative of the camel

1580

Spaniards found the city of Buenos Aires in Argentina.

1770s

The first coffee plantations are established in Brazil.

1997

Brazil establishes the world's largest rain forest reserve.

2004

South America's population reaches 350 million.

South America Physical Map
National capitals
Towns
Population
Over 1,000,000
250,000 – 1,000,000
Under 250,000
International boundary
Land elevation
3,000 meters — 9,840 feet
2,000 meters — 6,560 feet
1,000 meters — 3,280 feet
500 meters — 1,640 feet
200 meters — 656 feet
0 Sea level — 0 Sea level
Water depth
0 Sea level — 0 Sea level
200 meters — 656 feet
2,000 meters — 6,560 feet
0 200 400 600 800 1000 Miles
0 300 600 900 1200 1500 Kilometers
GULF OF MEXICO
Yucatan Channel
CUBA
Greater Antilles
HAITI
DOMINICAN REPUBLIC
NORTH AMERICA
JAMAICA
PUERTO RICO (U.S.)
Lesser Antilles
MEXICO
BELIZE
HONDURAS
GUATEMALA
EL SALVADOR
NICARAGUA
COSTA RICA
PANAMA
Golfo de Panamá
CARIBBEAN SEA
Punta Gallinas
Pico Cristóbal Colón
18,947 ft.
5,775 m.
Lago de Maracaibo
Caracas
TRINIDAD AND TOBAGO
Boca Grande
Orinoco
Llanos
VENEZUELA
Angel Falls
Pakaraima Mts.
GUYANA
SURINAME
FRENCH GUIANA (FR.)
Cabo Orange
ATLANTIC OCEAN
Magdalena
Bogotá
COLOMBIA
Nev. del Huila
18,865 ft.
5,750 m.
Punta Galera
ECUADOR
Chimborazo
20,702 ft.
6,310 m.
Galapagos Islands (Ec.)
Equator
Putumayo
Japurá
Negro
Manaus
Amazon
Ilha de Marajó
Xingu
Tocantins
Tapajós
Madeira
Amazon Basin
Juruá
Selvas
BRAZIL
Punta Pariñas
Ucayali
Andes
PERU
Cabo de São Roque
Recife
Represa de Sobradinho
Nev. Huascarán
22,133 ft.
6,746 m.
Lima
Planalto do Mato Grosso
São Francisco
Punta Carreta
Lago Titicaca
Nev. Illampu
21,066 ft.
6,421 m.
La Paz
Cordillera Real
BOLIVIA
Brasília
Serra do Espinhaço
PACIFIC OCEAN
Nev. Sajama
21,463 ft.
6,542 m.
Gran Chaco
Paraná
PARAGUAY
Cabo de São Tomé
São Paulo
Rio de Janeiro
Iguassu Falls
Atacama Desert
Tropic of Capricorn
Tropic of Cancer
Isla San Ambrosio (Chile)
Isla San Felix (Chile)
Nev. Ojos del Salado
22,615 ft.
6,893 m.
Uruguay
Lagoa dos Patos
URUGUAY
Lagoa Mirim
Archipiélago Juan Fernández (Chile)
Cerro Aconcagua
22,831 ft.
6,959 m.
Santiago
Buenos Aires
Río de la Plata
Pampas
CHILE
ARGENTINA
Punta Lavapié
N
W
E
S
Golfo San Matías
Península Valdés
Isla Grande de Chiloé
Archipiélago de los Chonos
Patagonia
Cabo Dos Bahías
Golfo San Jorge
Cabo Tres Puntas
Isla Wellington
Bahía Grande
FALKLAND ISLANDS (U.K.)
West Falkland
East Falkland
Strait of Magellan
Isla Santa Inés
Tierra del Fuego
Cape Horn
South Georgia (U.K.)
Drake Passage
South Shetland Islands (U.K.)
South Orkney Islands (U.K.)
South Sandwich Islands (U.K.)
© Rand McNally
Made in U.S.A.

A B C D E F G H I

1 90° 2 80° 3 70° 4 60° 5 50° 6 40° 7 30°

Tropic of Cancer

GULF OF MEXICO
Havana
CUBA

NORTH AMERICA

MEXICO
BELIZE
GUATEMALA
HONDURAS
EL SALVADOR
NICARAGUA

COSTA RICA
PANAMA

HAITI
DOMINICAN REPUBLIC
JAMAICA
PUERTO RICO (U.S.)

CARIBBEAN SEA

ATLANTIC OCEAN

Barranquilla
Cartagena
Maracaibo
Caracas
Barquisimeto
Valencia
Cúcuta
Bucaramanga
Medellín
Manizales
Bogotá
Cali
COLOMBIA

VENEZUELA

Ciudad Guayana
Orinoco
TRINIDAD AND TOBAGO
Georgetown
GUYANA
Paramaribo
SURINAME
Cayenne
FRENCH GUIANA (FR.)
Boa Vista
Macapá

Galapagos Islands (Ec.)
Equator
Quito
ECUADOR
Guayaquil
Iquitos
Amazon
Negro
Manaus
Amazon
Belém
Santarem
São Luis
Equator

Chiclayo
Trujillo
PERU
Ucayali
Madeira
Porto Velho
B R A Z I L
Imperatriz
Teresina
Fortaleza
Natal
João Pessoa
Recife
Maceió

Lima
Huancayo
Cusco
Lago Titicaca
BOLIVIA
La Paz
Cochabamba
Santa Cruz
Cuiabá
Goiânia
Brasília
Montes Claros
Feira de Santana
Aracaju
Salvador

PACIFIC OCEAN

Arequipa
Arica
Sucre
Uberlândia
Belo Horizonte

Antofagasta
Campo Grande
PARAGUAY
Paraná
Ribeirão Preto
Campinas
Uberlândia
Rio de Janeiro
Tropic of Capricorn

Isla San Ambrosio (Chile)
Salta
San Miguel de Tucumán
Asunción
São Paulo
Curitiba

Isla San Félix (Chile)
Resistencia
Caxias do Sul
Porto Alegre

Archipiélago Juan Fernández (Chile)
Córdoba
Mendoza
Rosario
Santa Fe
URUGUAY
Valparaíso
Santiago
CHILE
ARGENTINA
Paraná
Buenos Aires
La Plata
Rio de la Plata
Montevideo

Concepción
Bahía Blanca
Mar del Plata

Puerto Montt

Archipiélago de los Chonos
Comodoro Rivadavia

N
W E
S

ATLANTIC OCEAN

FALKLAND ISLANDS (U.K.)

Río Gallegos
Strait of Magellan
Punta Arenas
Tierra del Fuego

South Georgia (U.K.)

Drake Passage
South Shetland Islands (U.K.)
South Orkney Islands (U.K.)
South Sandwich Islands (U.K.)

© Rand McNally
Made in U.S.A.
M-100129-·-1-1-1

South America Political Map

National capitals	Towns	Population
✪	■	Over 1,000,000
◉	▣	250,000 – 1,000,000
○	•	Under 250,000
	▬▬▬	International boundary

200 400 600 800 1000 Miles
300 600 900 1200 1500 Kilometers

Natural Hazards

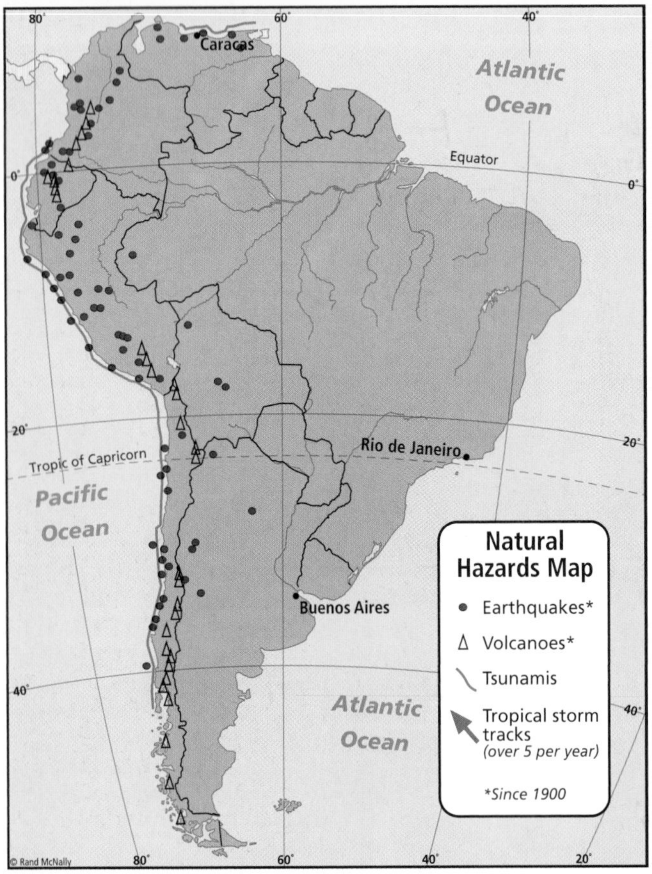

Climate

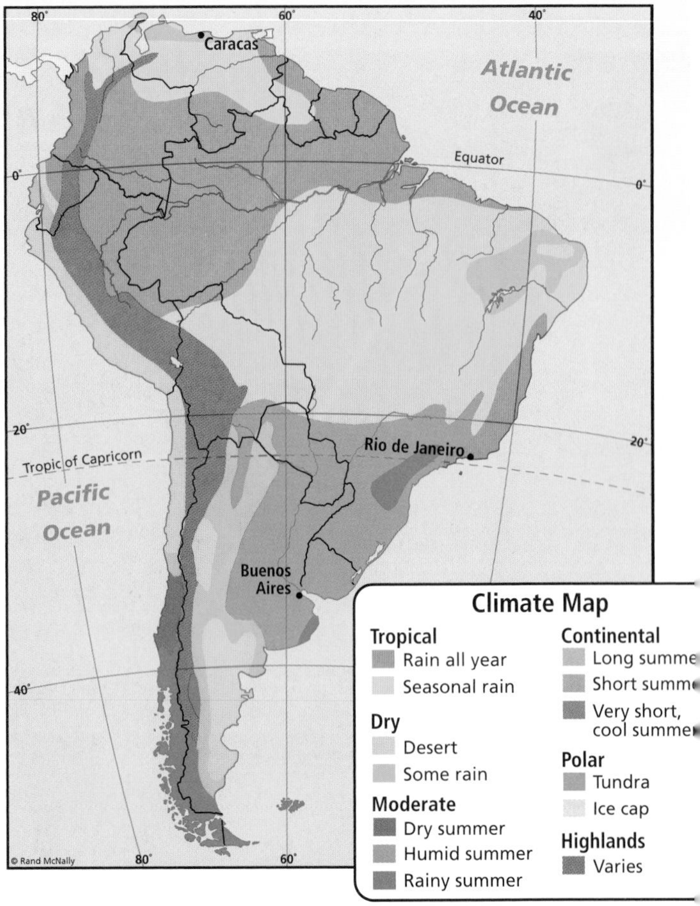

Environments

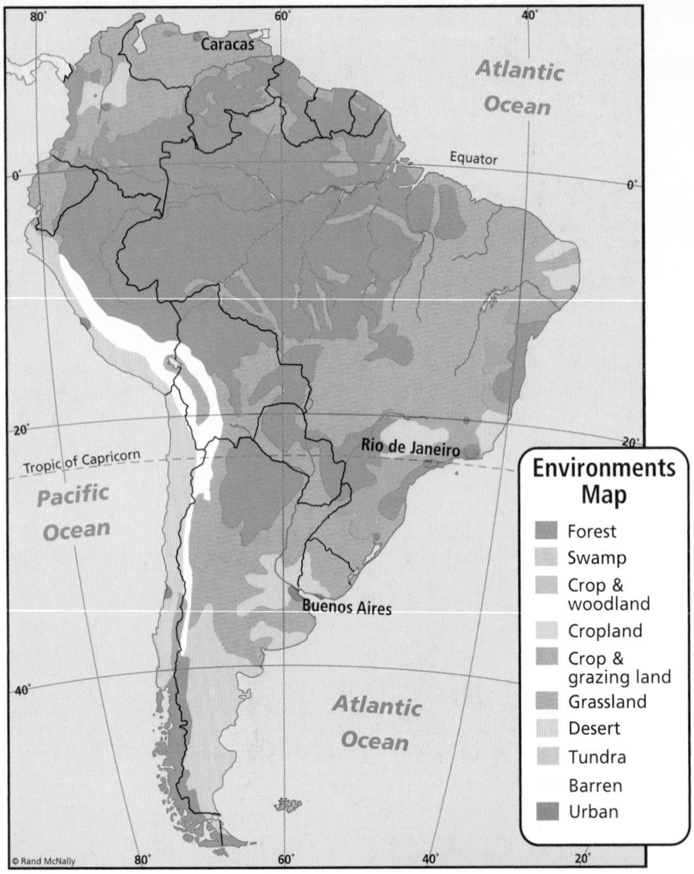

The Amazon rain forest supports almost half of Earth's animal and plant species.

What If?

What could happen if all of the rain forests in South America are destroyed?

Population

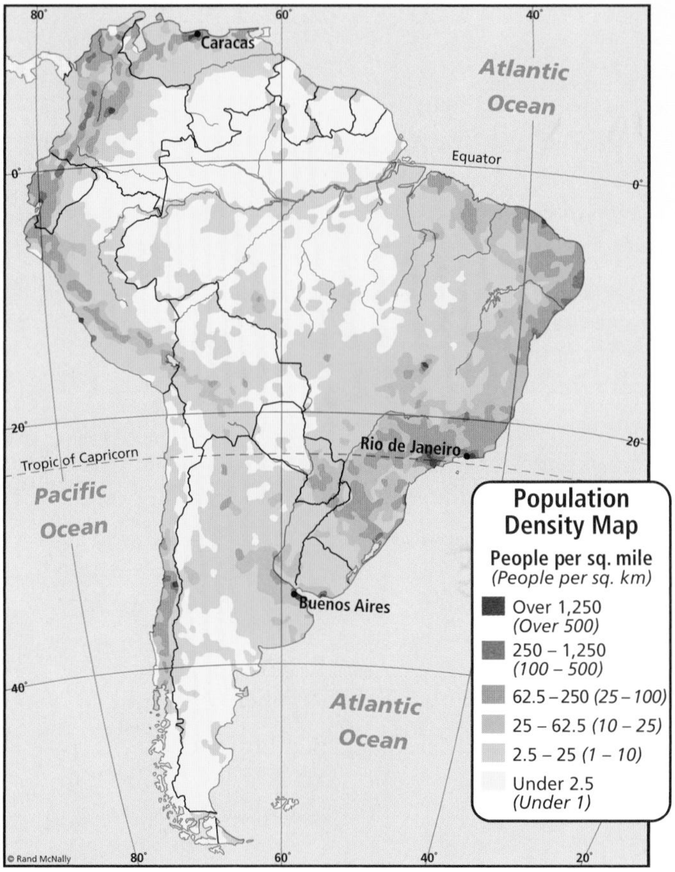

Most Brazilians live in large cities such as Rio de Janeiro.

Roughly two out of five South Americans are under the age of 20.

Did You Know?

São Paulo, Brazil, is South America's most populous city.

Cusco, Peru, was once capital of the Incan empire.

Dense vegetation is a barrier to settlement in the Amazon River basin.

Economic Activities

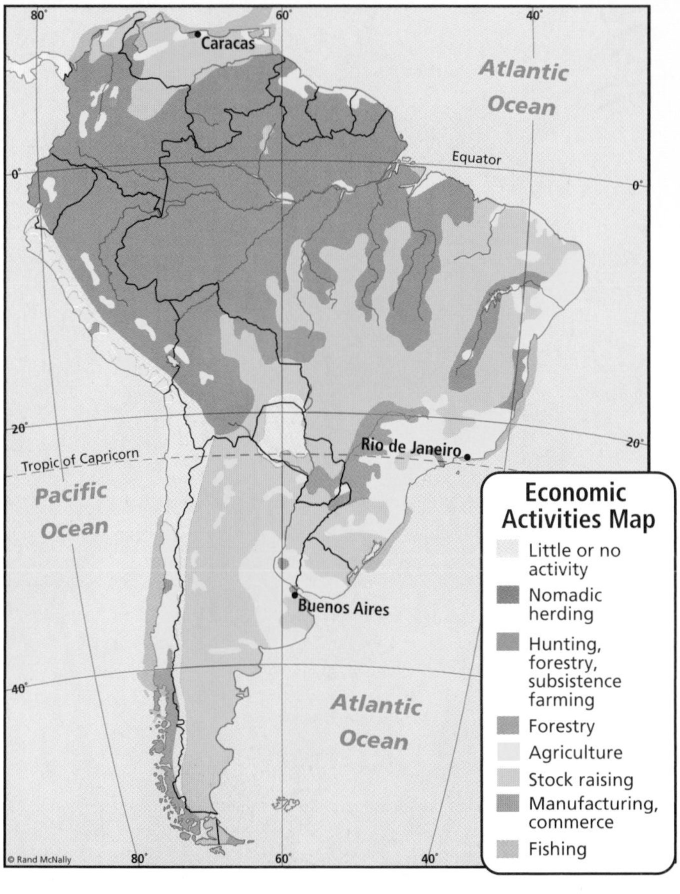

Coffee plants thrive in the tropical climates of South America.

World Coffee Production

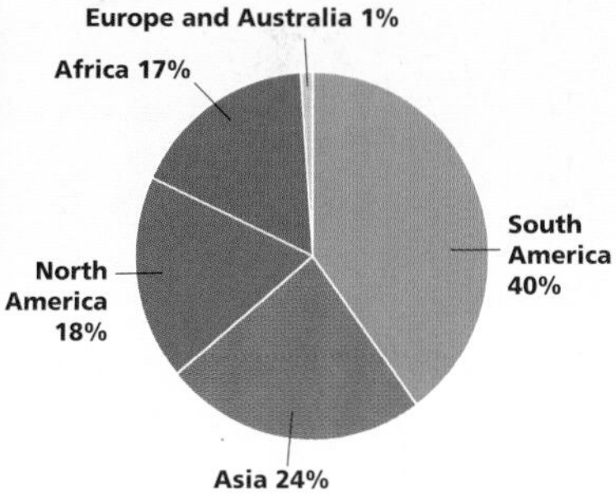

Gross Domestic Product (GDP) in billions of U.S. dollars

Gross Domestic Product is the total value of all goods and services produced by a country in one year.

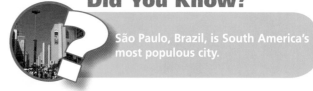

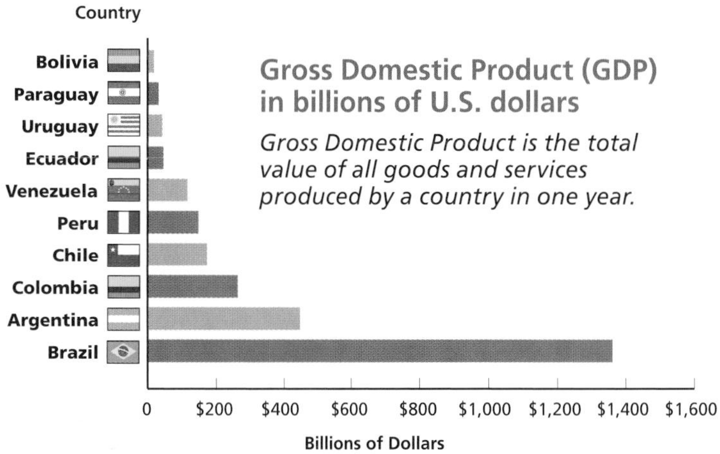

Europe

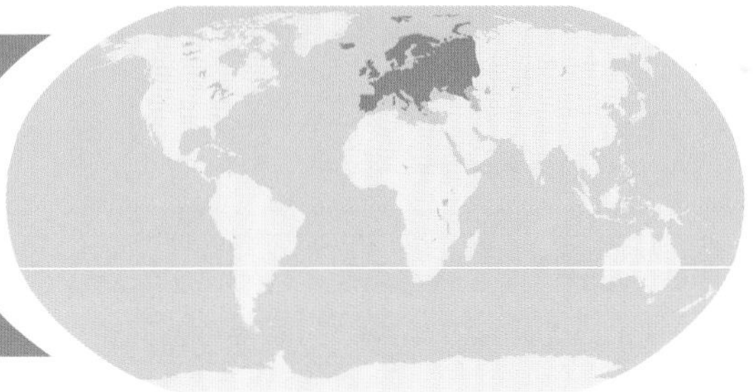

Prague, Czech Republic

Do you know what a *lago* is? A *lac*? A *loch*? These are just some of the words for "lake" in Europe. Europe is the world's second-smallest continent, but it has many countries and many languages.

Only the giant continents of Asia and Africa have more people than Europe. Because more than 729,000,000 live in the small continent of Europe, it is one of the most densely populated regions in the world.

The two smallest countries in the world are in Europe. Vatican City and Monaco are each less than one square mile (2.6 square kilometers) in size.

In recent decades, there have been great changes in Europe. East and West Germany were reunited in 1990 after being separated for 45 years. In 1991, the Soviet Union split up into 15 different countries. The following year, Czechoslovakia peacefully divided into two new countries: the Czech Republic and Slovakia.

Slovenia, Croatia, Macedonia, and Bosnia and Herzegovina broke away from Yugoslavia in 1991-92 to become independent countries. In 2003, Yugoslavia changed its name to Serbia and Montenegro. Then, in 2006, Montenegro split from Serbia to become an independent country. In 2008, a region known as Kosovo declared its independence from Serbia.

Church in the Alps of Austria

Hilltop village in Spain

Donkey and farmhouse, Aran Islands, Ireland

Did You Know?

Five European countries—Iceland, Norway, Sweden, Finland, and Russia—lie partly within the Arctic Circle.

A Historical Look At Europe

Circa 2200 B.C. Erecting of Stonehenge pillars begins in Great Britain.

776 B.C. The first recorded Olympic Games are held in Greece.

753 B.C. Rome is founded.

A.D. 874 Iceland is settled by Norse seafarers.

The European Union

Twenty-seven nations have joined the European Union to form a single, powerful market for business and trade.

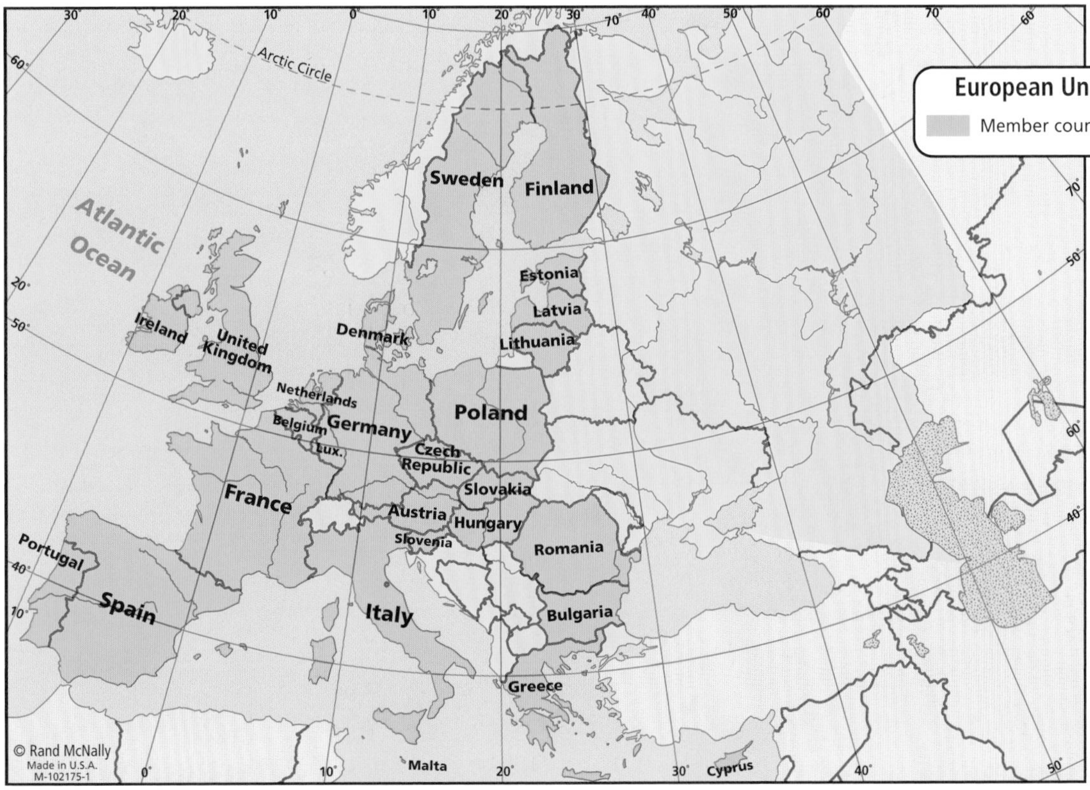

The headquarters of the European Union is in Brussels, Belgium.

Some countries of the European Union use the euro as their currency.

Because Europe has so many languages, there are 23 official languages of the European Union.

The European Union has its own passports. Citizens of all countries can move freely around the entire area.

1163–1200

The great gothic Notre Dame Cathedral is built in Paris.

The period known as the Renaissance marks a rebirth in art and science.

1300s–1500s

Circa 1750

The Industrial Revolution begins in England.

Romania and Bulgaria join the European Union.

2007

ICELAND

Horn
Fontur
Surtsey

20°
1
2
10°
3
0°
4
10°
5

A

B

Arctic Circle

NORWEGIAN
SEA

Lofoten Islands

Vestfjorden

Kebnekaise
6,926 ft.
2,111 m.

60°

30°

FAROE ISLANDS
(Den.)

SWEDEN

NORWAY

Galdhøpiggen △
8,100 ft.
2,469 m.

N
W E
S

Shetland
Islands

Vänern

Gotland

Gulf of

Dalälven

Umeälven

30°

ATLANTIC

OCEAN

Hebrides

Orkney
Islands

Ben Nevis △
4,406 ft.
1,343 m.

Moray
Firth

Kinnaird Head

Grampian
Mts.

Lindesnes

Skagerrak

Kattegat

Vänern

Vättern

Öland

BALTIC

British
Isles

UNITED

Firth of Forth

Cheviot
Hills

DENMARK

Sjælland

Bornholm
(Den.)

R

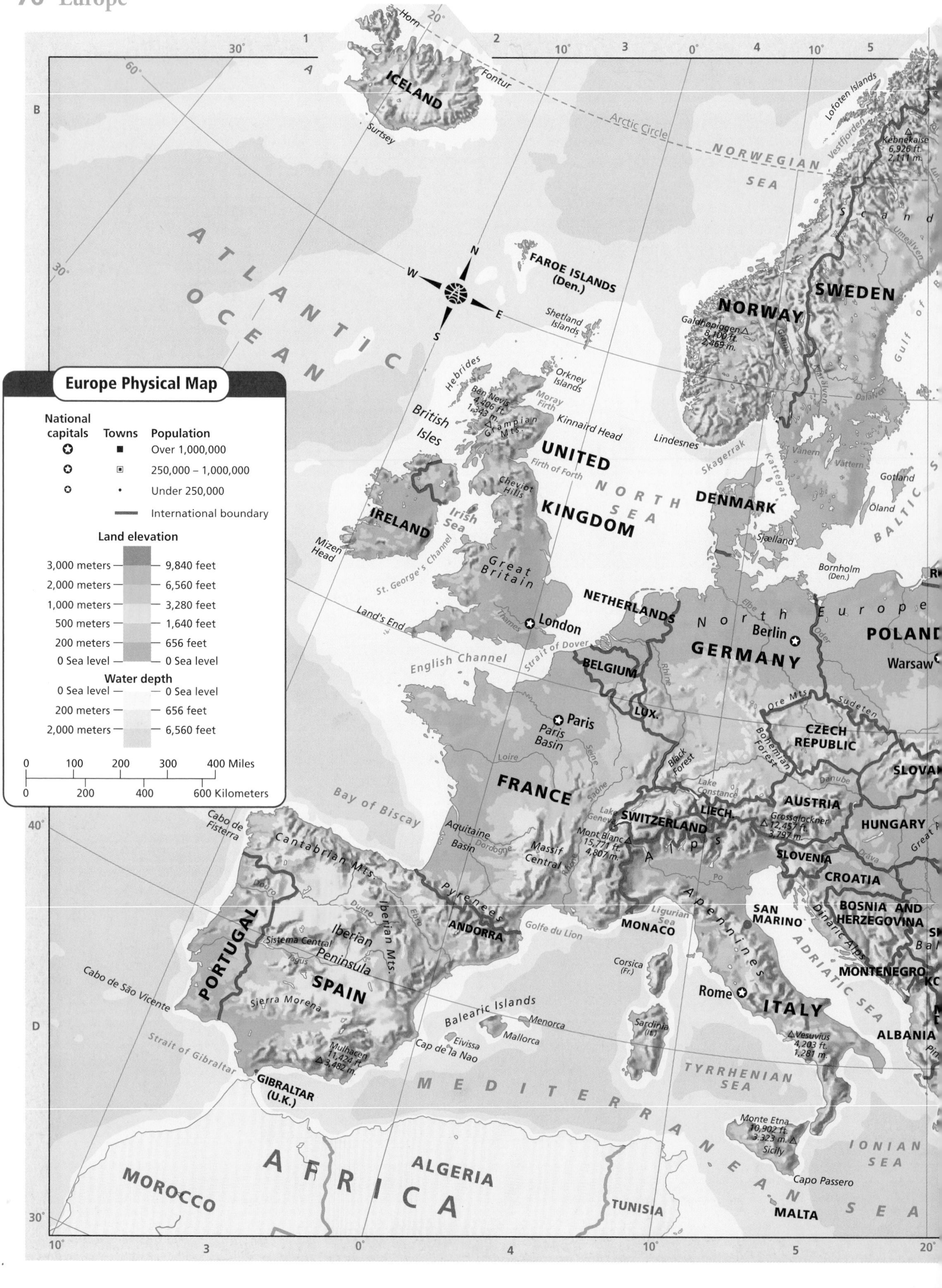

Europe Physical Map

National
capitals
⊛
⊛
⊛

Towns
■
▣
•

Population
Over 1,000,000
250,000 – 1,000,000
Under 250,000
International boundary

KINGDOM

IRELAND

Irish
Sea

NORTH

SEA

Elbe

North

Europe

POLAND

Land elevation

3,000 meters ― 9,840 feet
2,000 meters ― 6,560 feet
1,000 meters ― 3,280 feet
500 meters ― 1,640 feet
200 meters ― 656 feet
0 Sea level ― 0 Sea level

Mizen
Head

Great
Britain

NETHERLANDS

Berlin ⊛

Warsaw

Water depth

0 Sea level ― 0 Sea level
200 meters ― 656 feet
2,000 meters ― 6,560 feet

St. George's Channel

Land's End

English Channel

BELGIUM

Strait of Dover

London ⊛

Thames

GERMANY

Rhine

LUX.

Ore Mts.

Sudeten

CZECH
REPUBLIC

Bohemian
Forest

Danube

SLOVA

0 100 200 300 400 Miles
0 200 400 600 Kilometers

40°

Cabo de
Fisterra

Bay of Biscay

Paris ⊛
Paris
Basin

Seine

Loire

FRANCE

Saône

Black
Forest

Lake
Constance

AUSTRIA

Grossglockner △
12,457 ft.
3,797 m.

HUNGARY

Cantabrian Mts.

Aquitaine
Basin

Dordogne

Pyrenees

Massif
Central

Rhône

SWITZERLAND

Mont Blanc △
15,771 ft.
4,807 m.

LIECH.

Alps

Po

SLOVENIA

Drava

Great

Miño

Duero

Iberian
Peninsula

Iberian Mts.

ANDORRA

Golfe du Lion

MONACO

Ligurian
Sea

Apennines

SAN
MARINO

Dinaric Alps

CROATIA

BOSNIA AND
HERZEGOVINA

Bal

PORTUGAL

Sistema Central

Tagus

SPAIN

Sierra Morena

Mulhacén
11,424 ft.
△ 3,482 m.

Balearic Islands

Eivissa

Mallorca

Menorca

Cap de la Nao

Corsica
(Fr.)

Sardinia
(It.)

Rome ⊛

△ Vesuvius
4,203 ft.
1,281 m.

MONTENEGRO

KO

ITALY

ALBANIA

Pin

D

Cabo de São Vicente

Strait of Gibraltar

GIBRALTAR
(U.K.)

TYRRHENIAN
SEA

M E D I T E R R A N E A N

Monte Etna △
10,902 ft.
3,323 m.

Sicily

IONIAN
SEA

30°

MOROCCO

A F R I C A

ALGERIA

Capo Passero

TUNISIA

MALTA

SEA

10°
3

0°
4

10°
5

Murmansk
Kola Peninsula
Ponoy
WHITE SEA
Timan Ridge
Pechora
Gora Narodnaya 6,214 ft. 1,894 m.
Mezen'
Ural Mountains
Ob'
Irtysh
Severnaya Dvina
Onega
Lake Onega
Lake Ladoga
Sukhona
Severnyye Uvaly (Hills)
Kama
Kama Resevoir
RUSSIA
Rybinsk Res.
Gorki Res.
Kuybyshev Res.
Lake Peipus
Volga
Valdai Hills
Moscow
Oka
Oka-Don Plain
Central Russian Upland
Don
Khoper
Volga Upland
Volgograd Res.
Ural
KAZAKHSTAN
Caspian Depression
Aral Sea
UZBEKISTAN
Amu Darya
ASIA
BELARUS
Nëman
Prypjac'
Dnieper Lowland
Kiev
UKRAINE
Dnieper
Donets Basin
Tsymlyansk Res.
MOLDOVA
Sea of Azov
Crimean Peninsula
Caucasus
Gora El'brus 18,510 ft. 5,642 m.
CASPIAN SEA
TURKMENISTAN
BLACK SEA
GEORGIA
ARMENIA
AZERBAIJAN
AZER.
BULGARIA
Danube
İstanbul
Sea of Marmara
AEGEAN SEA
TURKEY
IRAN
Tigris
IRAQ
SYRIA
Euphrates
CYPRUS
LEBANON
Rhodes
Sea of Crete
Crete
© Rand McNally
Made in U.S.A.
M-100138-2

Europe Political Map

National capitals	State capitals	Towns	Population
✪	✪	■	Over 1,000,000
✪	✪	▣	250,000 – 1,000,000
✪	✪	•	Under 250,000

International boundary
State boundary

0 100 200 300 400 Miles
0 200 400 600 Kilometers

ICELAND
Reykjavík

Arctic Circle

NORWEGIAN SEA

ATLANTIC OCEAN

FAROE ISLANDS (Den.)

SWEDEN
NORWAY
Trondheim
Umeå
Bergen
Oslo
Stockholm
Göteborg
Vänern
Vättern

N
W E
S

DENMARK
Copenhagen
Skagerrak
Kattegat

BALTIC SEA
LITHU
Kaliningrad
Gdańsk
Szczecin

NORTH SEA

SCOTLAND
Aberdeen
Glasgow
Edinburgh
NORTHERN IRELAND
Belfast
UNITED KINGDOM
Dublin
IRELAND
Irish Sea
Cork
Liverpool
Manchester
WALES
ENGLAND
Birmingham
Cardiff
St. George's Channel
Plymouth
Thames
London
English Channel
Strait of Dover
Le Havre
Brest

NETHERLANDS
Amsterdam
The Hague
Antwerp
Brussels
BELGIUM
Luxembourg
LUX.

GERMANY
Hamburg
Berlin
Essen
Cologne
Bonn
Frankfurt
Dresden
Stuttgart
Munich

POLAND
Warsaw
Łódź
Wrocław
Katowice
Kra

CZECH REPUBLIC
Prague

SLOVAK
Vienna
Bratislava
AUSTRIA
Graz

FRANCE
Paris
Nantes
Loire
Strasbourg
Rhine
Bordeaux
Toulouse
Lyon
Rhône
Seine

SWITZERLAND
Zürich
Bern
Geneva
LIECH.
Danube

SLOVENIA
Ljubljana
HUNGARY
Budapest

Bay of Biscay

A Coruña
Gijón
Porto
Bilbao
PORTUGAL
Lisbon
Tagus
Valladolid
ANDORRA
Zaragoza
Ebro
Madrid
SPAIN
València
Córdoba
Seville
Alacant
Palma
Málaga
GIBRALTAR (U.K.)
Strait of Gibraltar
Barcelona

Marseille
Golfe du Lion
MONACO
Nice
Turin
Milan
Venice
Genoa
Bologna
CROATIA
Zagreb
Ligurian Sea
Corsica
Florence
SAN MARINO
Split
Sardinia
ITALY
Rome
VATICAN CITY
Naples
Bari
Cagliari
TYRRHENIAN SEA
Palermo
Messina
Sicily
Catania

ADRIATIC SEA
BOSNIA AND HERZEGOVINA
Sarajevo
SER
MONTENEGRO
Podgorica
Pr
ALBANIA
Tiranë
Sko
GRE
IONIAN SEA

MEDITERRANEAN SEA

Algiers
MOROCCO
ALGERIA
AFRICA
TUNISIA
MALTA

60°
50°
40°
30°
30°
60°
20°
10°
0°
10°
30°

1 2 10° 3 0° 4 10° 5
A
B
D

RUSSIA
ASIA
KAZAKHSTAN
UZBEKISTAN
TURKMENISTAN
BELARUS
UKRAINE
MOLDOVA
GEORGIA
ARMENIA
AZERBAIJAN
AZER.
TURKEY
SYRIA
IRAQ
IRAN
LEBANON
CYPRUS
BULGARIA
WHITE SEA
BLACK SEA
CASPIAN SEA
Sea of Azov
Aral Sea
Sea of Marmara
AEGEAN SEA
Crete
Murmansk
Arkhangel'sk
Severnaya Dvina
Pechora
Ukhta
Syktyvkar
Berezniki
Perm'
Kirov
Izhevsk
Naberezhnye Chelny
Ufa
Petrozavodsk
Lake Onega
Lake Ladoga
Saint Petersburg
Cherepovets
Rybinsk Res.
Gorki Res.
Yaroslavl'
Ivanovo
Nizhniy Novgorod
Kazan'
Kuybyshev Res.
Tver'
Moscow
Samara
Ryazan'
Oka
Penza
Volga
Tula
Vicebsk
Minsk
Bryansk
Lipetsk
Don
Saratov
Volgograd Res.
Ural
Homel'
Voronezh
Volgograd
Atyrau
Chornobyl'
Kiev
Kharkiv
Luhans'k
Tsymlyansk Res.
Astrakhan'
Vinnytsia
Dnieper
Dnipro-petrovs'k
Donets'k
Rostov-na-Donu
Kryvyi Rih
Zaporizhzhia
Mariupol'
Iași
Chișinău
Odesa
Krasnodar
Stavropol'
Vladikavkaz
Simferopol'
Sevastopol'
Galați
Bucharest
Constanța
Tbilisi
Baku
Yerevan
Varna
Plovdiv
İstanbul
Ankara
Tehrān
Baghdad
Finland
Lake Peipus
LAND
sinki
inn
NIA
ATVIA
-Napoca
MANIA
aiova
ofia
ssaloniki
hens
70°
40°
50°
60°
80°
30°
B
C
D
6
7
8
9
10
11
© Rand McNally
Made in U.S.A.
M-100128-

Climate

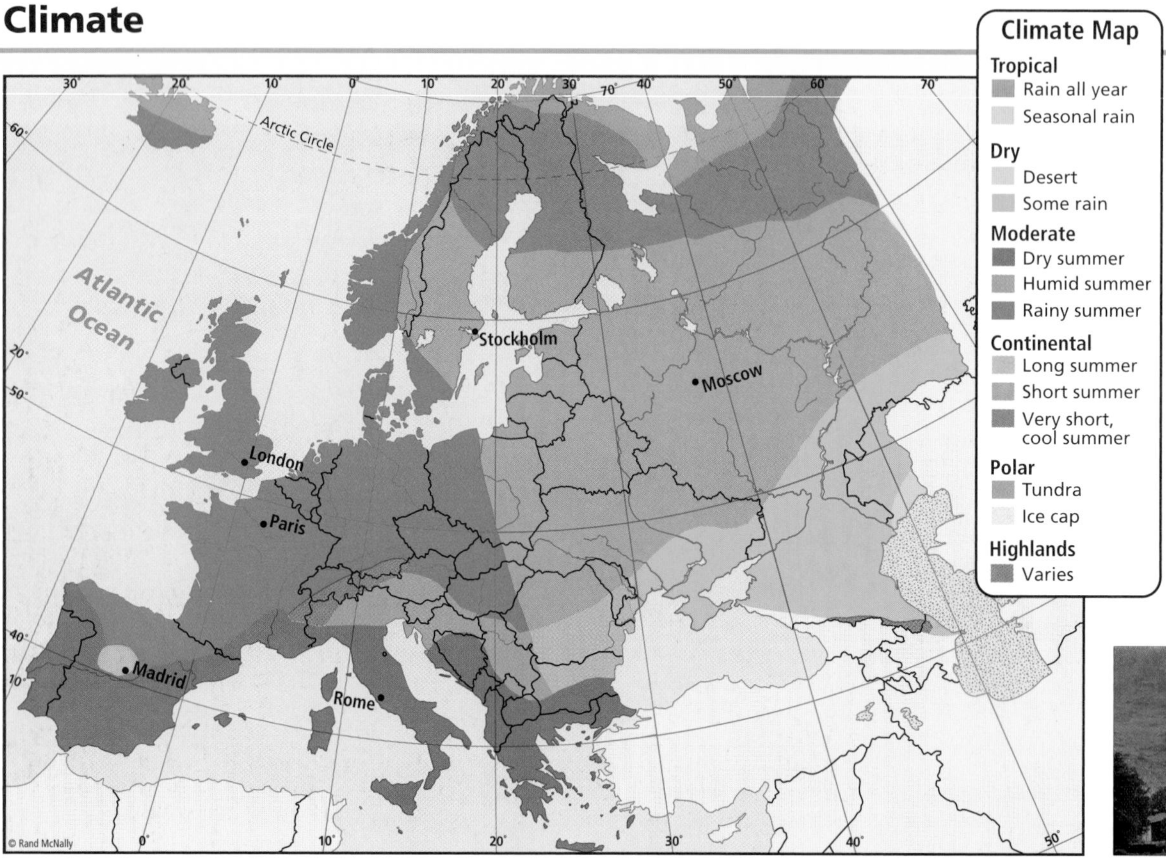
Climate Map
Tropical
Rain all year
Seasonal rain
Dry
Desert
Some rain
Moderate
Dry summer
Humid summer
Rainy summer
Continental
Long summer
Short summer
Very short, cool summer
Polar
Tundra
Ice cap
Highlands
Varies
Arctic Circle
Atlantic Ocean
Stockholm
Moscow
London
Paris
Madrid
Rome
© Rand McNally

Western Europe has a mild, rainy climate.

Population

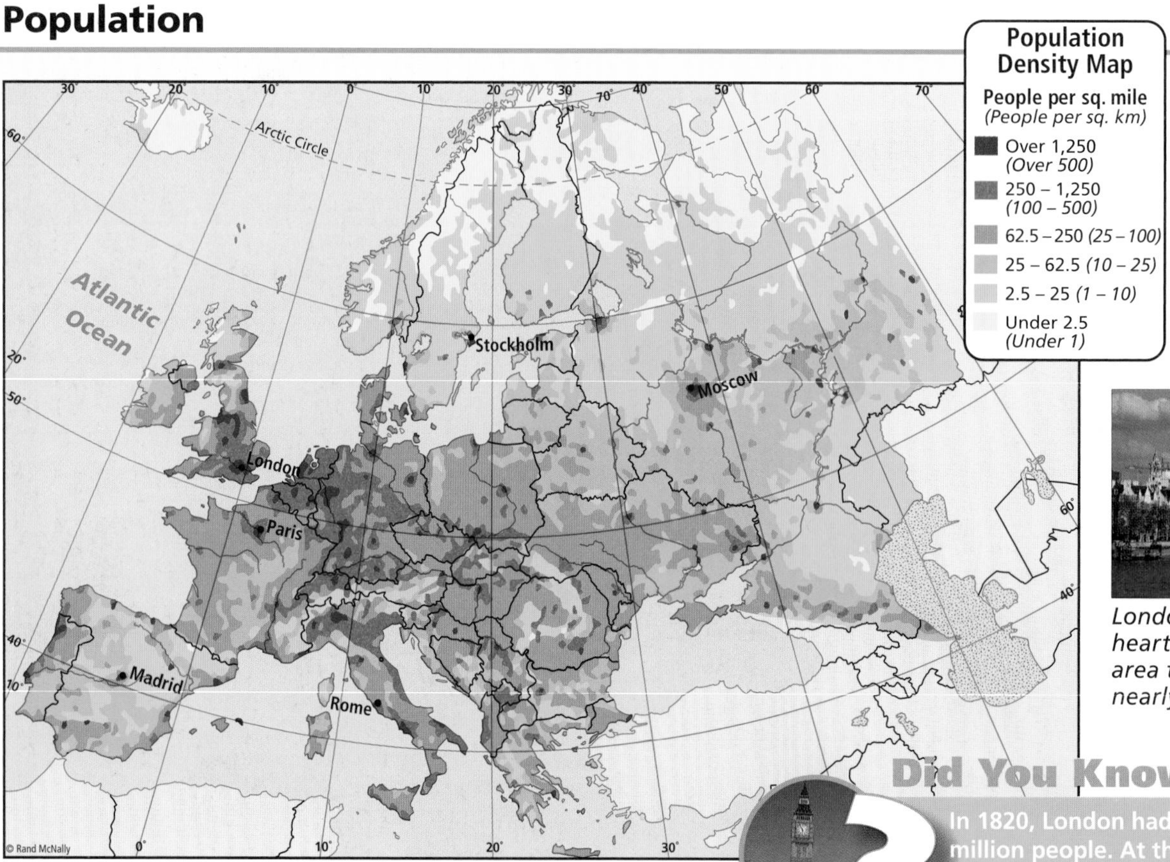
Population Density Map
People per sq. mile
(People per sq. km)
Over 1,250 (Over 500)
250 – 1,250 (100 – 500)
62.5 – 250 (25 – 100)
25 – 62.5 (10 – 25)
2.5 – 25 (1 – 10)
Under 2.5 (Under 1)
Arctic Circle
Atlantic Ocean
Stockholm
Moscow
London
Paris
Madrid
Rome
© Rand McNally

London, England, is the heart of a metropolitan area that is home to nearly 13 million people.

Did You Know?

In 1820, London had more than one million people. At the same time, New York City had just 124,000 people, and Denver had not even been founded yet.

Environments

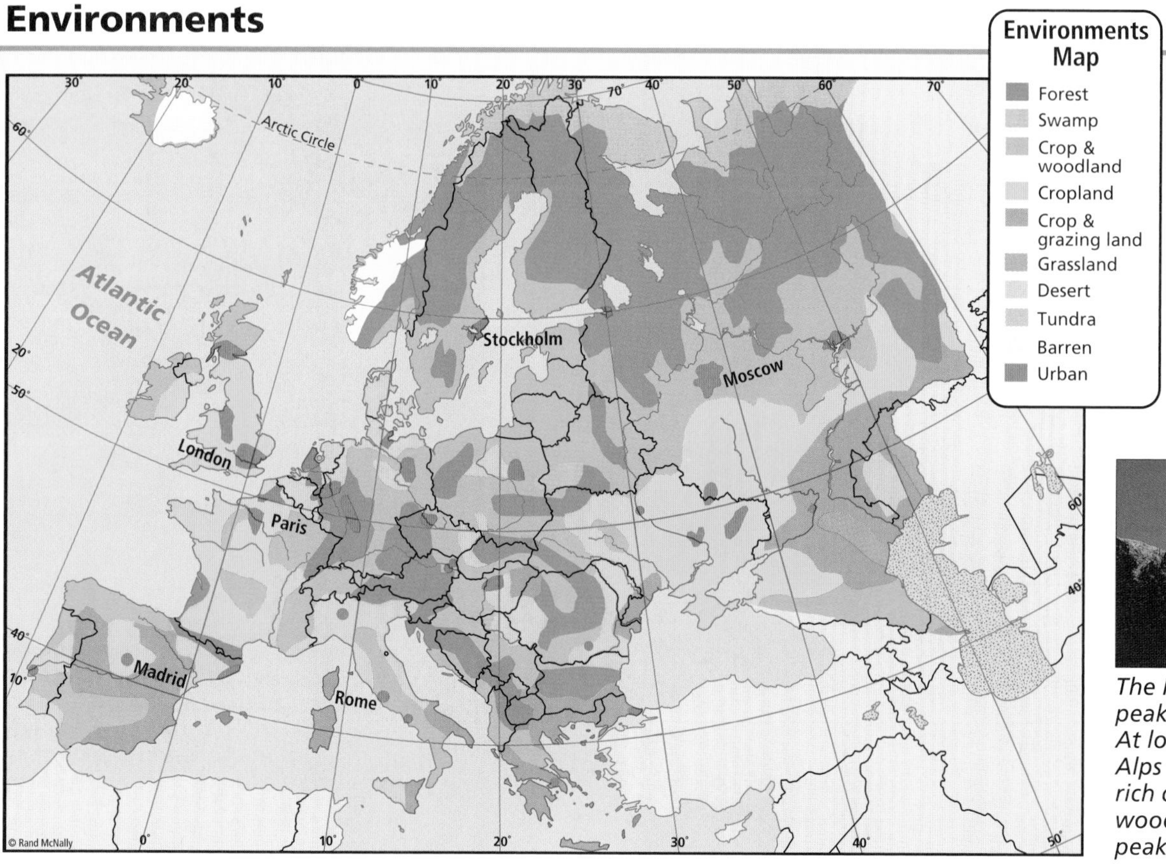

The Matterhorn is a peak in the Swiss Alps. At lower elevations, the Alps are covered with rich cropland and woodland. The higher peaks are barren.

Economic Activities

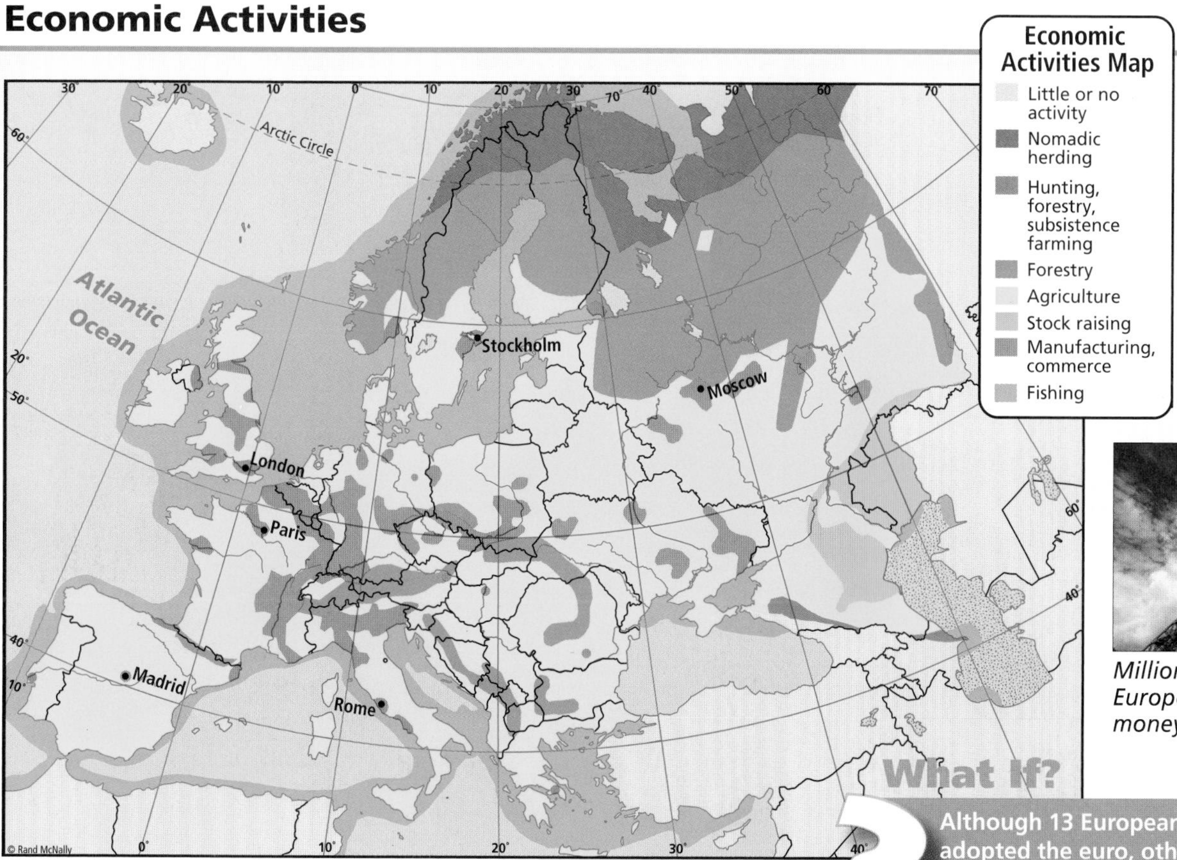

Millions of tourists visit Europe each year, bringing money to local economies.

What If?

Although 13 European countries have adopted the euro, others still have their own kind of money. What would it be like if each U.S. state had its own currency?

Natural Hazards

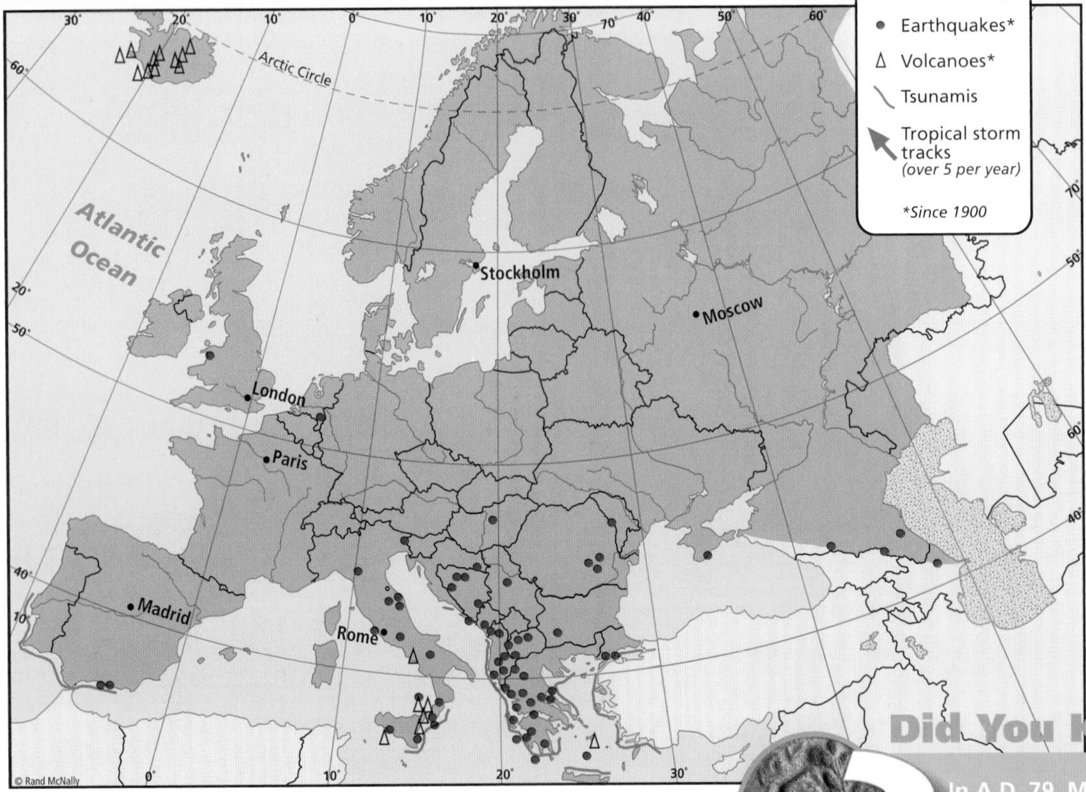

Lisbon, the capital of Portugal, was devastated by an earthquake in 1755.

Volcanic eruptions are a natural hazard in Italy. This photo shows Mt. Etna on the island of Sicily.

Did You Know?

In A.D. 79, Mt. Vesuvius erupted and buried the ancient city of Pompeii, Italy, under 20 feet (6 meters) of volcanic ash.

Transportation

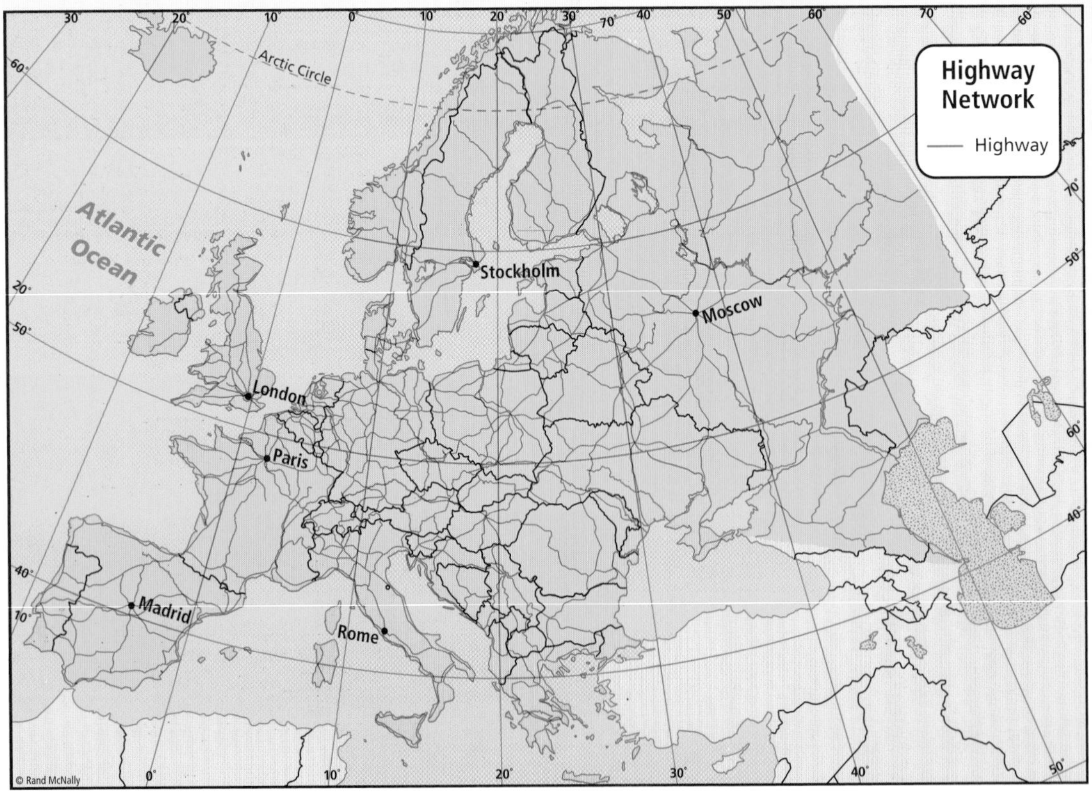

A canal boat is a modern means of transportation in Amsterdam, the Netherlands.

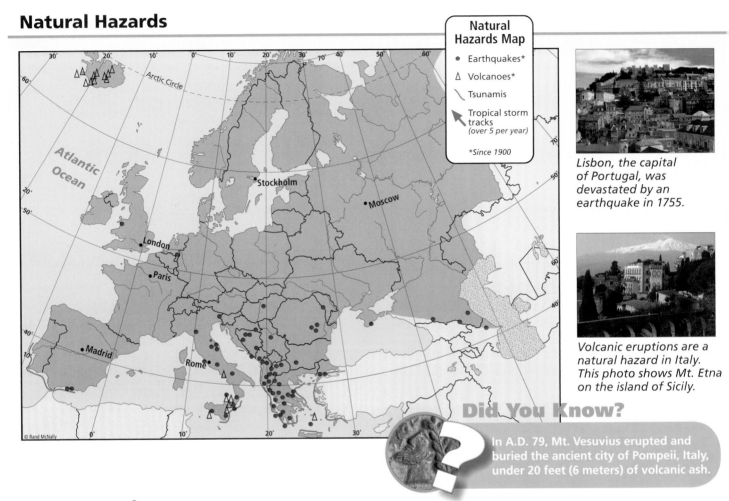

High-speed rail systems connect many European cities.

Energy

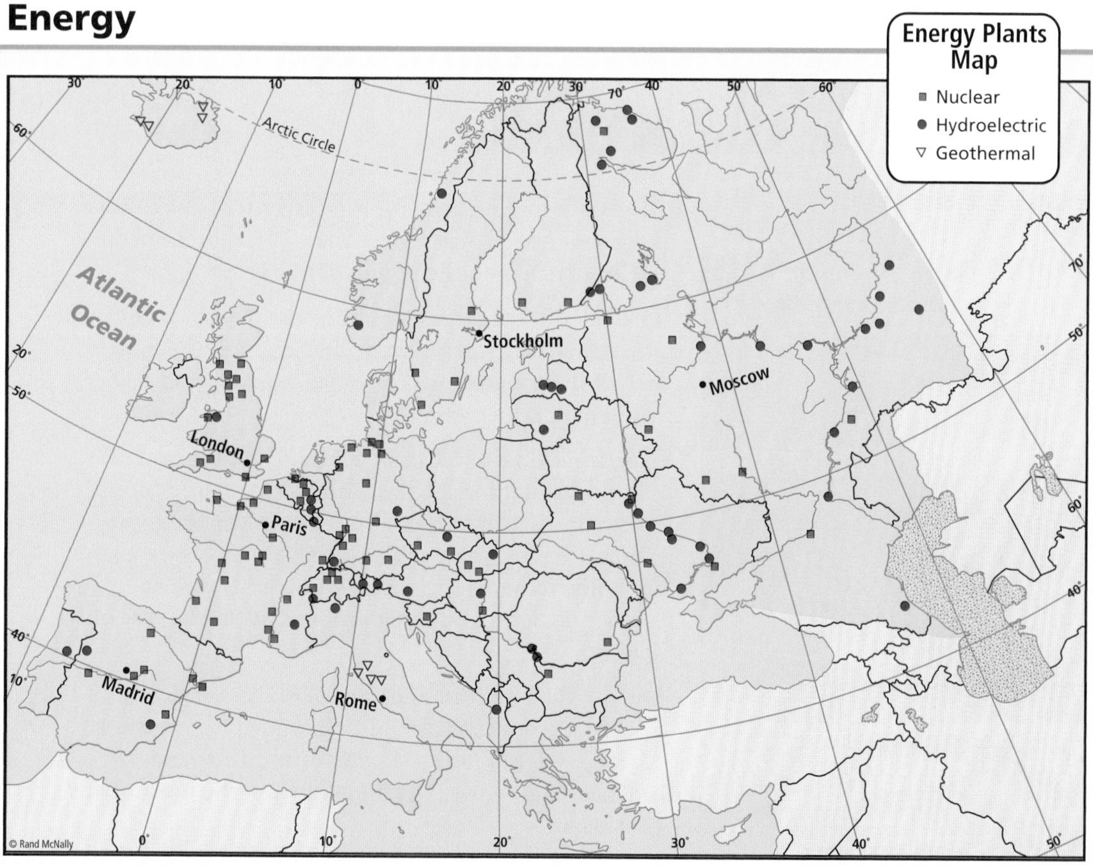
Energy Plants Map
Nuclear
Hydroelectric
Geothermal
Atlantic Ocean
Arctic Circle
Stockholm
Moscow
London
Paris
Madrid
Rome
© Rand McNally

In Iceland, water from hot springs heats homes and fuels geothermal plants.

Hydroelectric power is important in some parts of Europe. This dam is in Switzerland.

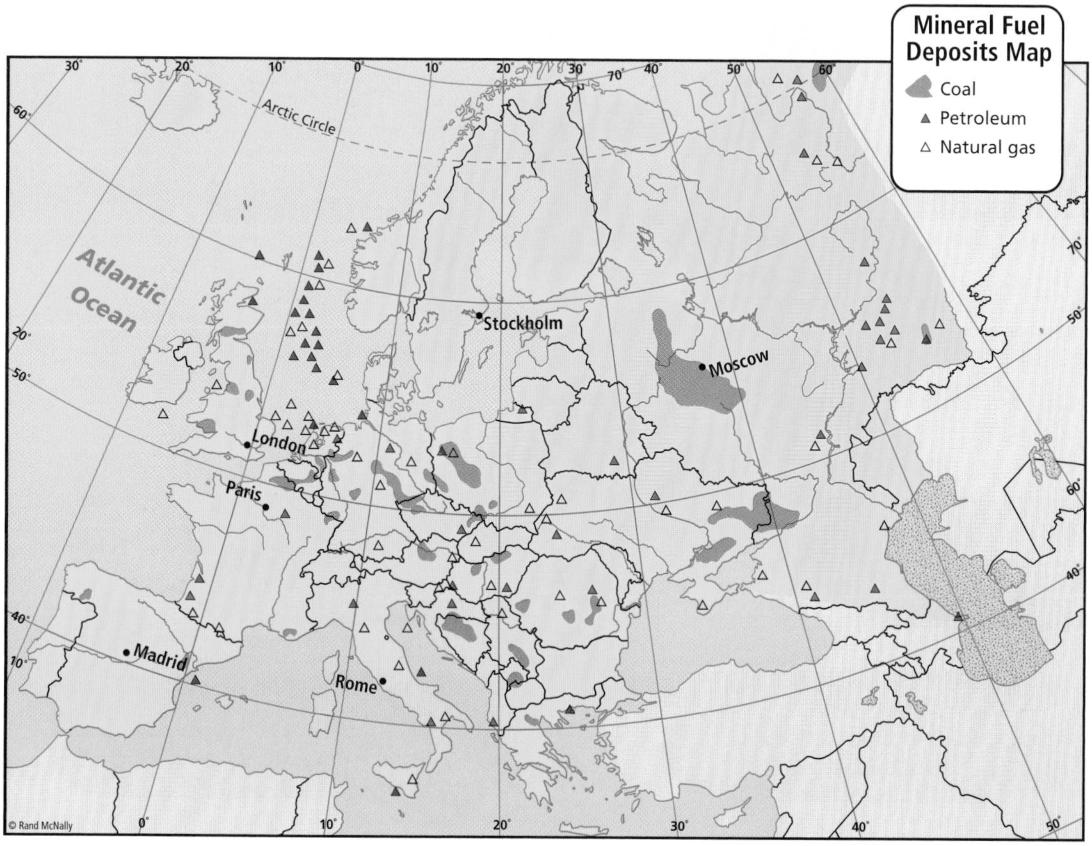
Mineral Fuel Deposits Map
Coal
Petroleum
Natural gas
Atlantic Ocean
Arctic Circle
Stockholm
Moscow
London
Paris
Madrid
Rome
© Rand McNally

North Sea oil and gas are important sources of energy for the United Kingdom and Norway.

Coal was the first fuel for modern factories, but today it is less favored because it is so polluting.

Africa

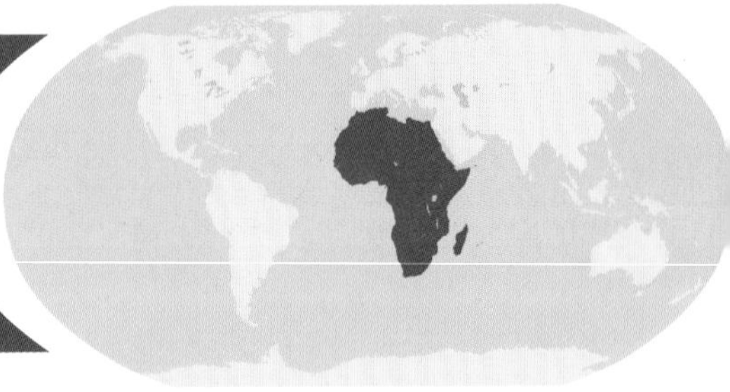

African elephant

Africa is a huge continent. It is larger than every other continent except Asia. More than 866 million people live in Africa, and the population is growing fast.

The Sahara, the largest desert in the world, covers most of northern Africa. South of the Sahara is the Sahel, an area of dry grasslands. The Sahel expands and recedes with changes in climate.

The tropical rain forests of central Africa provide a natural habitat for gorillas, chimpanzees, and monkeys. North and south of the rain forests and in eastern Africa are vast grassy plains, or savannas. These plains are home to herds of grazing animals, as well as elephants, lions, and other animals most of us see only in zoos.

During the late 19th and early 20th centuries, European countries occupied and governed most of Africa. Today, almost every country in Africa is independent. Africa has 54 countries, the most of any continent.

Many of Africa's people are poor, and they face great challenges in health care, literacy, and life expectancy. Terrible civil wars have torn apart several nations.

Nevertheless, Africa has many possibilities. Hydroelectric power from the Congo and other rivers, minerals such as iron and copper, and improved farming methods offer the hope of better lives to many Africans.

Did You Know?

Tectonic forces are slowly tearing Africa into two parts. The Rift Valley in eastern Africa marks the dividing line.

A Historical Look At Africa

Circa 140,000 B.C.

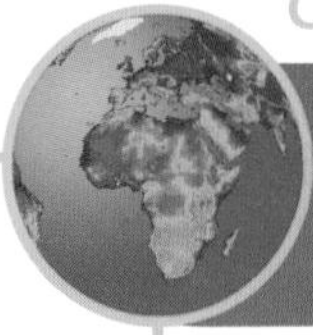

The first people live in Africa.

Permanent fishing communities are established along many lakes and rivers.

Circa 8000 B.C.

3000 B.C.–400 A.D.

The Nile River valley is home to thriving civilizations.

The kingdom of Ghana flourishes in the Sahel.

500–1076

African Independence

In the late 19th and early 20th centuries, European countries colonized in almost all of Africa. As recently as 1950, only four African countries were independent: Egypt, Ethiopia, Liberia, and South Africa. During the following decades, anti-colonial movements gathered strength across the continent. By the end of the 1970s, a total of 43 countries had become independent. Today, the only African country that is not independent is Western Sahara, which is under the control of Morocco.

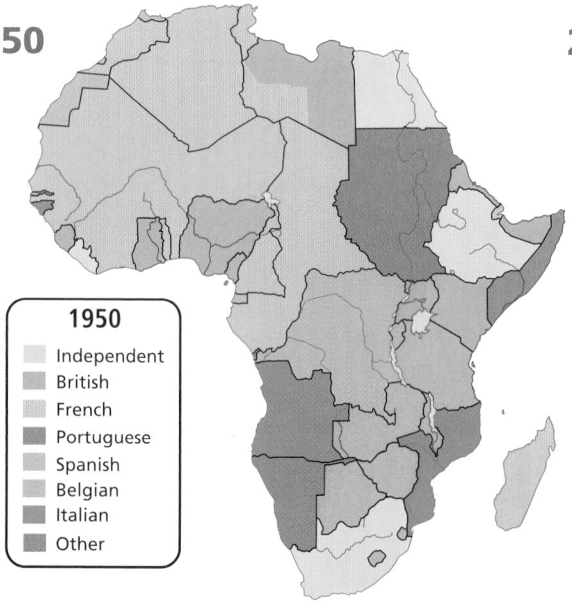
1950
1950
Independent
British
French
Portuguese
Spanish
Belgian
Italian
Other

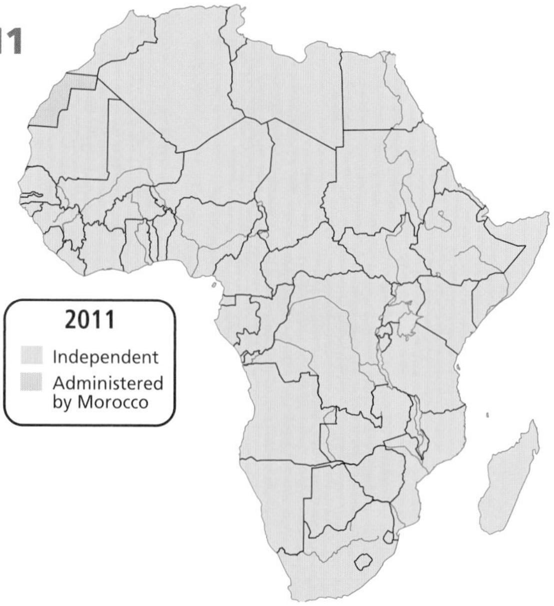
2011
2011
Independent
Administered by Morocco

The People of Africa

There are more than 800 ethnic groups in Africa. It is estimated that the people of Africa speak between 800 and 1,600 different languages.

Children from Egypt

Girl from Ethiopia

Women from Mauritius

Shepherd from the Sahel

1847

Liberia, founded as a refuge for freed slaves returning to Africa, gains independence.

1885

European countries divide Africa into colonies.

1950–1979

Most African countries become independent.

1991

South Africa ends apartheid, the official policy of racial segregation.

2011

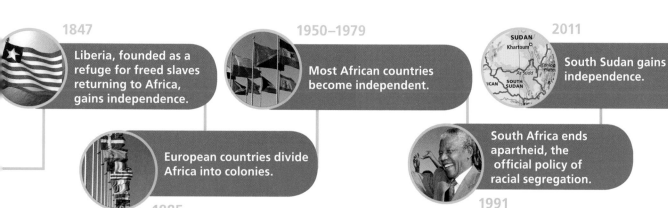

South Sudan gains independence.

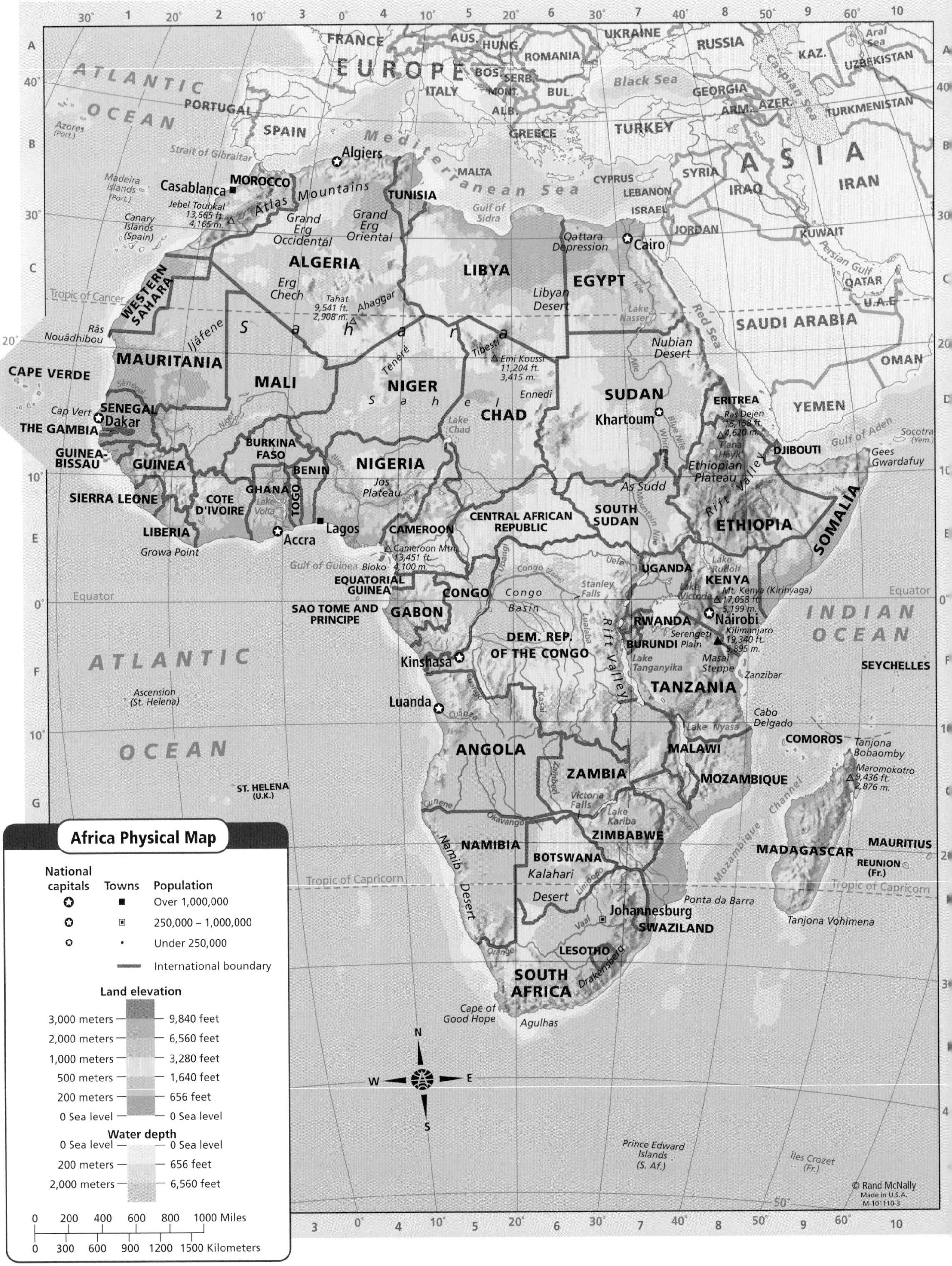
Africa Physical Map
National capitals
Towns
Population
Over 1,000,000
250,000 – 1,000,000
Under 250,000
International boundary
Land elevation
3,000 meters — 9,840 feet
2,000 meters — 6,560 feet
1,000 meters — 3,280 feet
500 meters — 1,640 feet
200 meters — 656 feet
0 Sea level — 0 Sea level
Water depth
0 Sea level — 0 Sea level
200 meters — 656 feet
2,000 meters — 6,560 feet
0 200 400 600 800 1000 Miles
0 300 600 900 1200 1500 Kilometers
N
W
E
S
EUROPE
FRANCE
AUS.
HUNG.
UKRAINE
RUSSIA
ROMANIA
BOS.
SERB.
MONT.
ALB.
BUL.
ITALY
PORTUGAL
SPAIN
GREECE
TURKEY
Black Sea
GEORGIA
ARM.
AZER.
KAZ.
UZBEKISTAN
TURKMENISTAN
Aral Sea
Caspian Sea
ASIA
SYRIA
IRAQ
IRAN
CYPRUS
LEBANON
ISRAEL
JORDAN
KUWAIT
Persian Gulf
QATAR
U.A.E.
SAUDI ARABIA
OMAN
YEMEN
Gulf of Aden
Socotra (Yem.)
ATLANTIC OCEAN
Azores (Port.)
Strait of Gibraltar
Madeira Islands (Port.)
Canary Islands (Spain)
Mediterranean Sea
MALTA
Algiers
Casablanca
MOROCCO
TUNISIA
Atlas Mountains
Jebel Toubkal 13,665 ft. 4,165 m.
Grand Erg Occidental
Grand Erg Oriental
Gulf of Sidra
ALGERIA
LIBYA
EGYPT
Cairo
Qattara Depression
Libyan Desert
Nile
Lake Nasser
Red Sea
Tropic of Cancer
WESTERN SAHARA
Erg Chech
Tahat 9,541 ft. 2,908 m.
Ahaggar
Sahara
Râs Nouâdhibou
MAURITANIA
Ijâfene
MALI
NIGER
Ténéré
Tibesti
Emi Koussi 11,204 ft. 3,415 m.
Nubian Desert
CAPE VERDE
Sahel
Ennedi
SUDAN
Khartoum
Blue Nile
White Nile
ERITREA
Ras Dejen 15,158 ft. 4,620 m.
Tana Hayk'
DJIBOUTI
Gees Gwardafuy
Sénégal
Cap Vert
SENEGAL
Dakar
THE GAMBIA
CHAD
Lake Chad
GUINEA-BISSAU
GUINEA
BURKINA FASO
BENIN
NIGERIA
Niger
Jos Plateau
Benue
Ethiopian Plateau
Rift Valley
As Sudd
SOUTH SUDAN
Mountain Nile
ETHIOPIA
SOMALIA
SIERRA LEONE
COTE D'IVOIRE
GHANA
TOGO
Lake Volta
LIBERIA
Accra
Lagos
CAMEROON
CENTRAL AFRICAN REPUBLIC
Growa Point
Cameroon Mtn. 13,451 ft. 4,100 m.
Gulf of Guinea
Bioko
EQUATORIAL GUINEA
Ubangi
Congo (Zaire)
Uele
UGANDA
Lake Rudolf
KENYA
Lake Victoria
Mt. Kenya (Kirinyaga) 17,058 ft. 5,199 m.
Equator
CONGO
Congo Basin
Stanley Falls
SAO TOME AND PRINCIPE
GABON
Nairobi
RWANDA
BURUNDI
Serengeti Plain
Kilimanjaro 19,340 ft. 5,895 m.
INDIAN OCEAN
DEM. REP. OF THE CONGO
Lualaba
Rift Valley
Lake Tanganyika
Masai Steppe
Zanzibar
SEYCHELLES
Kinshasa
TANZANIA
Ascension (St. Helena)
Luanda
Cuango
Cuanza
Kasai
Cabo Delgado
Lake Nyasa
COMOROS
Tanjona Bobaomby
ANGOLA
MALAWI
Zambezi
ZAMBIA
MOZAMBIQUE
Maromokotro 9,436 ft. 2,876 m.
ST. HELENA (U.K.)
Victoria Falls
Lake Kariba
Mozambique Channel
Cunene
Okavango
ZIMBABWE
NAMIBIA
Namib Desert
BOTSWANA
Kalahari Desert
Limpopo
MADAGASCAR
MAURITIUS
REUNION (Fr.)
Tropic of Capricorn
Ponta da Barra
Tanjona Vohimena
Johannesburg
Vaal
SWAZILAND
Orange
LESOTHO
Drakensberg
SOUTH AFRICA
Cape of Good Hope
Agulhas
Prince Edward Islands (S. Af.)
Îles Crozet (Fr.)
© Rand McNally
Made in U.S.A.
M-101110-3

ATLANTIC OCEAN

FRANCE
AUS. HUNG.
EUROPE
BOS. ROMANIA
SERB.
ITALY BUL.
Rome ALB.
GREECE
Athens
MALTA

PORTUGAL
Madrid
SPAIN
Strait of Gibraltar
Azores (Port.)
Madeira Islands (Port.)

Algiers
Oran
Constantine
Tunis
TUNISIA
Tripoli
Ghardaïa

UKRAINE
RUSSIA
KAZ.
Aral Sea
UZBEKISTAN

Black Sea
GEORGIA
ARM. AZER.
TURKMENISTAN
TURKEY
CYPRUS
SYRIA
LEBANON
ISRAEL
JORDAN

ASIA
IRAQ
IRAN
KUWAIT
Persian Gulf
QATAR
U.A.E.

Casablanca
Rabat
MOROCCO
Marrakech
Canary Islands (Spain)
Laayoune
WESTERN SAHARA
Tropic of Cancer

ALGERIA
Tamanrasset

LIBYA
Sabhā
Gulf of Sidra
Banghāzi
Tripoli

Alexandria
Cairo Suez
Asyût
EGYPT
Aswân
Lake Nasser

Riyadh
SAUDI ARABIA
OMAN

MAURITANIA
Nouakchott
PE VERDE
Tombouctou
Sénégal
Dakar
SENEGAL
HE GAMBIA
Bamako
GUINEA-BISSAU
Conakry
GUINEA
Freetown
SIERRA LEONE
Monrovia
LIBERIA
Abidjan

MALI
Gao
Niger
BURKINA FASO
Ouagadougou
Niamey
Zinder
Lake Chad
N'Djamena
Kano
BENIN
NIGERIA
Abuja
TOGO
GHANA
Lake Volta
Cotonou
Accra
Ibadan
Lagos

NIGER
CHAD
Abéché
SUDAN

Omdurman
Khartoum
Blue Nile
White Nile
ERITREA
Asmara
YEMEN
Socotra (Yem.)

Port Sudan
Red Sea

DJIBOUTI
Djibouti
Lake Tana
SOUTH SUDAN
Juba
Addis Ababa
Dire Dawa
ETHIOPIA
Gulf of Aden

CAMEROON
Douala
Malabo
Yaoundé
EQUATORIAL GUINEA
SAO TOME AND PRINCIPE
Libreville
GABON
CONGO
Brazzaville
Kinshasa

CENTRAL AFRICAN REPUBLIC
Bangui
Congo (Zaïre)
Kisangani
DEM. REP. OF THE CONGO
Kigali
Bujumbura
Mbuji-Mayi

UGANDA
Kampala
Lake Victoria
RWANDA
BURUNDI
Dodoma
Lake Tanganyika

SOMALIA
Mogadishu
KENYA
Nairobi
INDIAN OCEAN

Equator

ATLANTIC
OCEAN
Ascension (St. Helena)

Luanda
Lobito
ANGOLA
Huambo

ST. HELENA (U.K.)

Kolwezi
Lubumbashi
Ndola
Zambezi

Mombasa
TANZANIA
Dar es Salaam
SEYCHELLES

Lake Nyasa
MALAWI
Lilongwe
ZAMBIA
Lusaka
Harare
ZIMBABWE
Bulawayo
MOZAMBIQUE
Beira
COMOROS
MAYOTTE (FR.)
Antsirañana
Antananarivo
MADAGASCAR
MAURITIUS
Fianarantsoa
REUNION (Fr.)

NAMIBIA
Walvis Bay
Windhoek
BOTSWANA
Gaborone
Limpopo
Pretoria (Tshwane)
Johannesburg
Maputo
SWAZILAND
Orange
Maseru
LESOTHO
Durban
SOUTH AFRICA
Cape Town
Port Elizabeth

Tropic of Capricorn
Mozambique Channel

Capitals not shown on map

Country	Capital
Benin	Porto-Novo
Cape Verde	Praia
Comoros	Moroni
Cote d'Ivoire	Yamoussoukro
Guinea-Bissau	Bissau
Mauritius	Port Louis
Mayotte (Fr.)	Mamoutzou
Réunion (Fr.)	Saint-Denis
St. Helena (U.K.)	Jamestown
Sao Tome and Principe	São Tomé
Seychelles	Victoria
Swaziland	Lobamba, Mbabane
The Gambia	Banjul
Togo	Lomé

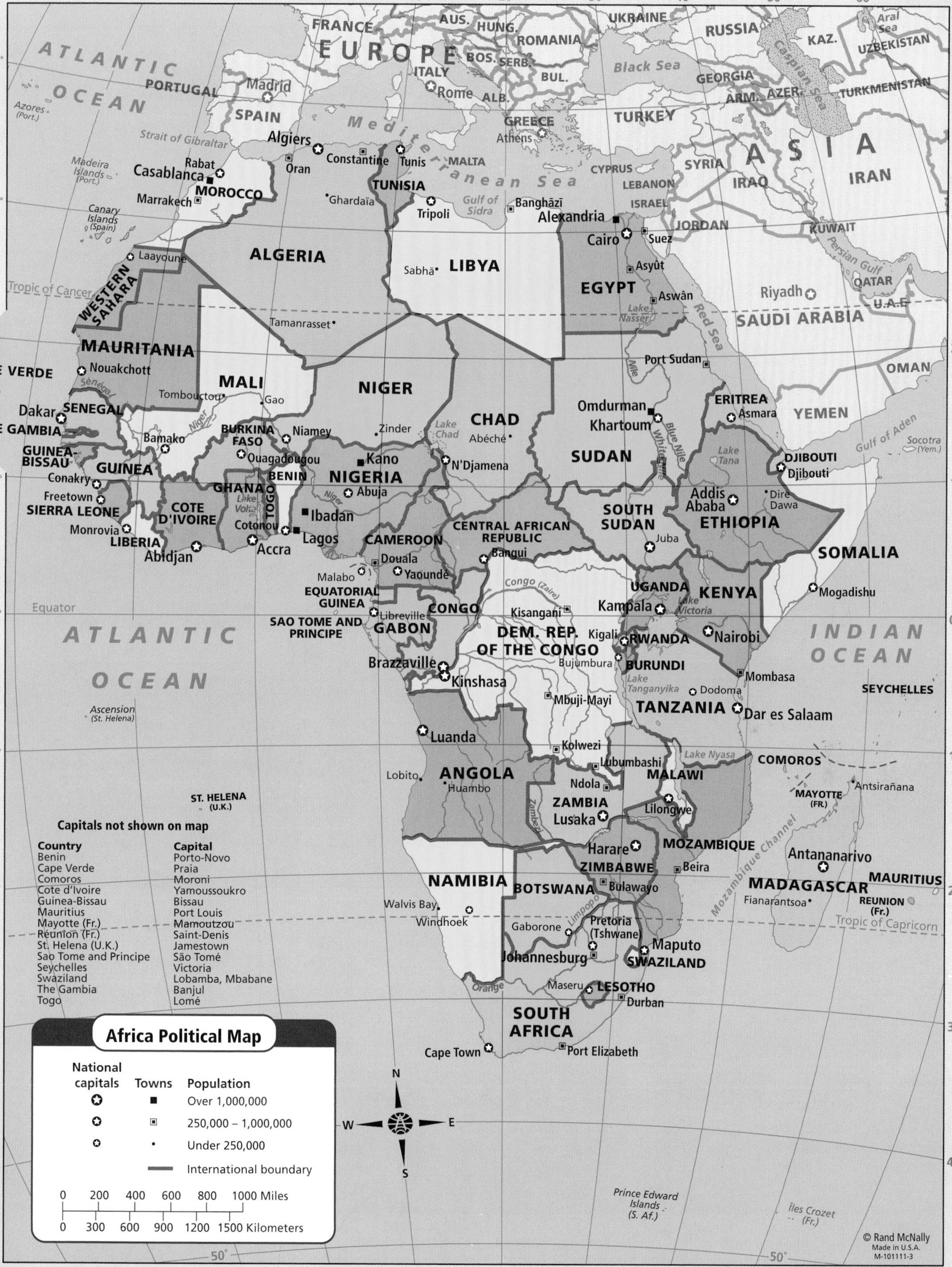

Africa Political Map

National capitals	Towns	Population
⊛	■	Over 1,000,000
⊛	▣	250,000 – 1,000,000
⊛	•	Under 250,000
—		International boundary

N W E S

| 0 | 200 | 400 | 600 | 800 | 1000 Miles |
| 0 | 300 | 600 | 900 | 1200 | 1500 Kilometers |

Prince Edward Islands (S. Af.)
Îles Crozet (Fr.)

© Rand McNally
Made in U.S.A.
M-101111-3

Environments

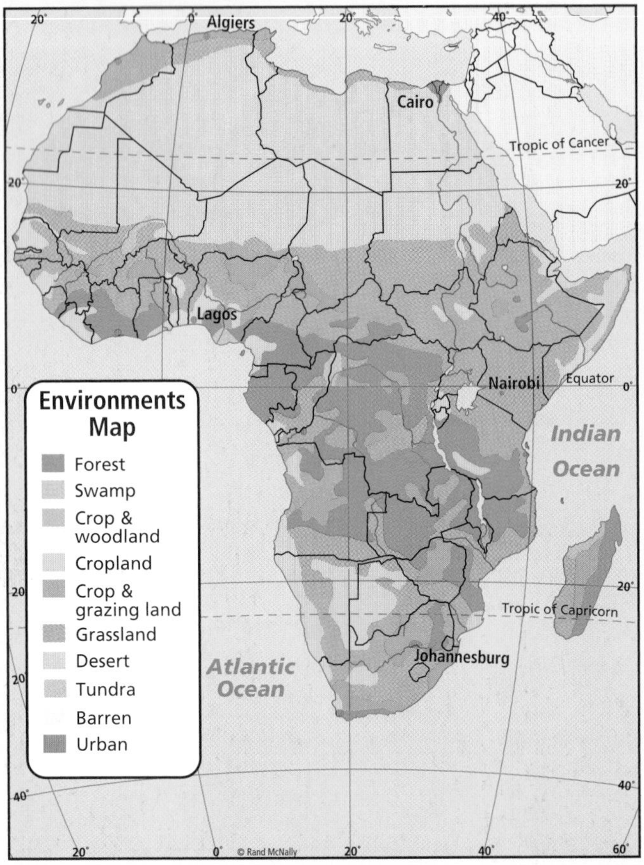

Tropical rain forests of central Africa are hot and humid. Jungles are areas of dense, tangled plant growth in these forests.

An erg is a large area of sand dunes in a desert. Deserts cover about one-third of Africa.

Savannas, areas of grassland with few trees, cover about two-fifths of Africa's land area. Similar areas in North America are called prairies.

The region known as the Sahel borders the Sahara on the south. Overfarming, overgrazing, and droughts have caused parts of the Sahel to become desert.

An oasis in a desert is found where underground water comes to the surface.

Although many Africans still live in the countryside, Africa has large, modern cities. This is a view of Johannesburg, South Africa.

Africa's most fertile cropland is found along its rivers. This farm is in Egypt's Nile River valley.

Climate

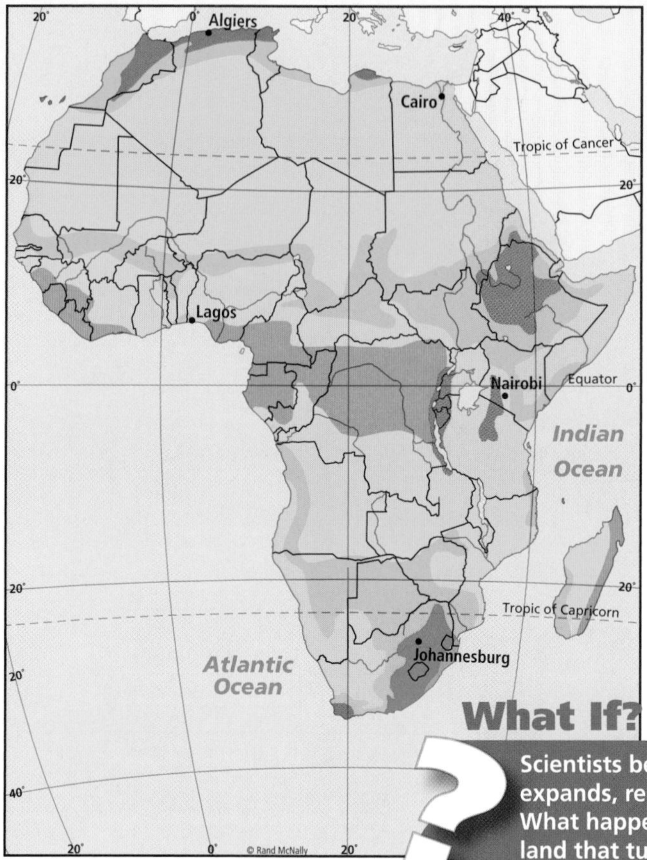

Climate Map

Tropical
- Hot with rain all year
- Hot with seasonal rain

Dry
- Desert
- Some rain

Moderate (Rainy Winter)
- Hot, dry summer
- Hot, humid summer
- Mild, rainy summer

Continental (Snowy Winter)
- Long, warm, humid summer
- Short, cool, humid summer
- Very short, cool, humid summer

Polar
- Tundra – very cold and dry
- Ice cap

Highlands
- Varies with altitude

The Sahara

The Sahara is the largest hot desert in the world. It covers about two-and-a-half million square miles (six million square kilometers). The name "Sahara" comes from the Arabic word for desert.

The highest temperature ever recorded in the world was in the Sahara: 136° F (58° C). But the Sahara can be very cold at night because the dry air does not hold much heat. The daytime and nighttime temperatures can differ by as much as 100° F (56° C).

On average, rainfall in the Sahara is less than 10 inches (25 centimeters) per year. There may be no rain at all for years at a time.

Besides sand, the Sahara has vast areas of gravel, rocky plateaus, and volcanic mountains.

What If?

Scientists believe that the Sahara expands, recedes, and expands again. What happens if people settle on fertile land that turns back into desert?

Animals of the Savanna

African elephants

Lion

Thomson's gazelles

White rhinoceroses

Cheetah and cubs

Zebras

Natural Hazards

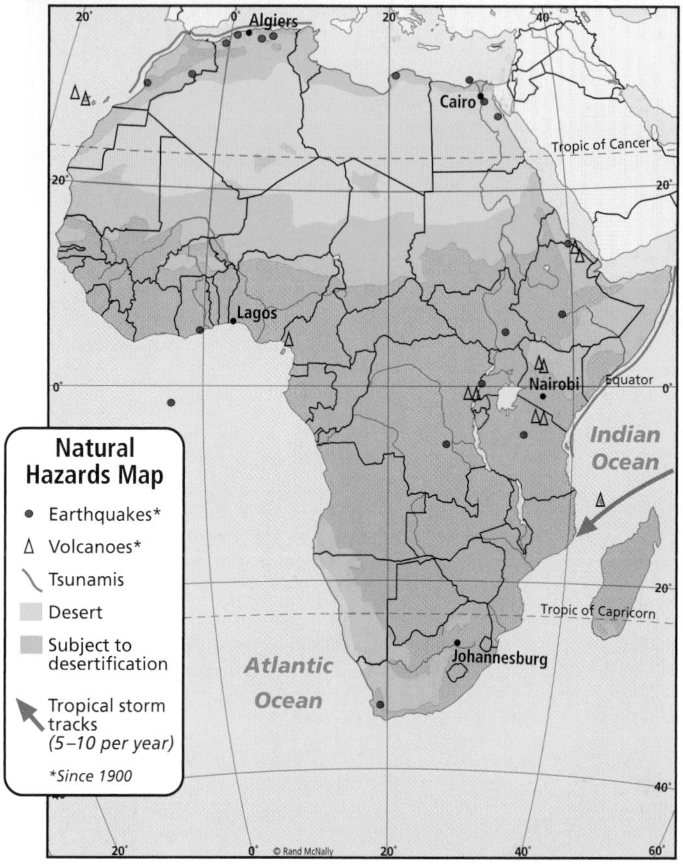

Population

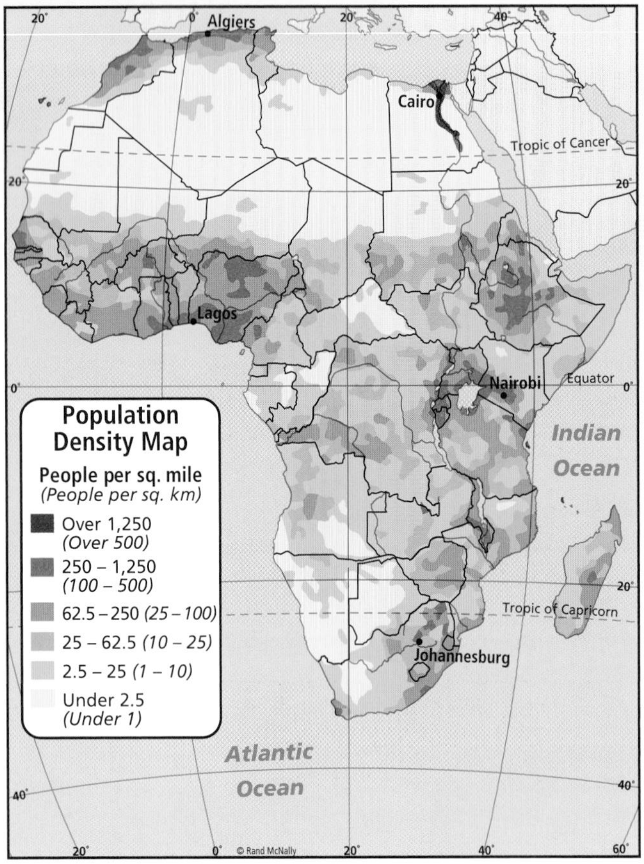

Life Expectancy

Life expectancy varies widely across Africa. In recent decades, the deadly disease AIDS has shortened the average life span of people in many African countries, especially those south of the Sahara Desert.

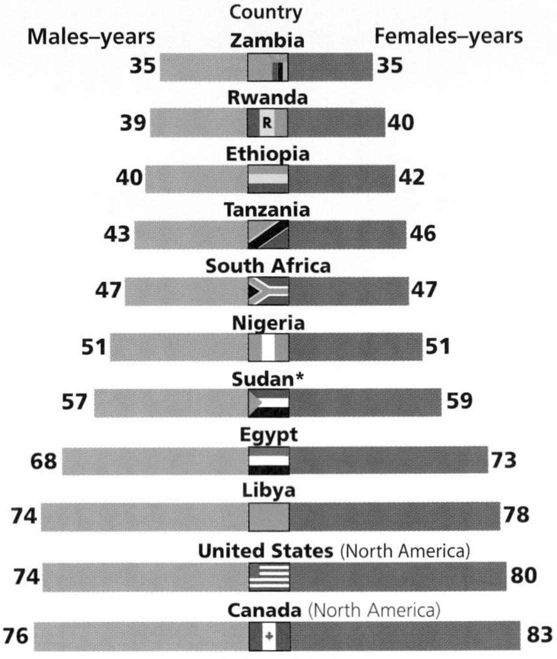

Transportation

Did You Know?

During the 1967 war with Israel, Egypt sank ships in the Suez Canal to block traffic. The canal stayed closed for eight years.

Fewer than 10% of the roads in Africa are paved.

Camels are still used to transport goods across the desert. Their heavy-lidded eyes and closeable nostrils offer protection in sandstorms, and they can travel long distances without water.

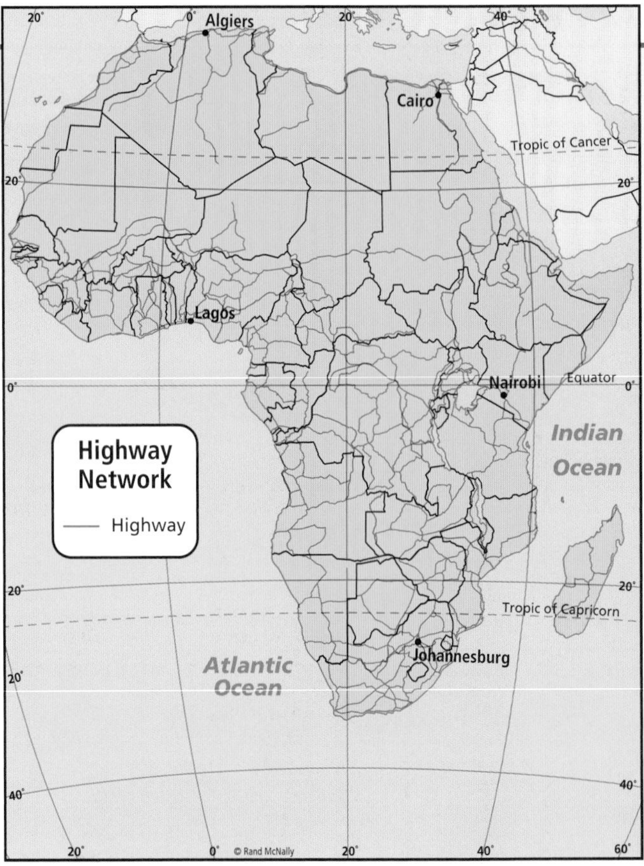

Economic Activities

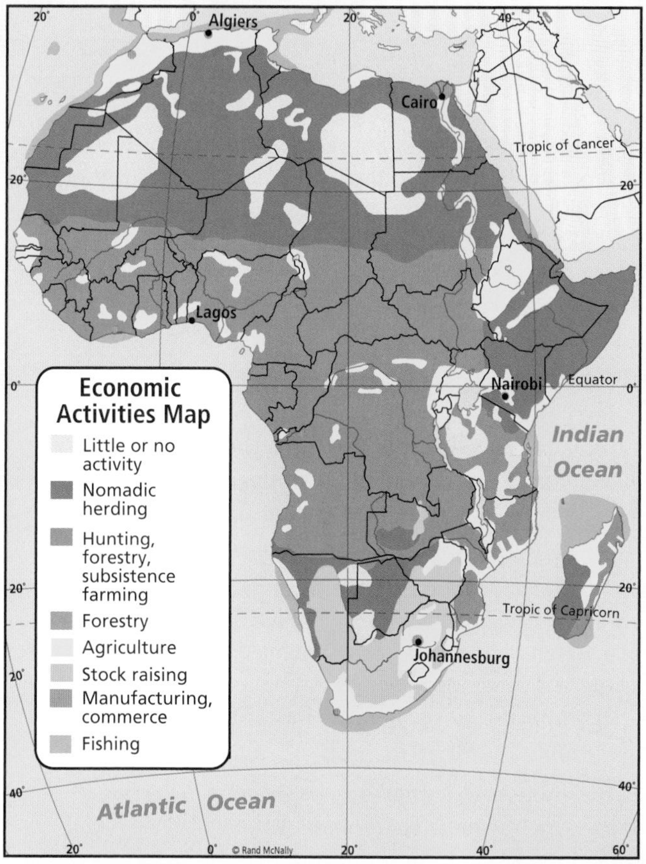

Per Capita Income

Per capita income measures the relative wealth of countries. Most African countries have per capita incomes far below those of the three wealthy non-African countries included in this graph: Sweden, Canada, and the United States.

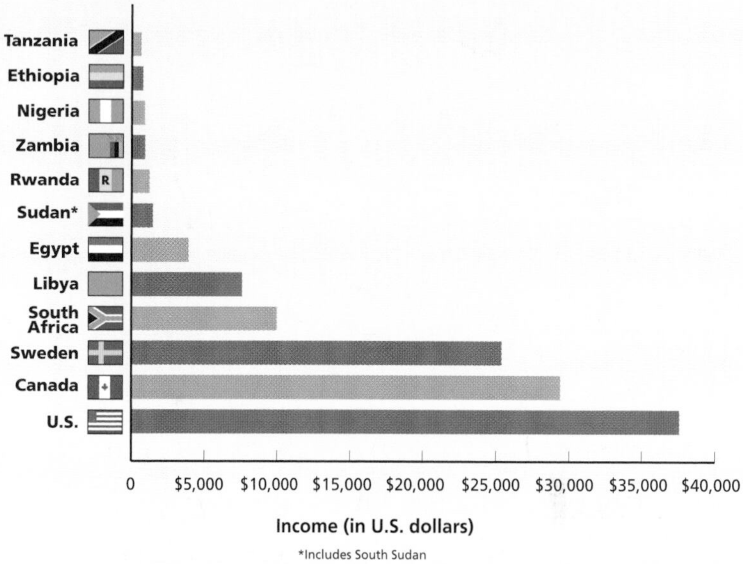

In many parts of Africa, nomadic herding is the way of life for most people.

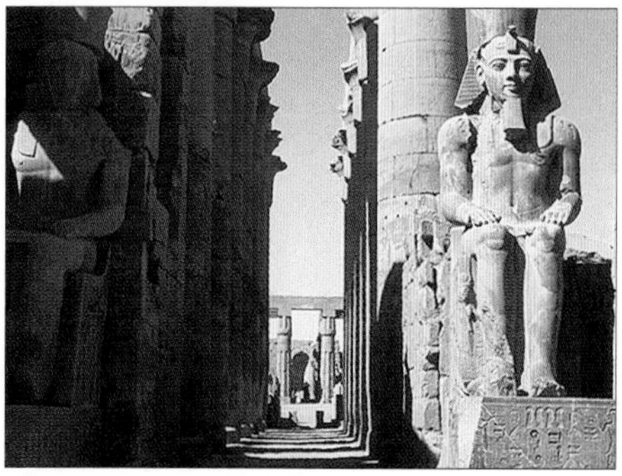

The monuments of ancient Egypt attract millions of visitors each year. Tourism revenue is an important contributor to Egypt's economy.

About three-quarters of all Africans make a living by farming.

World Gold Production

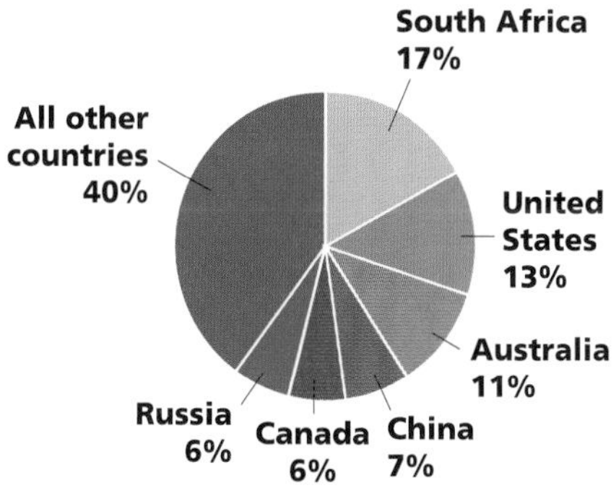
South Africa 17%
United States 13%
Australia 11%
China 7%
Canada 6%
Russia 6%
All other countries 40%

World Platinum Production

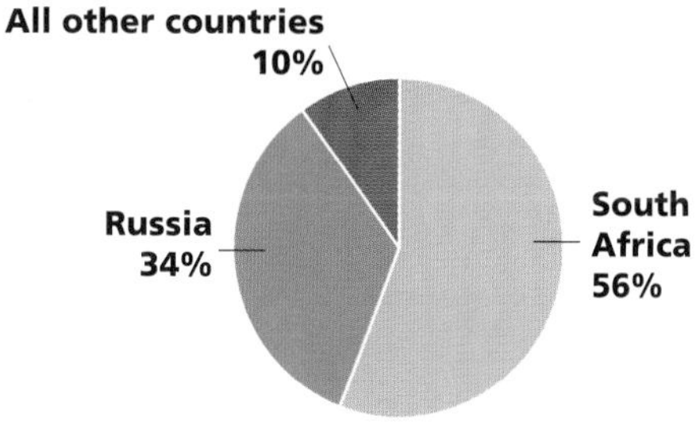
All other countries 10%
Russia 34%
South Africa 56%

World Diamond Production

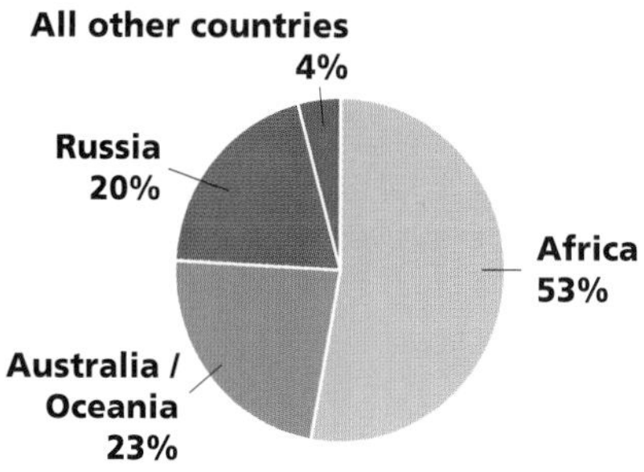
All other countries 4%
Russia 20%
Africa 53%
Australia / Oceania 23%

One reason for the high annual per capita income for South Africa is that it is rich in gold, platinum, and diamonds. Discovery of these precious mineral resources in the 1800s brought many Europeans to settle in South Africa.

Asia

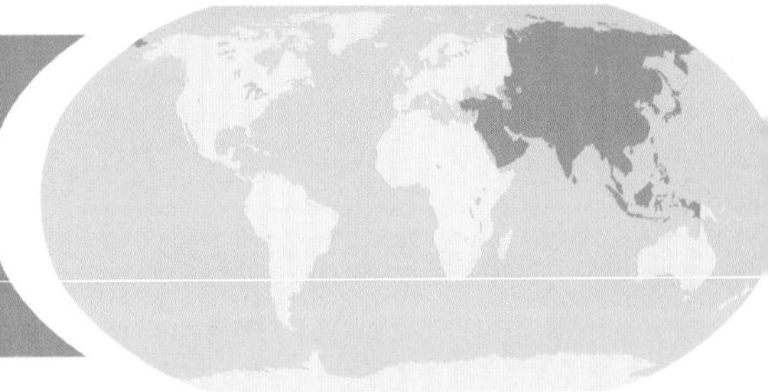

Terraced rice field in Bali, Indonesia

Asia is the world's largest continent, and it is immense. It covers more than 17 million square miles (44 million square kilometers). It stretches from the sands of the Middle Eastern deserts in the west to the island country of Japan in the east. In the north, Siberian Russia extends beyond the Arctic Circle, while in the south Indonesia reaches the equator.

Asia is home to some of the world's oldest civilizations. Farming, cities, and writing began in Mesopotamia, in the Indus River valley, and in China thousands of years ago. Asians also invented many things that we use today, such as the idea of zero, paper, the printing press, and the magnetic compass.

Many countries in Asia are working to develop their economies, and their people still have difficult lives. Other Asian countries such as Japan, Taiwan, and Singapore are economic powers. The fortunes of the oil-rich countries of the Middle East depend on the value of their oil exports.

Asia has more people than any other continent: 3.8 billion, which is more than 60% of the world's people. China alone has 1.3 billion people, and India has passed one billion. Eastern China is as densely populated as the New York City urban area.

Mt. Fuji in Japan

Limestone pinnacles along the Li River in China

Did You Know?

The highest point in the world (Mt. Everest) and the lowest point (the Dead Sea) are both in Asia.

A Historical Look At Asia

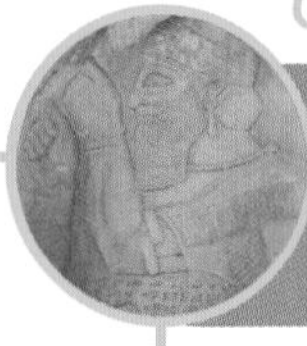

Circa 3500 B.C.
Sumerian civilization begins in Mesopotamia (modern Iraq).

214 B.C.
Construction of the Great Wall of China begins.

A.D. 618–907
The T'ang Dynasty rules China.

1631–1648
The Taj Mahal is built in India.

The Regions of Asia

Asia has six distinct regions. Use the political map on pages 96 and 97 to determine the countries in each region.

Central Asia

Central Asia is rugged and dry. Farming in most places is difficult, and many people make a living as nomadic herders. The region has large deposits of oil.

Southwest Asia

Most of Southwest Asia is desert and semi-desert. The region has the world's richest deposits of oil.

South Asia

India and neighboring countries make up South Asia. The Himalayas border the northeastern part of this region.

North Asia

North Asia has long, bitterly cold winters. Despite its mineral resources, fewer people live in North Asia than in any other part of the continent.

East Asia

Eastern China and its neighbors make up East Asia. About one quarter of the world's people live in East Asia.

Southeast Asia

The southeast part of the Asian mainland and many islands make up Southeast Asia. Most of the region has a tropical climate.

Central Asia

Southwest Asia

South Asia

North Asia

East Asia

Southeast Asia

1854

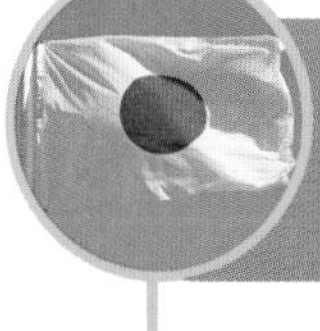

Japan begins trading with the United States.

Circa 1900

Britain begins developing oil fields in southwestern Iran.

1947

India is divided into two countries, India and Pakistan, and both become independent from British rule..

2004

Powerful tsunamis devastate coastal areas of Southeast and South Asia.

Mt. Everest, which rises along the border between Nepal and China, is the world's highest mountain. It is 29,028 feet (8,848 meters) high.

The Dead Sea located between Isreal and Jordan, is the lowest point on earth. Its shore is 1,339 feet (408 meters) below sea level.

Lake Baikal in Russia is the deepest lake in the world. Its greatest depth is slightly more than a mile.

Russia's Kamchatka Peninsula is one of the most volcanically active places in the world.

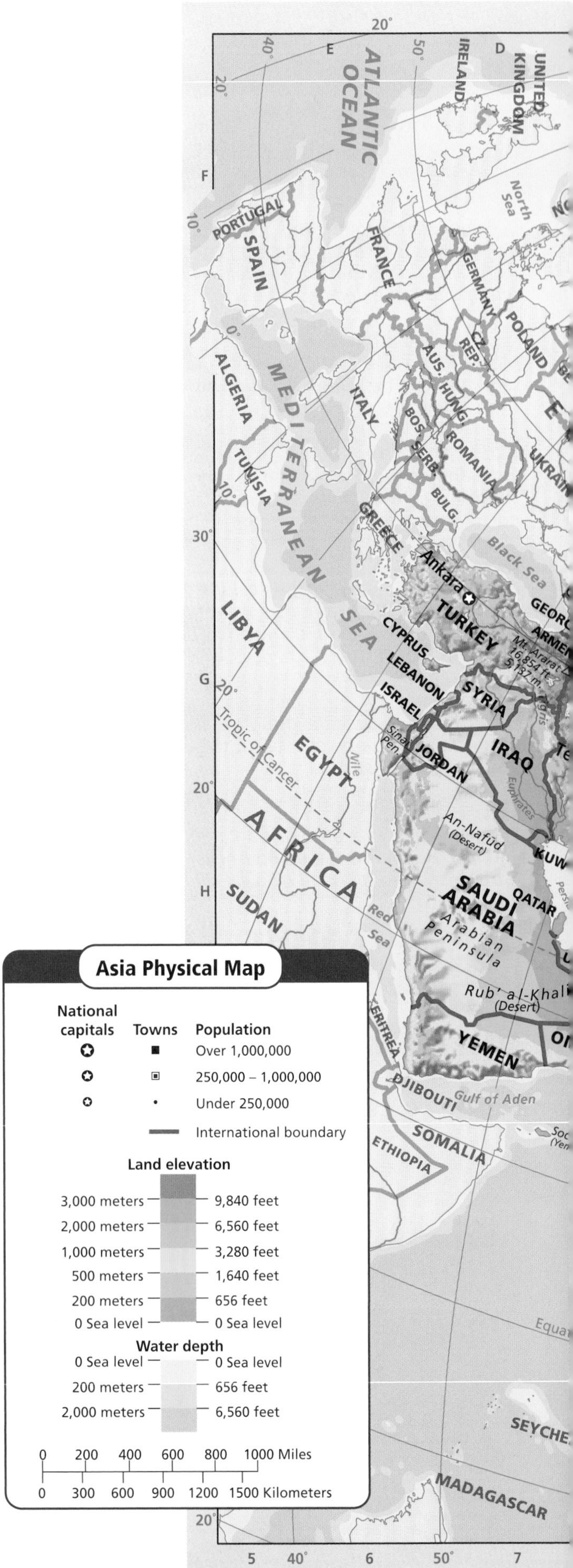

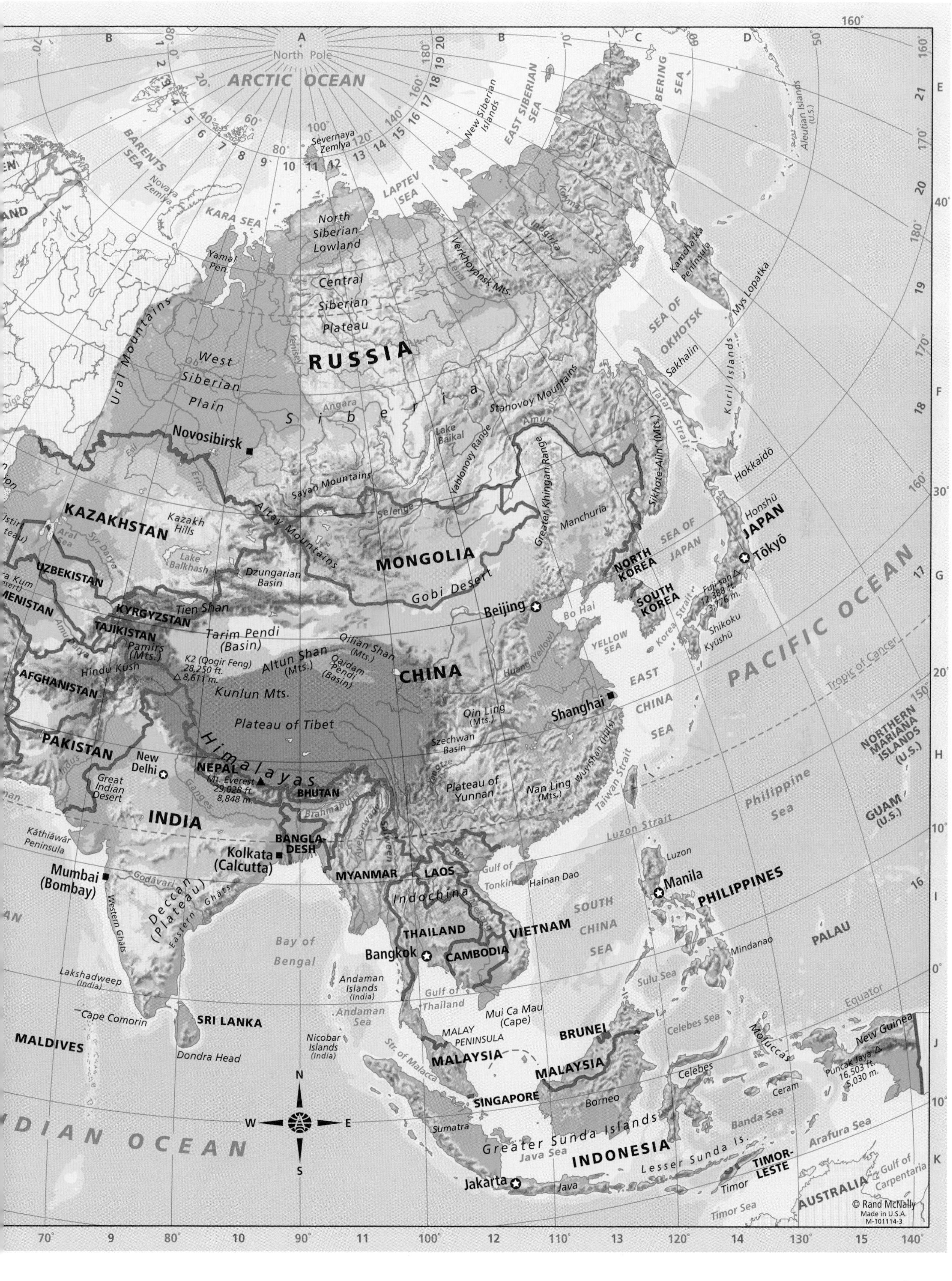
North Pole
ARCTIC OCEAN
BARENTS SEA
KARA SEA
LAPTEV SEA
EAST SIBERIAN SEA
BERING SEA
Severnaya Zemlya
New Siberian Islands
Novaya Zemlya
Yamal Pen.
North Siberian Lowland
Central Siberian Plateau
West Siberian Plain
Ural Mountains
RUSSIA
Siberia
Verkhoyansk Mts.
Kamchatka Peninsula
Mys Lopatka
Aleutian Islands (U.S.)
SEA OF OKHOTSK
Sakhalin
Kuril Islands
Stanovoy Mountains
Lake Baikal
Yablonovy Range
Sayan Mountains
Novosibirsk
Altay Mountains
KAZAKHSTAN
Kazakh Hills
Lake Balkhash
Dzungarian Basin
UZBEKISTAN
KYRGYZSTAN
TAJIKISTAN
Tien Shan
Tarim Pendi (Basin)
Pamirs (Mts.)
Hindu Kush
AFGHANISTAN
K2 (Qogir Feng) 28,250 ft. 8,611 m.
Kunlun Mts.
Altun Shan (Mts.)
Qilian Shan (Mts.)
Qaidam Pendi (Basin)
Plateau of Tibet
MONGOLIA
Gobi Desert
CHINA
Beijing
Manchuria
Greater Khingan Range
Sikhote-Alin' (Mts.)
Tatar Strait
Hokkaidō
Honshū
JAPAN
Tōkyō
Fuji san 12,388 ft. 3,776 m.
Shikoku
Kyūshū
NORTH KOREA
SOUTH KOREA
SEA OF JAPAN
Korea Strait
Bo Hai
YELLOW SEA
EAST CHINA SEA
Shanghai
Qin Ling (Mts.)
Szechwan Basin
Plateau of Yunnan
Nan Ling (Mts.)
Wuyishan (Hills)
Taiwan Strait
PACIFIC OCEAN
Tropic of Cancer
NORTHERN MARIANA ISLANDS (U.S.)
GUAM (U.S.)
Philippine Sea
Luzon Strait
Luzon
Manila
PHILIPPINES
Mindanao
PALAU
PAKISTAN
New Delhi
Great Indian Desert
NEPAL
Mt. Everest 29,028 ft. 8,848 m.
Himalayas
BHUTAN
INDIA
Ganges
Brahmaputra
BANGLADESH
Kolkata (Calcutta)
Kāthiāwār Peninsula
Mumbai (Bombay)
Godāvari
Deccan (Plateau)
Western Ghāts
Eastern Ghāts
Lakshadweep (India)
Cape Comorin
SRI LANKA
Dondra Head
MALDIVES
Bay of Bengal
Andaman Islands (India)
Andaman Sea
Nicobar Islands (India)
MYANMAR
LAOS
Indochina
Gulf of Tonkin
Hainan Dao
THAILAND
Bangkok
CAMBODIA
VIETNAM
Gulf of Thailand
Mui Ca Mau (Cape)
SOUTH CHINA SEA
Sulu Sea
Celebes Sea
MALAY PENINSULA
MALAYSIA
BRUNEI
Str. of Malacca
SINGAPORE
Sumatra
Borneo
Celebes
Moluccas
Ceram
New Guinea
Puncak Jaya 16,503 ft. 5,030 m.
Greater Sunda Islands
Java Sea
INDONESIA
Jakarta
Java
Lesser Sunda Is.
Timor
TIMOR-LESTE
Banda Sea
Arafura Sea
Timor Sea
Gulf of Carpentaria
AUSTRALIA
INDIAN OCEAN
Equator
© Rand McNally
Made in U.S.A.
M-101114-3

Indonesia is an island nation located in Southeast Asia. It has a larger population than all but two of the world's countries: China and India.

China is the world's most populous country. It is home to more than 1.3 billion people.

Kyrgyzstan is located in Central Asia. It became a country when the Soviet Union broke up in 1991.

Turkey is Asia's westernmost country. Istanbul, Turkey's largest city, lies along the Bosporus Strait, which divides Asia and Europe.

Asia Political Map

National capitals	Towns	Population
✪	■	Over 1,000,000
✪	▣	250,000 – 1,000,000
✪	•	Under 250,000
—		International boundary

0 200 400 600 800 1000 Miles

0 300 600 900 1200 1500 Kilometers

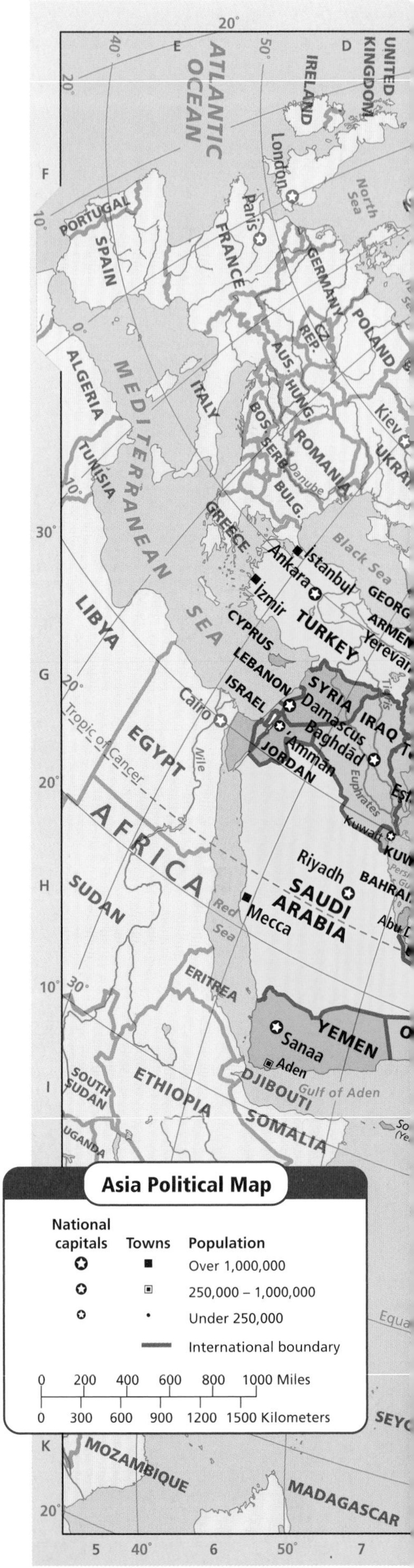

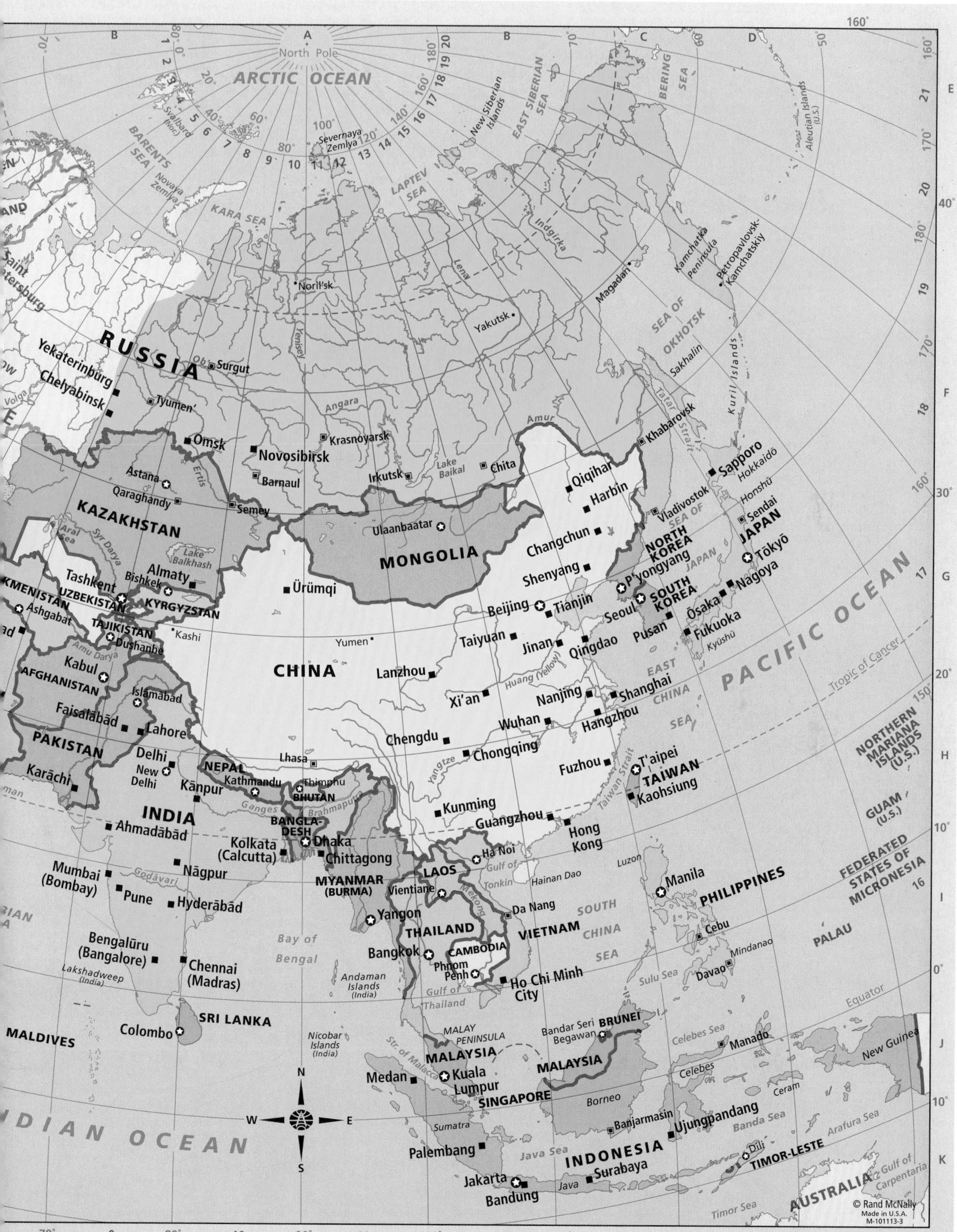
North Pole
ARCTIC OCEAN
Svalbard (Nor.)
BARENTS SEA
Novaya Zemlya
KARA SEA
Severnaya Zemlya
LAPTEV SEA
New Siberian Islands
EAST SIBERIAN SEA
BERING SEA
Aleutian Islands (U.S.)
Indigirka
Lena
Kamchatka Peninsula
Petropavlovsk-Kamchatskiy
Magadan
Noril'sk
Yakutsk
SEA OF OKHOTSK
Sakhalin
Kuril Islands
Tatar Strait
Saint Petersburg
RUSSIA
Yekaterinburg
Chelyabinsk
Volga
Ob'
Surgut
Yenisey
Tyumen'
Angara
Amur
Khabarovsk
Omsk
Novosibirsk
Krasnoyarsk
Ertis
Barnaul
Irkutsk
Lake Baikal
Chita
Astana
Qaraghandy
Semey
KAZAKHSTAN
Aral Sea
Syr Darya
Lake Balkhash
Almaty
Bishkek
Tashkent
UZBEKISTAN
KYRGYZSTAN
TURKMENISTAN
Ashgabat
TAJIKISTAN
Dushanbe
Kashi
Amu Darya
Kabul
AFGHANISTAN
Islāmābād
Faisalābād
Lahore
PAKISTAN
Karāchi
Ulaanbaatar
MONGOLIA
Ürümqi
Qiqihar
Harbin
Changchun
Shenyang
Vladivostok
NORTH KOREA
P'yongyang
SEA OF JAPAN
Sapporo
Hokkaidō
Honshū
Sendai
JAPAN
Tōkyō
Nagoya
Ōsaka
Fukuoka
Kyūshū
SOUTH KOREA
Seoul
Pusan
Beijing
Tianjin
Taiyuan
Jinan
Qingdao
Yumen
CHINA
Lanzhou
Huang (Yellow)
Xi'an
Nanjing
Shanghai
Wuhan
Hangzhou
EAST CHINA SEA
PACIFIC OCEAN
Tropic of Cancer
Chengdu
Chongqing
Yangtze
Lhasa
Fuzhou
T'aipei
TAIWAN
Taiwan Strait
Kaohsiung
NORTHERN MARIANA ISLANDS (U.S.)
GUAM (U.S.)
FEDERATED STATES OF MICRONESIA
Delhi
New Delhi
NEPAL
Kathmandu
Thimphu
BHUTAN
Kānpur
Ganges
Brahmaputra
INDIA
BANGLA-DESH
Dhaka
Chittagong
Kunming
Guangzhou
Hong Kong
Ahmadābād
Kolkata (Calcutta)
Nāgpur
Godāvari
Mumbai (Bombay)
Pune
Hyderābād
Ha Noi
Gulf of Tonkin
Hainan Dao
LAOS
Luzon
MYANMAR (BURMA)
Vientiane
Mekong
Manila
PHILIPPINES
Yangon
Da Nang
SOUTH CHINA SEA
THAILAND
VIETNAM
Cebu
PALAU
Bay of Bengal
Bengalūru (Bangalore)
Chennai (Madras)
Lakshadweep (India)
Bangkok
CAMBODIA
Phnom Penh
Ho Chi Minh City
Andaman Islands (India)
Gulf of Thailand
Mindanao
Sulu Sea
Davao
SRI LANKA
Colombo
MALDIVES
Nicobar Islands (India)
MALAY PENINSULA
Str. of Malacca
MALAYSIA
Bandar Seri Begawan
BRUNEI
Celebes Sea
Manado
Equator
New Guinea
Medan
Kuala Lumpur
SINGAPORE
Celebes
Borneo
Ceram
INDIAN OCEAN
Sumatra
Banjarmasin
Ujungpandang
Banda Sea
Arafura Sea
Palembang
INDONESIA
Java Sea
Dili
TIMOR-LESTE
Jakarta
Bandung
Java
Surabaya
Gulf of Carpentaria
AUSTRALIA
Timor Sea
N
S
E
W
© Rand McNally
Made in U.S.A.
M-101113-3

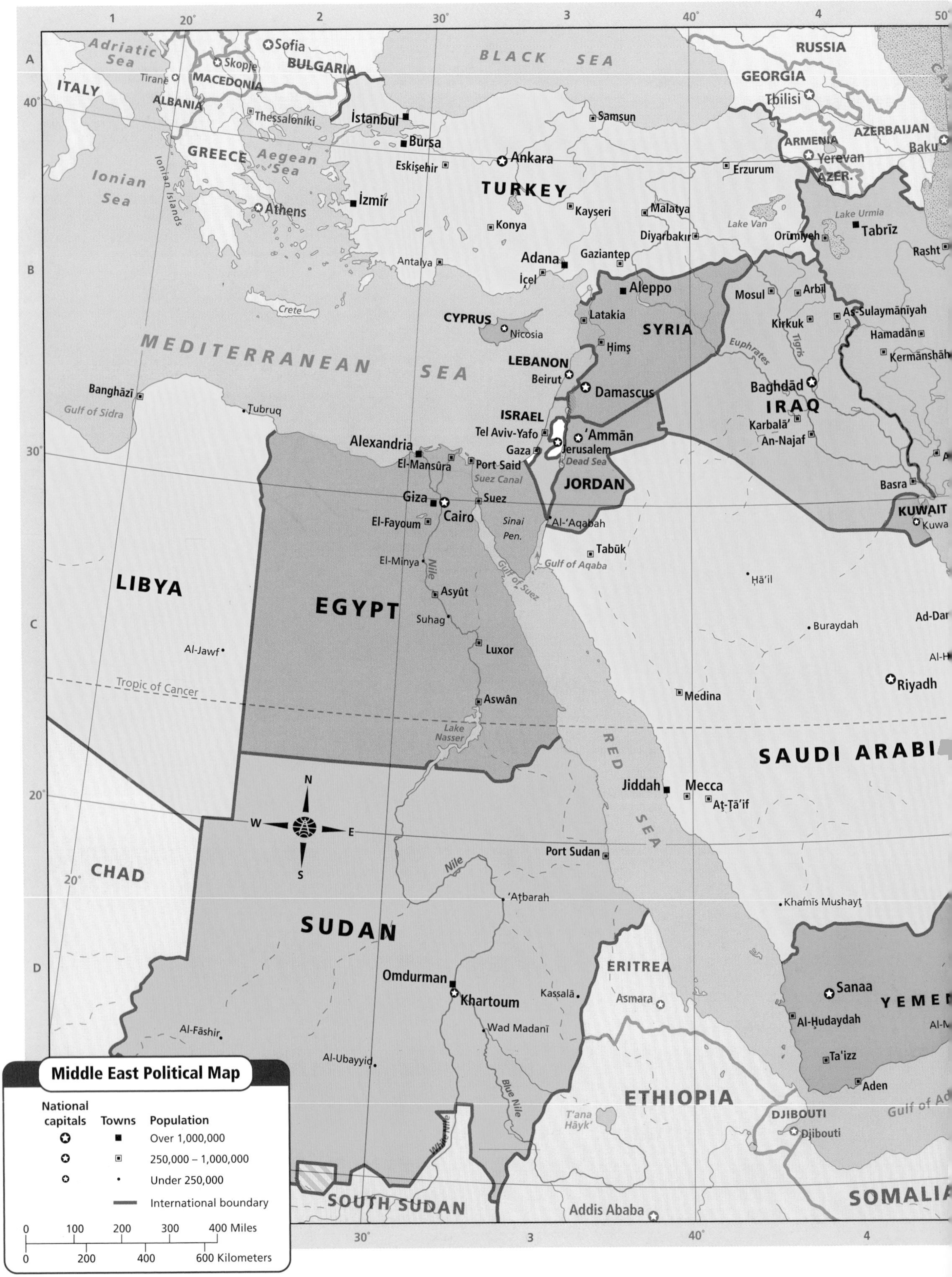
Middle East Political Map
National capitals
Towns
Population
Over 1,000,000
250,000 – 1,000,000
Under 250,000
International boundary
0 100 200 300 400 Miles
0 200 400 600 Kilometers
1
2
3
4
A
B
C
D
20°
30°
40°
50°
Adriatic Sea
Sofia
BULGARIA
Skopje
MACEDONIA
Tirane
ITALY
ALBANIA
BLACK SEA
RUSSIA
GEORGIA
Tbilisi
AZERBAIJAN
Baku
ARMENIA
Yerevan
AZER.
Thessaloniki
İstanbul
Bursa
Samsun
GREECE
Aegean Sea
Eskişehir
Ankara
Erzurum
Ionian Sea
Ionian Islands
TURKEY
Athens
İzmir
Kayseri
Malatya
Lake Van
Lake Urmia
Tabrīz
Konya
Diyarbakır
Orūmīyeh
Rasht
Antalya
Adana
Gaziantep
İçel
Aleppo
Crete
Mosul
Arbīl
As-Sulaymānīyah
CYPRUS
Nicosia
Latakia
SYRIA
Kirkuk
Hamadān
Ḥimṣ
Euphrates
Tigris
Kermānshāh
MEDITERRANEAN SEA
LEBANON
Beirut
Damascus
Baghdād
Banghāzī
Gulf of Sidra
Tubruq
ISRAEL
IRAQ
Tel Aviv-Yafo
'Ammān
Karbalā'
An-Najaf
Alexandria
Gaza
Jerusalem
Dead Sea
El-Mansûra
Port Said
Suez Canal
JORDAN
Basra
Giza
Cairo
Suez
KUWAIT
El-Fayoum
Sinai Pen.
Al-'Aqabah
Tabūk
Gulf of Aqaba
El-Minya
Nile
Gulf of Suez
Ḥā'il
LIBYA
Asyût
EGYPT
Suhag
Buraydah
Ad-Dar
Al-Jawf
Luxor
Al-H
Tropic of Cancer
Riyadh
Aswân
Medina
Lake Nasser
RED SEA
SAUDI ARABI
Jiddah
Mecca
Aṭ-Ṭā'if
N
W
E
S
Port Sudan
CHAD
Nile
'Aṭbarah
Khamīs Mushayṭ
SUDAN
ERITREA
Omdurman
Sanaa
Khartoum
Kassalā
Asmara
YEMEN
Al-Ḥudaydah
Al-Fāshir
Wad Madanī
Al-Ubayyid
Ta'izz
Aden
Blue Nile
White Nile
ETHIOPIA
T'ana Hāyk'
DJIBOUTI
Djibouti
Gulf of Ad
SOUTH SUDAN
Addis Ababa
SOMALIA

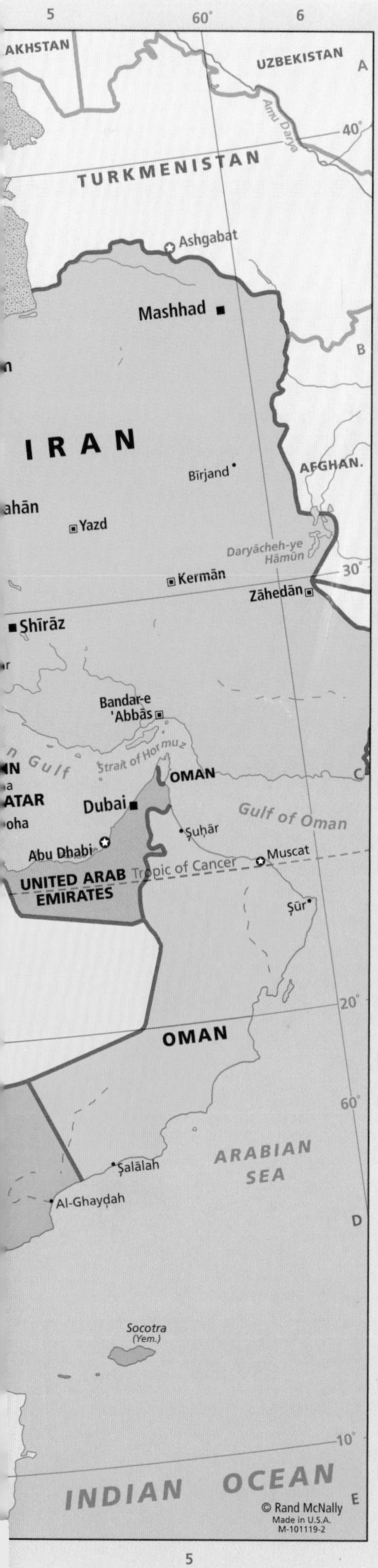

The Middle East

Africa, Asia, and Europe meet in the Middle East. Since ancient times, great powerful empires have fought to control these lands, their resources, and their trade routes. Today, the oil that many Middle Eastern countries produce is valuable to rich countries. There are also deep-rooted cultural conflicts among the peoples of the region.

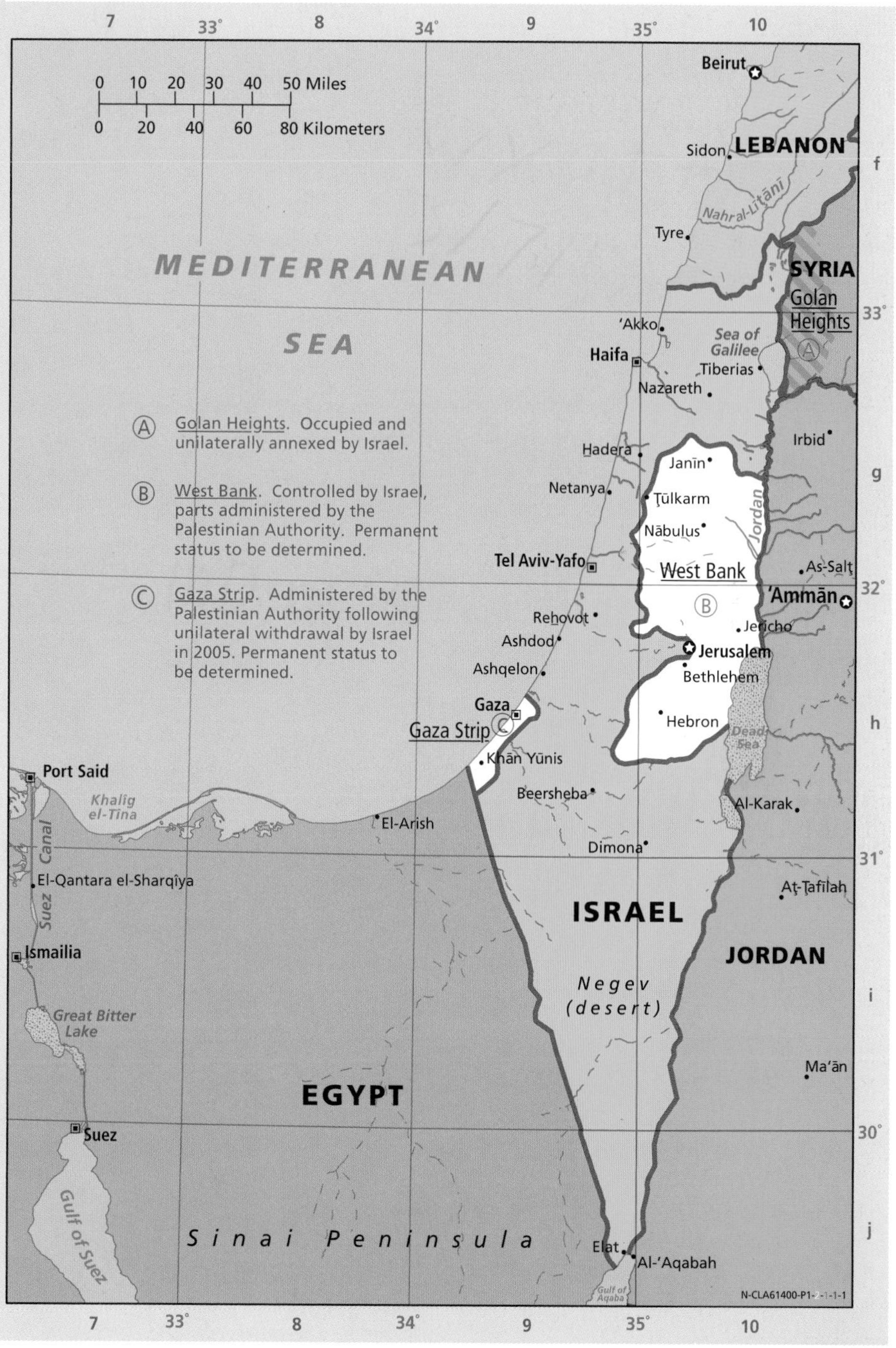

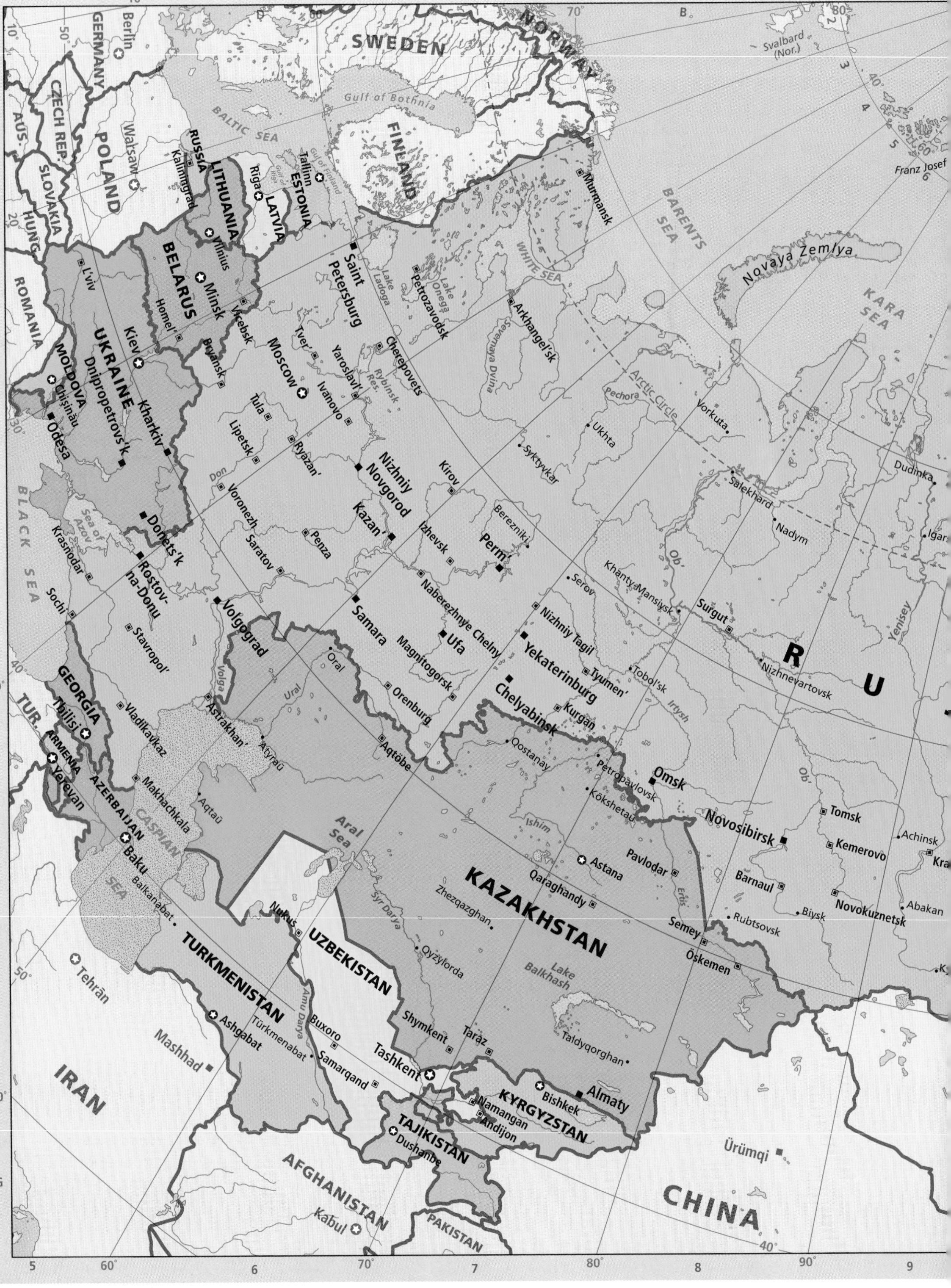
SWEDEN
NORWAY
FINLAND
RUSSIA
LITHUANIA
LATVIA
ESTONIA
BELARUS
UKRAINE
MOLDOVA
POLAND
GERMANY
CZECH REP.
SLOVAKIA
HUNG.
AUS.
ROMANIA
GEORGIA
ARMENIA
AZERBAIJAN
TUR.
KAZAKHSTAN
UZBEKISTAN
TURKMENISTAN
KYRGYZSTAN
TAJIKISTAN
AFGHANISTAN
PAKISTAN
IRAN
CHINA
R U
BALTIC SEA
Gulf of Bothnia
Gulf of Finland
Gulf of Riga
BARENTS SEA
WHITE SEA
KARA SEA
BLACK SEA
Sea of Azov
CASPIAN SEA
Aral Sea
Lake Balkhash
Lake Ladoga
Lake Onega
Rybinsk Res.
Arctic Circle
Novaya Zemlya
Svalbard (Nor.)
Franz Josef
Berlin
Warsaw
Kaliningrad
Vilnius
Riga
Tallinn
Minsk
Homel'
Vitebsk
Bryansk
L'viv
Kiev
Dnipropetrovs'k
Kharkiv
Chişinău
Odesa
Donets'k
Saint Petersburg
Petrozavodsk
Cherepovets
Murmansk
Arkhangel'sk
Severnaya Dvina
Moscow
Tver'
Yaroslavl'
Ivanovo
Tula
Ryazan'
Lipetsk
Voronezh
Don
Nizhniy Novgorod
Kazan'
Kirov
Izhevsk
Perm'
Berezniki
Syktyvkar
Ukhta
Pechora
Vorkuta
Salekhard
Nadym
Dudinka
Igar
Penza
Saratov
Krasnodar
Rostov-na-Donu
Sochi
Stavropol'
Volgograd
Volga
Samara
Naberezhnye Chelny
Ufa
Magnitogorsk
Orenburg
Oral
Ural
Astrakhan'
Atyraū
Vladikavkaz
Tbilisi
Yerevan
Makhachkala
Baku
Aqtaū
Aqtöbe
Serov
Nizhniy Tagil
Yekaterinburg
Chelyabinsk
Tyumen'
Kurgan
Tobol'sk
Irtysh
Khanty-Mansiysk
Surgut
Nizhnevartovsk
Ob'
Yenisey
Qostanay
Petropavlovsk
Omsk
Kökshetaū
Ishim
Astana
Pavlodar
Qaraghandy
Zhezqazghan
Ertis
Semey
Öskemen
Novosibirsk
Tomsk
Achinsk
Kemerovo
Barnaul
Novokuznetsk
Biysk
Rubtsovsk
Abakan
Syr Darya
Qyzylorda
Nukus
Balkanabat
Tehrān
Mashhad
Ashgabat
Türkmenabat
Amu Darya
Buxoro
Samarqand
Tashkent
Shymkent
Taraz
Taldyqorghan
Bishkek
Almaty
Namangan
Andijon
Dushanbe
Kabul
Ürümqi
10°
20°
30°
40°
50°
60°
70°
80°
90°
B
D
E
F
G
2
3
4
5
6
7
8
9

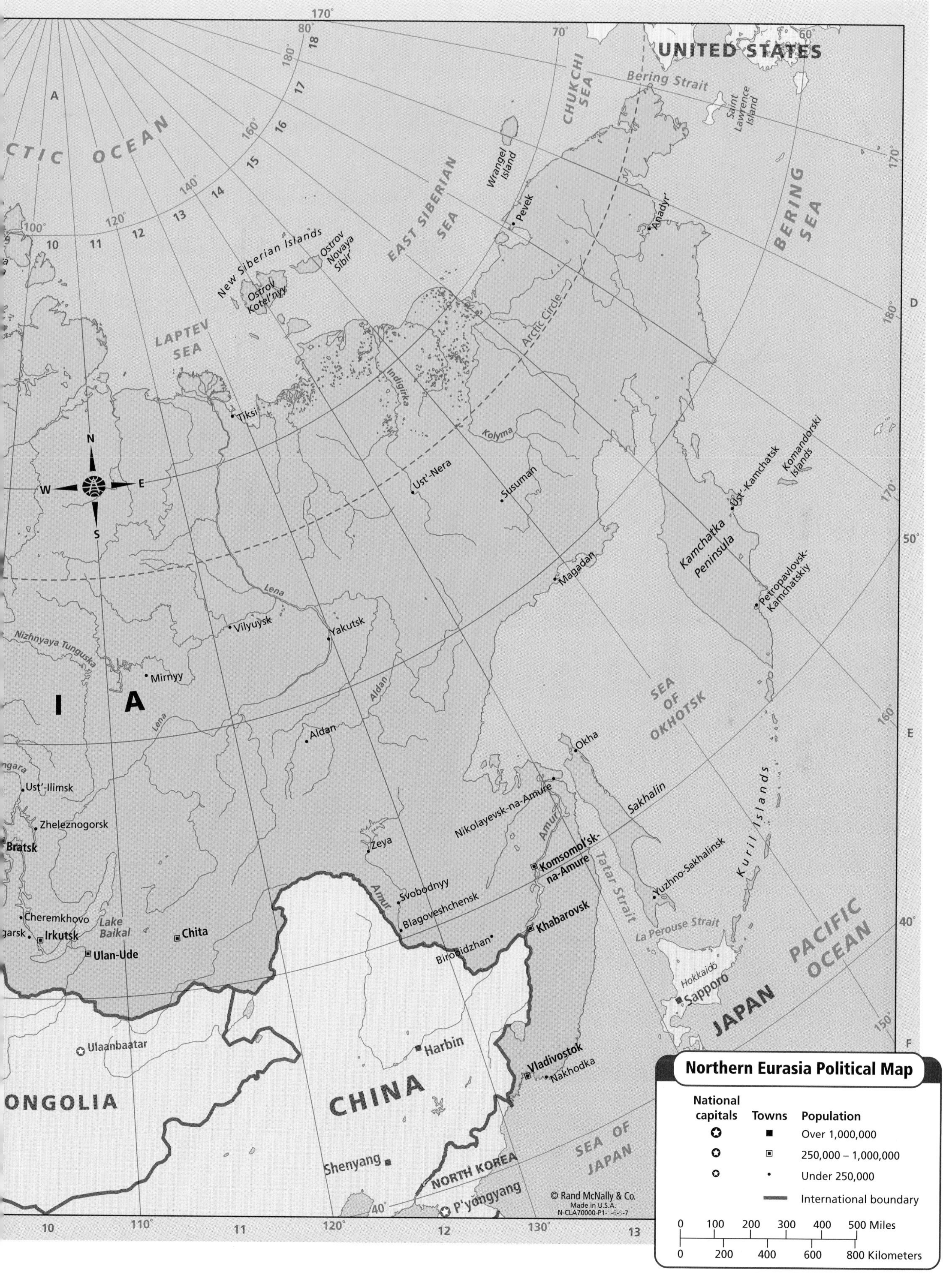

UNITED STATES

CHUKCHI SEA
Bering Strait

Saint Lawrence Island

BERING SEA

ARCTIC OCEAN

18
17
16
15
14
13
12
11
10

180°
170°
160°
140°
120°
100°
80°
70°
60°

Wrangel Island

Pevek

Anadyr

EAST SIBERIAN SEA

New Siberian Islands

Ostrov Novaya Sibir'

Ostrov Kotel'nyy

LAPTEV SEA

Arctic Circle

D
180°

Tiksi

Indigirka

Kolyma

Komandorski Islands

Ust'-Kamchatsk

170°

Ust'-Nera

Susuman

Kamchatka Peninsula

Petropavlovsk-Kamchatskiy

50°

N
W E
S

Lena

Vilyuysk

Yakutsk

Magadan

SEA OF OKHOTSK

Nizhnyaya Tunguska

Mirnyy

Aldan

160°

I A

Lena

Aldan

Okha

E

Ust'-Ilimsk

Zheleznogorsk

Bratsk

Zeya

Amur

Nikolayevsk-na-Amure

Amur

Sakhalin

Kuril Islands

Tatar Strait

Cheremkhovo

Lake Baikal

Chita

Svobodnyy

Blagoveshchensk

Komsomol'sk-na-Amure

Yuzhno-Sakhalinsk

40°

garsk

Irkutsk

Ulan-Ude

Birobidzhan

Khabarovsk

La Perouse Strait

PACIFIC OCEAN

Hokkaido

Sapporo

JAPAN

150°

Ulaanbaatar

Harbin

Vladivostok

Nakhodka

F

ONGOLIA

CHINA

Shenyang

NORTH KOREA

SEA OF JAPAN

P'yongyang

© Rand McNally & Co.
Made in U.S.A.
N-CLA70000-P1-·-6-5-7

40°

10
110°
11
120°
12
130°
13

Northern Eurasia Political Map

National capitals **Towns** **Population**

⊛ ■ Over 1,000,000

⊛ ▣ 250,000 – 1,000,000

⊛ • Under 250,000

—— International boundary

0 100 200 300 400 500 Miles

0 200 400 600 800 Kilometers

KAZAKHSTAN

Lake Balkhash

Bishkek

Almaty

KYRGYZSTAN

TAJIKISTAN

AFG.

PAKISTAN

Kashi

Shache

Hotan

Altay

Yining

Karamay

Shihezi

Ürümqi

Aksu

Korla

SINKIANG (XINJIANG UYGUR)

Hami

Dund-Us

Ulaangom

Ölgiy

Hyargas
Nuur

Har Us
Nuur

Uliastay

Altay

Hövsgöl
Nuur

Mörön

Ider

Selenge

Bulgan

Tsetserleg

Bayanhongor

Sühbaatar

Darhan

Ulaanbaatar

Arvayheer

MONGOLIA

Dalandzadagad

Irkutsk

Linhe

Wuhai

Yinchuan

NINGXIA
HUIZU

SH.

Ba

Yumen

Zhangye

Xining

Lanzhou

GANSU

Tongch

Baoji

Xi'a

Golmud

QINGHAI

Qinghai
Hu

Delhi

New Delhi

TIBET (XIZANG)

NEPAL

Zhongba

Xigazê

Kathmandu

Lhasa

Nagqu

Nam Co

Mekong

Qamdo

Salween

Brahmaputra

Yangtze

C H I N

SICHUAN

Chengdu

Leshan

Zigong

CHONGQING

Chongq

BHUTAN

Thimphu

Ganges

Brahmaputra

INDIA

Tropic of Cancer

BANGLADESH

Dhaka

Kolkata
(Calcutta)

Zhongdian

Panzhihua

GUIZHO

Guiyang

Baoshan

Kunming

YUNNAN

You

Gejiu

GUAN
ZHUAN

Nanning

VIETNAM

Mandalay

MYANMAR
(BURMA)

Red

Ha Noi

Hai Phong

Gulf
of
Ton

Bay of Bengal

THAILAND

LAOS

HA

Hainan Da

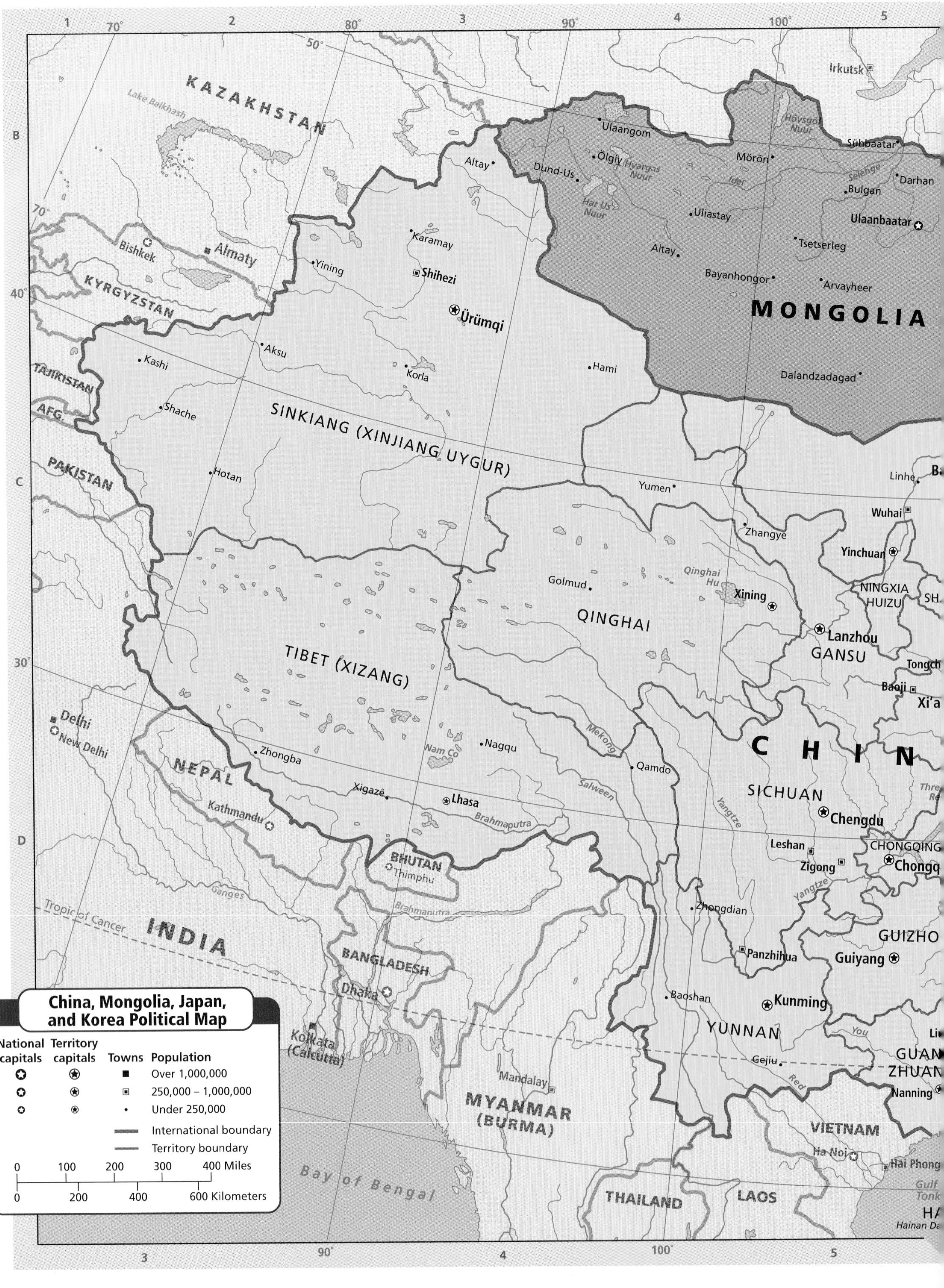

China, Mongolia, Japan, and Korea Political Map

National capitals	Territory capitals	Towns	Population
✪	✹	■	Over 1,000,000
✪	✹	▣	250,000 – 1,000,000
✪	✹	•	Under 250,000

International boundary

Territory boundary

0 100 200 300 400 Miles

0 200 400 600 Kilometers

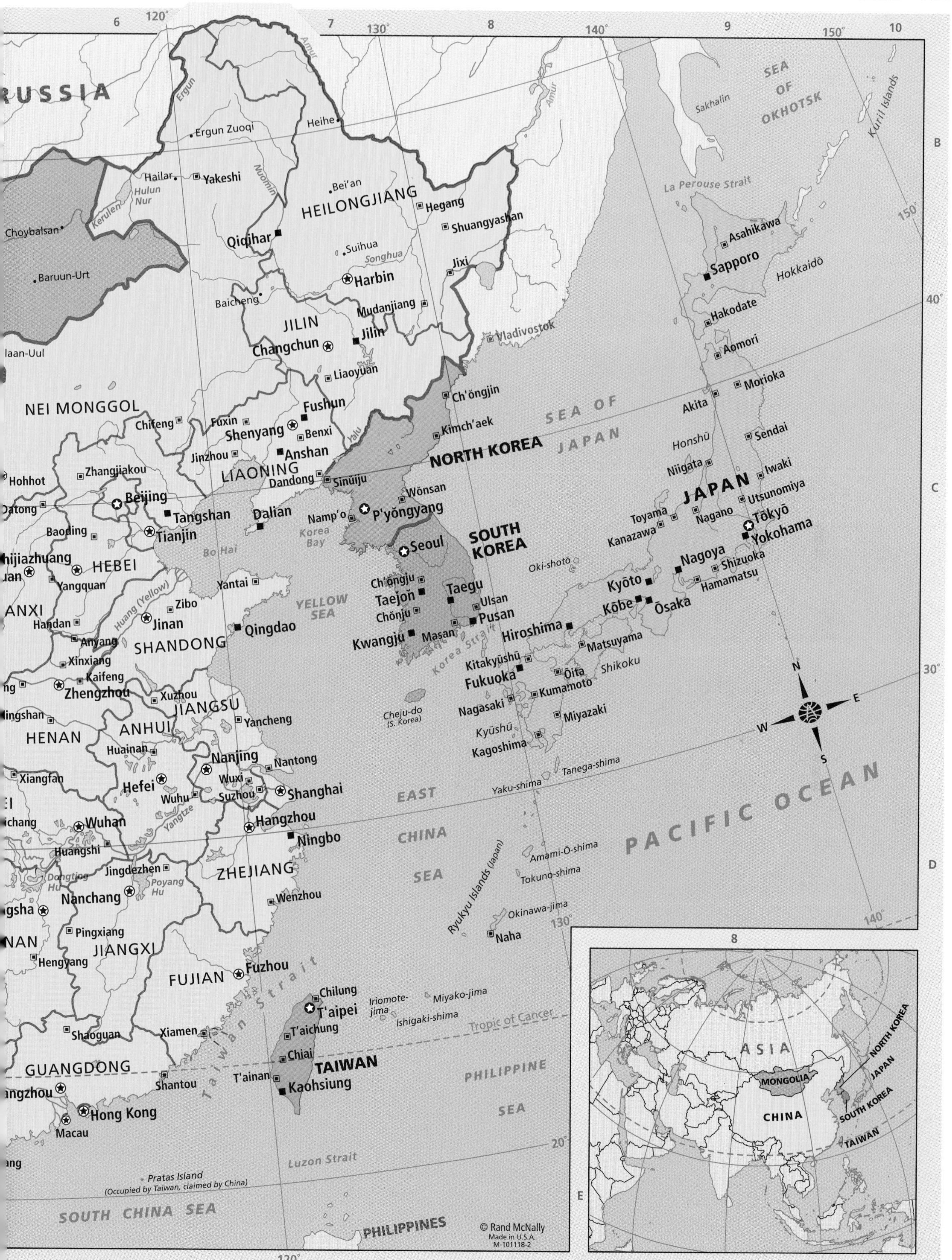
RUSSIA
SEA OF OKHOTSK
Sakhalin
Kuril Islands
La Perouse Strait
Amur
Ergun
Ergun Zuoqi
Heihe
Hailar
Yakeshi
Hulun Nur
Kerulen
Nuomin
Bei'an
HEILONGJIANG
Hegang
Shuangyashan
Choybalsan
Qiqihar
Suihua
Songhua
Jixi
Baruun-Urt
Harbin
Baicheng
Mudanjiang
JILIN
Jilin
Changchun
Vladivostok
laan-Uul
Liaoyuan
Asahikawa
Sapporo
Hokkaidō
Hakodate
Aomori
Morioka
Akita
Ch'ŏngjin
NEI MONGGOL
Fushun
Chifeng
Fuxin
Shenyang
Benxi
Kimch'aek
SEA OF JAPAN
Honshū
Sendai
Jinzhou
Anshan
Yalu
NORTH KOREA
Niigata
Iwaki
Zhangjiakou
LIAONING
Dandong
Sinŭiju
Hohhot
JAPAN
Utsunomiya
Wŏnsan
Beijing
Datong
Tangshan
Dalian
Namp'o
P'yŏngyang
Toyama
Nagano
Tōkyō
Kanazawa
Yokohama
Baoding
Tianjin
Korea Bay
SOUTH KOREA
Seoul
Bo Hai
Shijiazhuang
HEBEI
Oki-shotō
Nagoya
Shizuoka
Kyōto
Hamamatsu
Yangquan
Yantai
Ch'ŏngju
Taegu
Taejŏn
Ulsan
Kōbe
Ōsaka
ANXI
Huang (Yellow)
Zibo
YELLOW SEA
Chŏnju
Pusan
Handan
Jinan
Qingdao
Masan
Hiroshima
Kwangju
Korea Strait
Anyang
SHANDONG
Matsuyama
Kitakyūshū
Xinxiang
Ōita
Shikoku
Kaifeng
Fukuoka
Zhengzhou
Kumamoto
Xuzhou
JIANGSU
Nagasaki
Cheju-do (S. Korea)
Miyazaki
Yancheng
ANHUI
HENAN
Kyūshū
Kagoshima
Huainan
Nanjing
Nantong
Tanega-shima
Xiangfan
Hefei
Wuxi
Shanghai
Yaku-shima
Wuhu
Suzhou
EAST CHINA SEA
PACIFIC OCEAN
Yangtze
Hangzhou
Wuhan
Ningbo
Huangshi
Amami-Ō-shima
Dongting Hu
Jingdezhen
ZHEJIANG
Poyang Hu
Tokuno-shima
Ryukyu Islands (Japan)
Nanchang
Wenzhou
Okinawa-jima
Pingxiang
Naha
JIANGXI
Hengyang
Fuzhou
FUJIAN
Taiwan Strait
Chilung
Miyako-jima
Iriomote-jima
T'aipei
Ishigaki-shima
T'aichung
Tropic of Cancer
Shaoguan
Xiamen
Chiai
TAIWAN
GUANGDONG
T'ainan
PHILIPPINE SEA
Shantou
Kaohsiung
Hong Kong
Macau
Luzon Strait
Pratas Island
(Occupied by Taiwan, claimed by China)
SOUTH CHINA SEA
PHILIPPINES
© Rand McNally
Made in U.S.A.
M-101118-2
ASIA
MONGOLIA
CHINA
NORTH KOREA
JAPAN
SOUTH KOREA
TAIWAN
N
E
S
W
120°
130°
140°
150°
40°
30°
20°
6
7
8
9
10
B
C
D
E

Climate

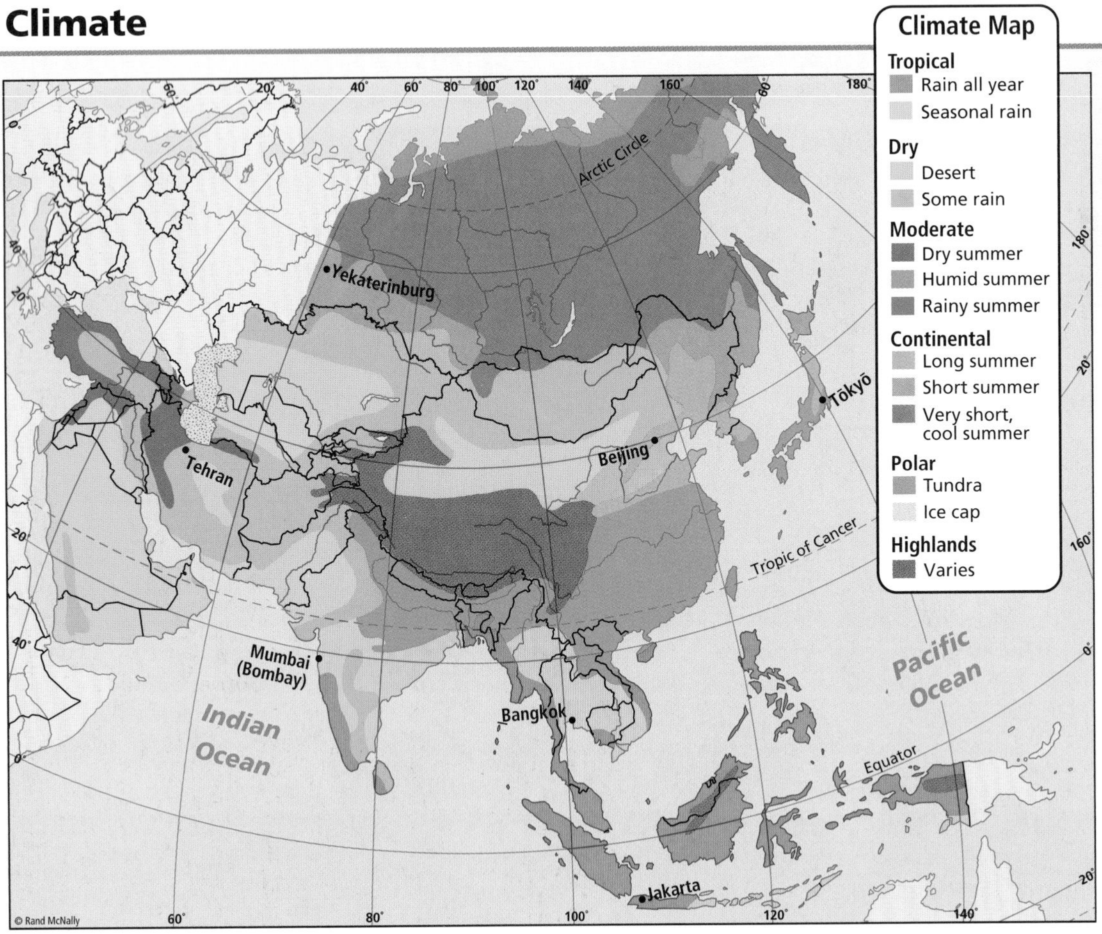

Rain forests thrive in the hot, rainy climate of Southeast Asia.

Eastern China has a moderate climate with humid summers. This is like the climate of the eastern United States.

Economic Activities

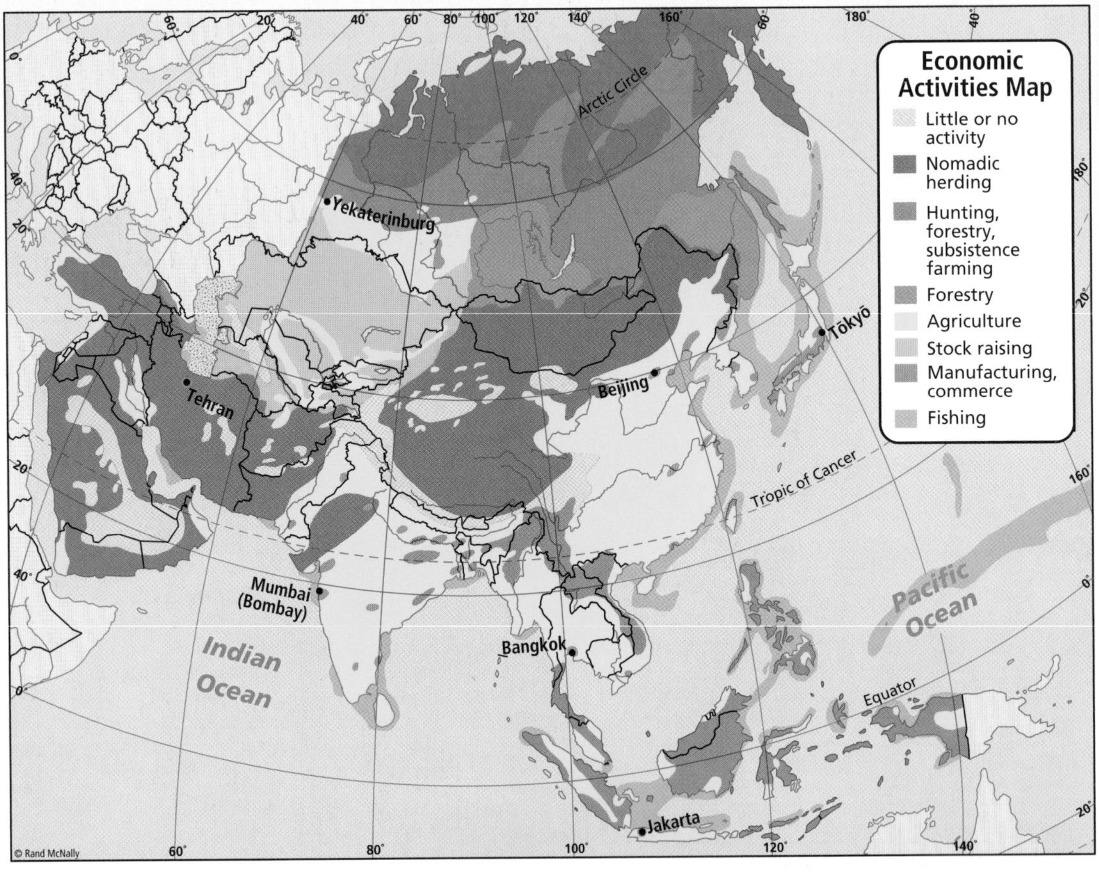

Rice is the most important food crop in Southeast Asia.

Japan sends many of its exports to the United States, but it trades with other countries, too. Trading with many countries helps a country continue to earn money if one trading partner has economic problems.

Populations

Population Density Map

People per sq. mile
(People per sq. km)

- Over 1,250 *(Over 500)*
- 250 – 1,250 *(100 – 500)*
- 62.5 – 250 *(25 – 100)*
- 25 – 62.5 *(10 – 25)*
- 2.5 – 25 *(1 – 10)*
- Under 2.5 *(Under 1)*

© Rand McNally

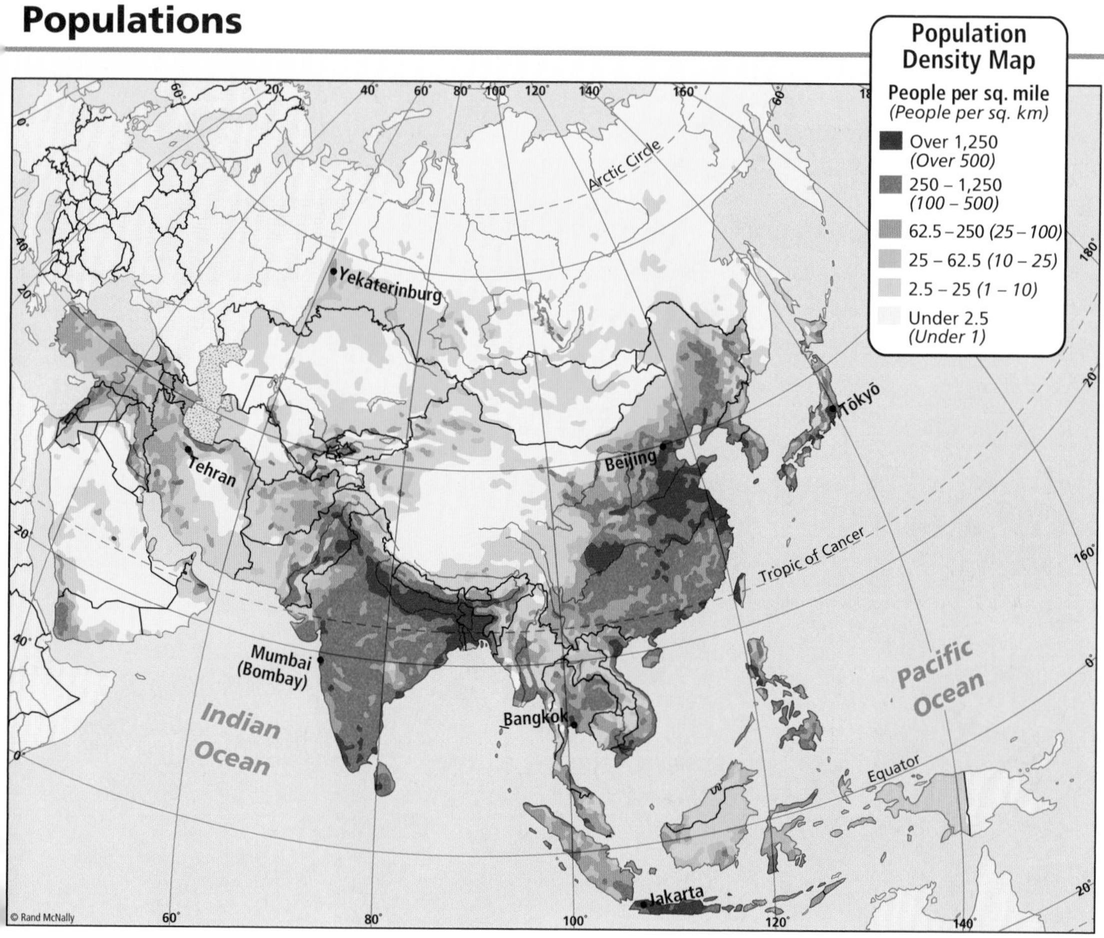

Seoul, South Korea, is home to more than 21 million people.

Bangladesh is one of most densely populated countries in the world.

Much of Mongolia is sparsely populated.

India and China

China and India are the world's population giants. Both have populations of more than one billion people. India's population, however, is growing faster. By 2040 it will be larger than China's. Since about 1980, China has brought down its rate of population growth by strictly limiting how many children a family may have.

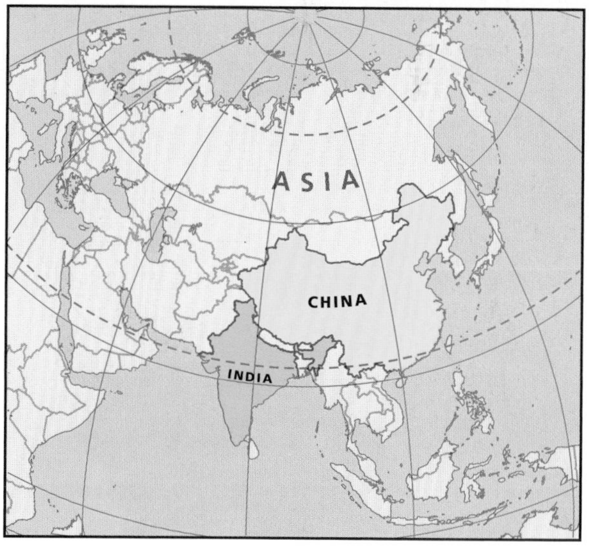

India and China Population Growth

- ○ China
- ○ India

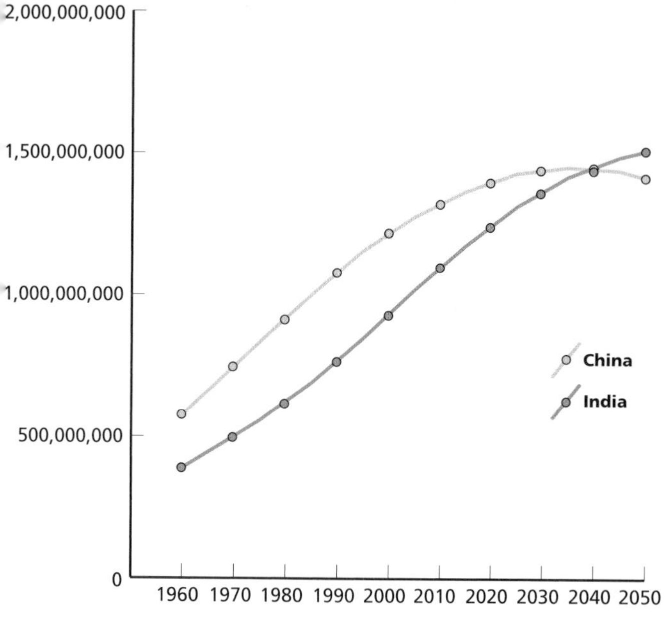

What If?

? What do you think life in India will be like if the population continues to grow rapidly?

Transportation

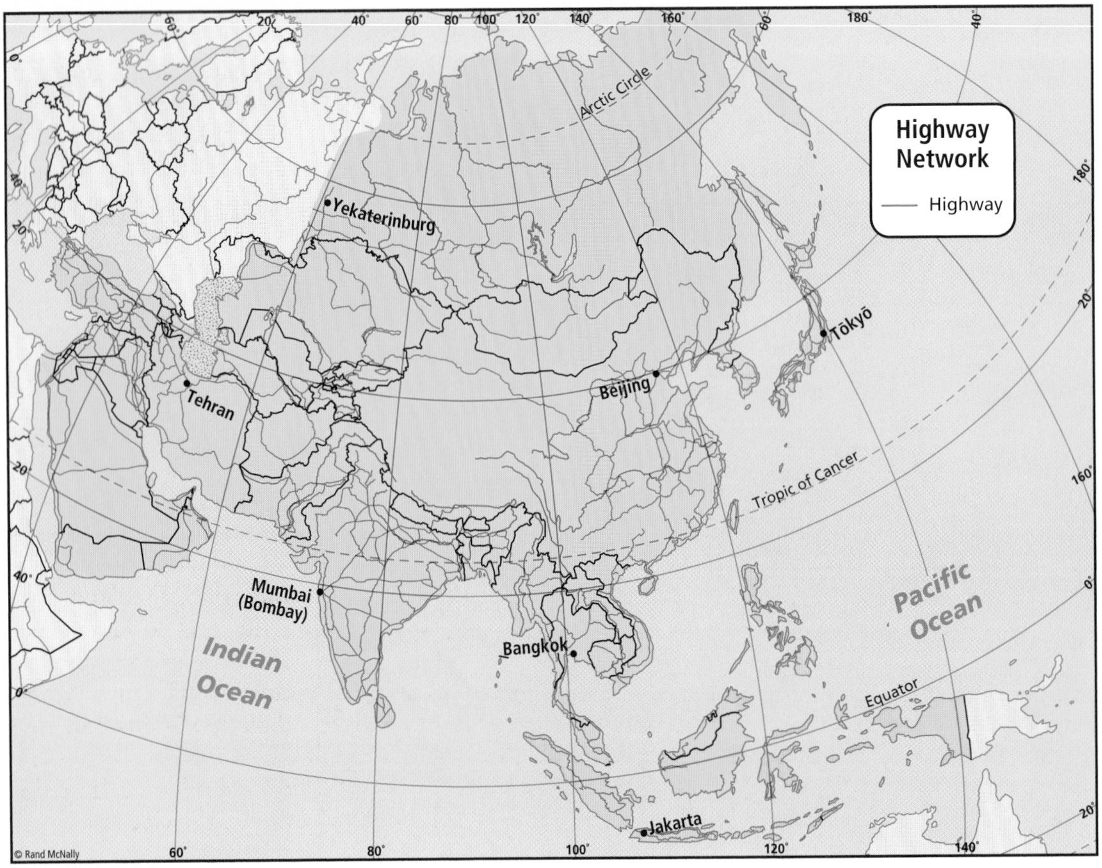

Japan's bullet trains can travel at speeds of up to 155 miles per hour (249 kilometers per hour).

Mountainous terrain makes road-building difficult in many parts of Asia.

Environments

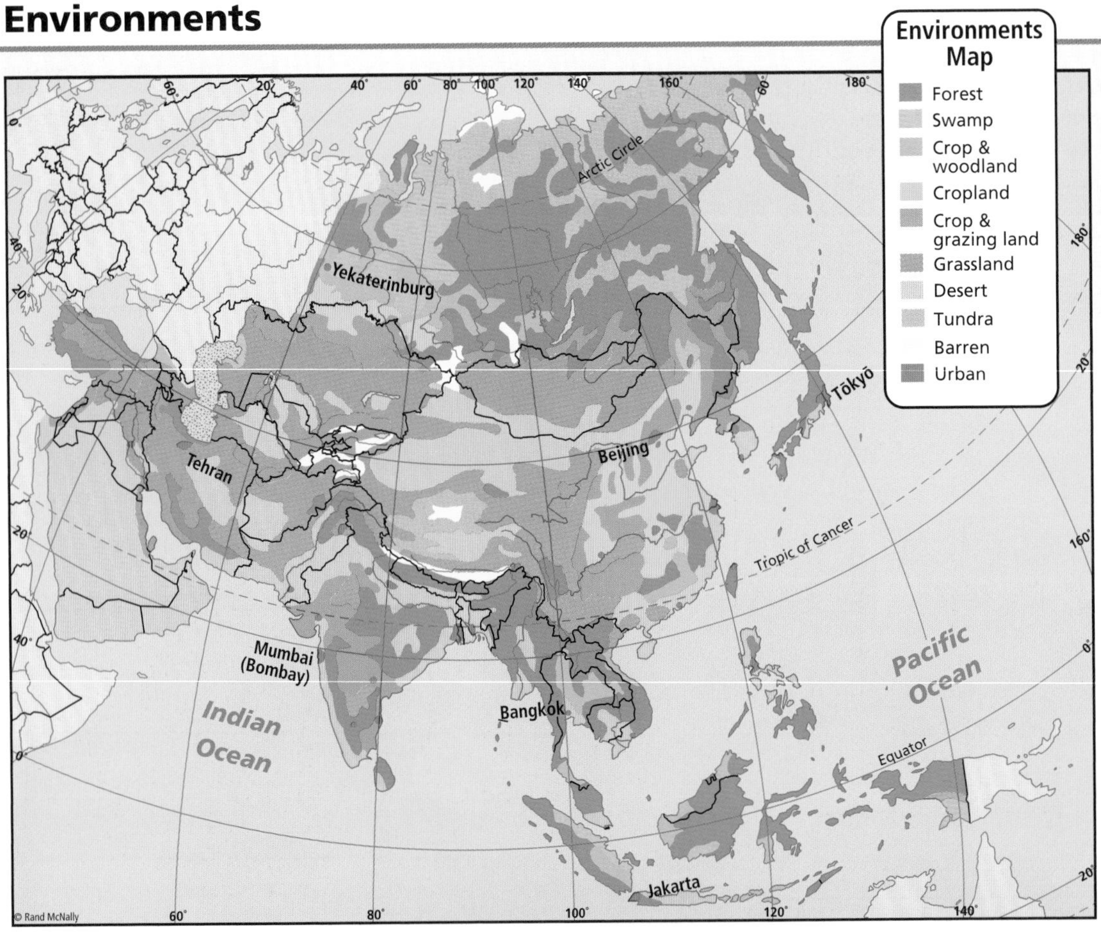

The country of Nepal lies along the southern edge of the Himalayas. Thick woodlands cover some of the lower elevations.

Grasslands called steppes cover much of Central Asia. This photo shows camels on a steppe in Mongolia.

Natural Hazards

Natural Hazards Map

- ● Earthquakes*
- △ Volcanoes*
- \ Tsunamis
- ➤ Tropical storm tracks
 (over 5 per year)

*Since 1900

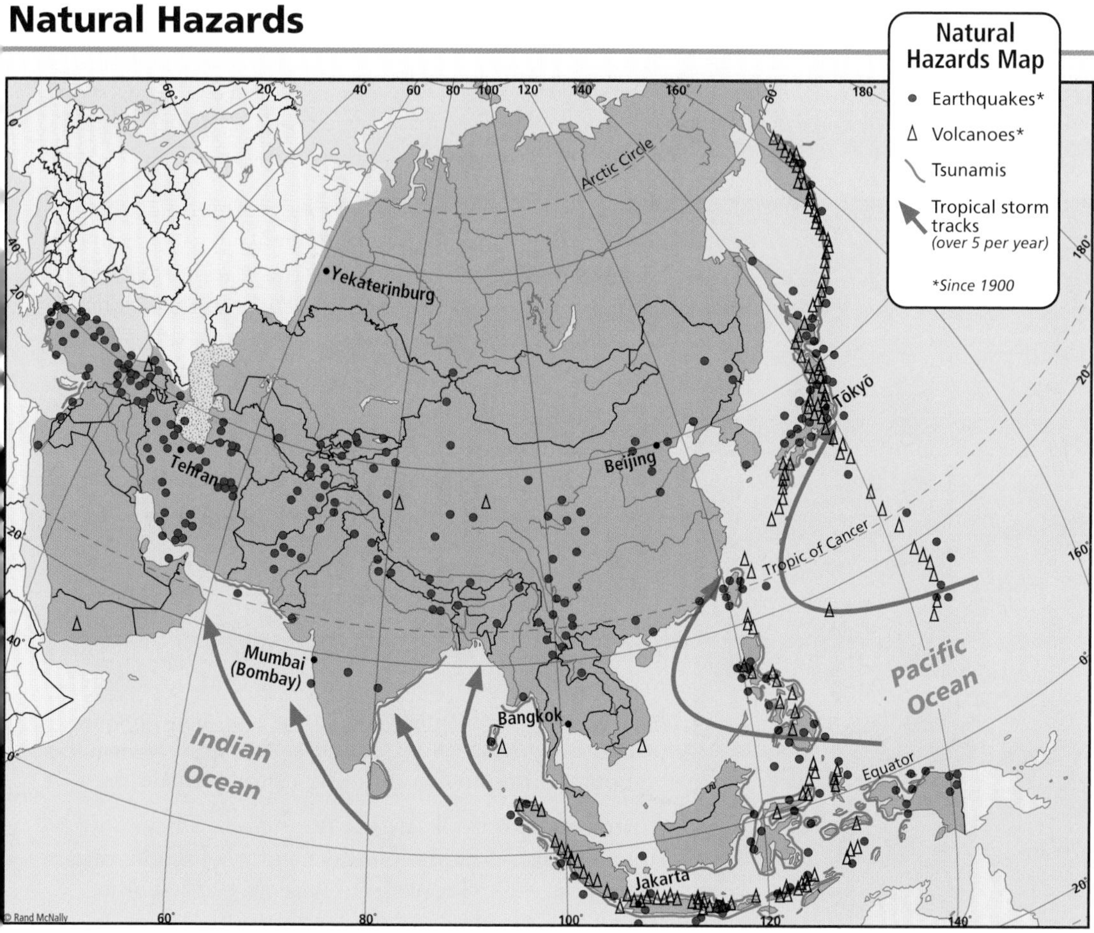

Tsunamis

Tsunamis are huge ocean waves caused by underwater earthquakes or volcanoes. They usually travel at speeds of about 300 miles per hour (500 km/hr).

Tsunamis that reach the shore can cause terrible damage to coastal areas. On December 26, 2004, a strong earthquake off the coast of Sumatra in Indonesia caused a tsunami that destroyed huge coastal areas in Indonesia, Thailand, India, and Sri Lanka and also hit Madagascar and continental Africa. More than 200,000 people were killed. Most other tsunamis have occurred in the Pacific Ocean.

Energy

On the Mineral Fuel Deposits map, note the cluster of symbols indicating petroleum deposits around the Persian Gulf, which is near the left edge of the map. This area is part of the Middle East, which produces one-third of the world's oil.

Mineral Fuel Deposits Map

- ◤ Coal
- ▲ Petroleum
- △ Natural gas

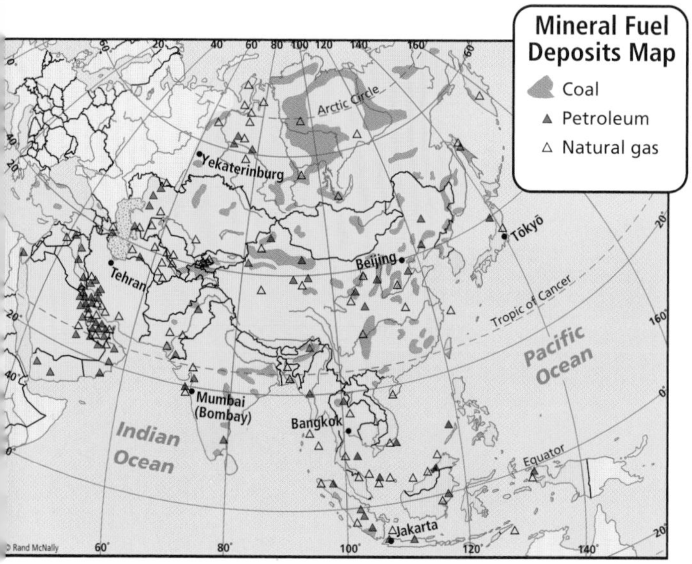

Oil exporting has brought great wealth to the countries in the Persian Gulf region of the Middle East. This photo shows an oil refinery in the United Arab Emirates.

A pipeline delivers oil to an oil tanker in Saudi Arabia

China produces more than one-fourth of the world's coal.

Australia and Oceania

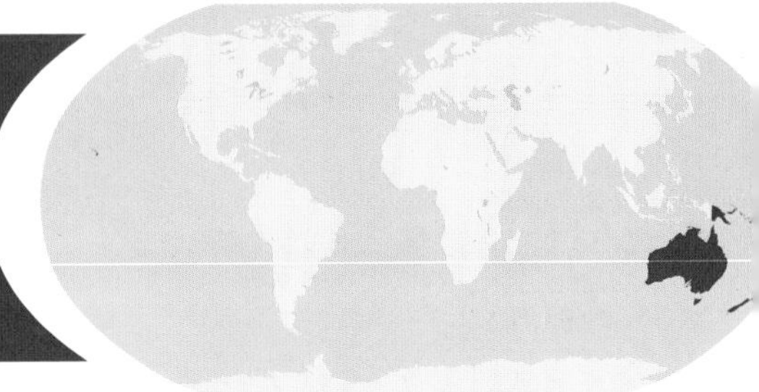

Uluru, also known as Ayers Rock, in central Australia.

Sydney, Australia

A dairy farm on New Zealand's South Island

Australia is the only continent except Antarctica that lies completely in the Southern Hemisphere. Oceania consists of New Zealand, part of the island of New Guinea, and thousands of other islands in the Pacific Ocean. Many of these islands are tiny coral atolls where no one lives. Others are the tops of volcanoes.

Australia is the smallest continent. It is about the size of the conterminous 48 U.S. states. It has a drier climate than every other continent except Antarctica. Because Australia is in the Southern Hemisphere, it is warmer in the north than in the south.

Australia's vast, dry interior is called the Outback. Few people live there. Much of the land is used for grazing cattle and sheep on huge ranches called "stations." For many years, children on stations have "gone to school" by two-way radio connection with their teachers and other students called the School of the Air. Today, computers also provide connections for such children.

Australia's first people are the Aborigines. They came to Australia from Asia thousands of years before the first Europeans came. People from Asia also settled other islands of Oceania. New Zealand was the last place they reached. English people started coming to Australia and New Zealand in the late 1700s. People from the British Isles still make up most of the population, but Asians and people from the Pacific Islands have joined them. In both Australia and New Zealand, most people live along the coasts in modern cities.

A Historical Look At Australia

Circa 40,000 B.C.–30,000 B.C.

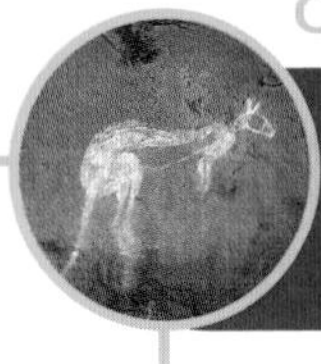

Aborigines arrive in Australia from Asia.

Circa A.D. 1432

Chinese settlers arrive in Northern Territory

1788

The British establish the first Australian penal colony in Sydney.

1851

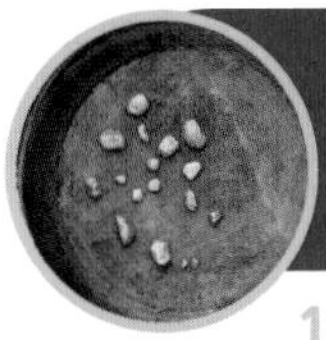

Gold is discovered in New South Wales and Victoria.

Australia's Extremes

Landforms Map

- Mountains
- Plains
- Hills and low tablelands

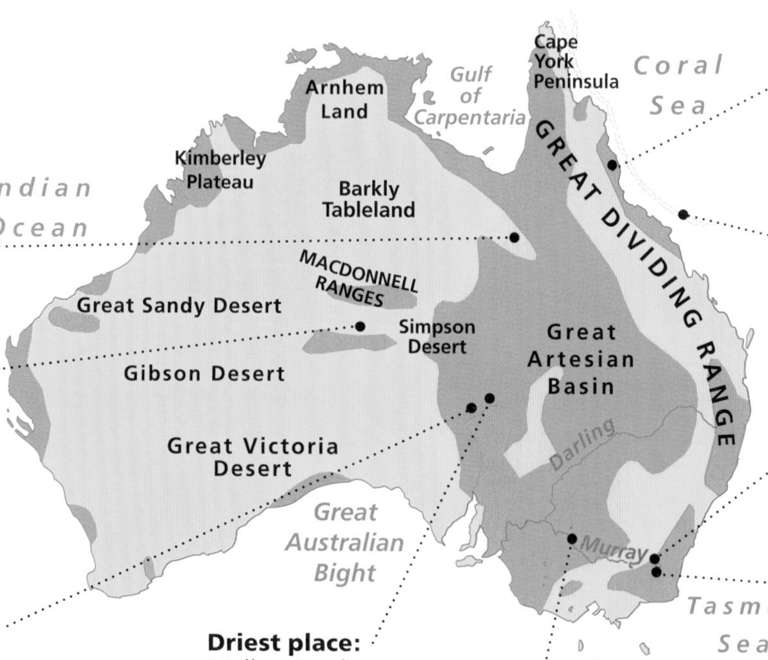
Cape York Peninsula
Gulf of Carpentaria
Coral Sea
Arnhem Land
Kimberley Plateau
Barkly Tableland
Indian Ocean
GREAT DIVIDING RANGE
MACDONNELL RANGES
Great Sandy Desert
Simpson Desert
Great Artesian Basin
Gibson Desert
Great Victoria Desert
Darling
Great Australian Bight
Murray
Tasman Sea
TASMANIA
© Rand McNally

Wettest place:
Bellenden Ker, Queensland
340 inches (863.6 cm) of precipitation a year

Longest coral reef:
Great Barrier Reef, northeast coast of Queensland
1,250 miles (2,000 km)

Hottest recorded temperature:
Cloncurry, Queensland
128° F (53° C)

Largest freestanding monolith:
Uluru (Ayers Rock), Northern Territory
1,141.7 feet (348 m) high above ground by 2.2 miles (3.6 km) long by 1.5 miles (2.4 km) wide

Highest point:
Mt. Kosciuszko, New South Wales
7,313 feet (2,229 m)

Coldest recorded temperature:
Charlotte Pass, New South Wales
-8° F (-22° C)

Lowest point:
Lake Eyre, South Australia
52 feet (16 m) below sea level

Driest place:
Mulka, South Australia
4.05 inches (10 cm)/year

Longest river:
Murray River, southeastern Australia
1,566 miles (2,520 km)

Largest island:
Tasmania
26,400 square miles (68,400 square km)

Koala

Wallabies

Tasmanian devil

Wombat

1893

New Zealand is the first country to give women the right to vote.

1901

Australia becomes a self-governing dominion within the British Empire.

1976

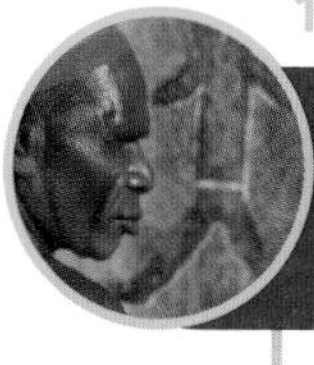

The First Aboriginal Land Rights Act is passed.

2000

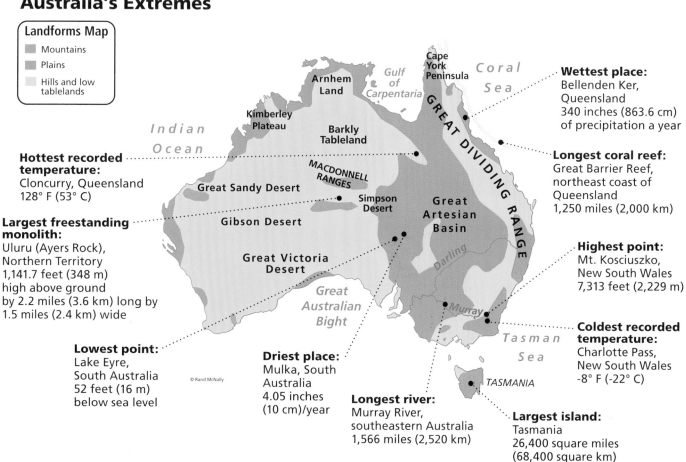

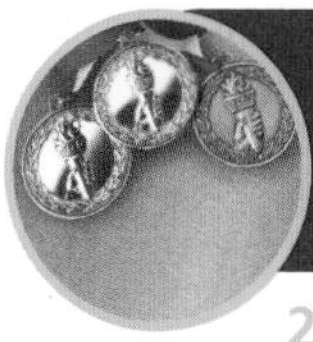

Sydney hosts the summer Olympic Games.

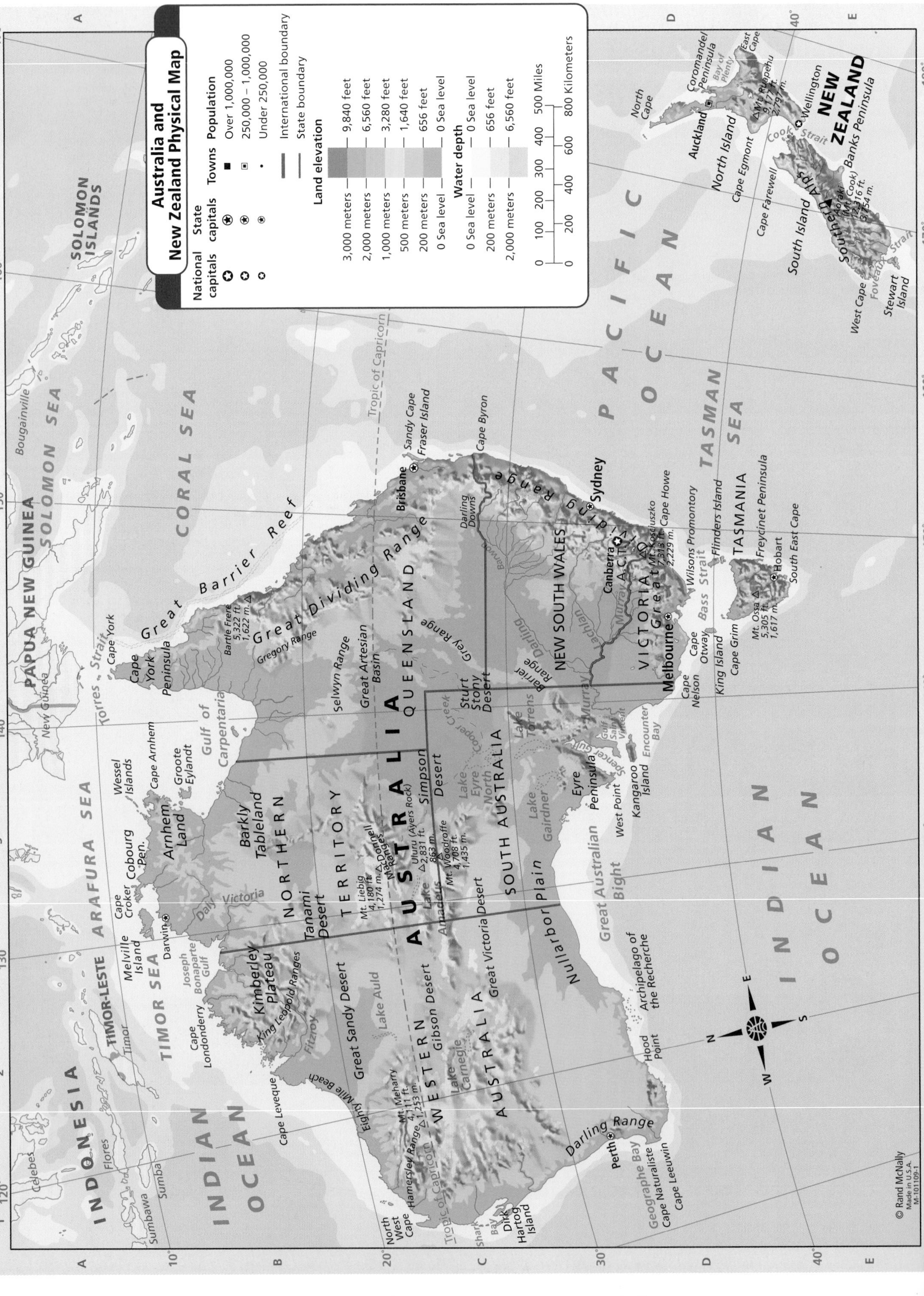
Australia and New Zealand Physical Map
National capitals
State capitals
Towns
Population
Over 1,000,000
250,000 – 1,000,000
Under 250,000
International boundary
State boundary
Land elevation
3,000 meters — 9,840 feet
2,000 meters — 6,560 feet
1,000 meters — 3,280 feet
500 meters — 1,640 feet
200 meters — 656 feet
0 Sea level — 0 Sea level
Water depth
0 Sea level — 0 Sea level
200 meters — 656 feet
2,000 meters — 6,560 feet
0 100 200 300 400 500 Miles
0 200 400 600 800 Kilometers
INDONESIA
PAPUA NEW GUINEA
SOLOMON ISLANDS
TIMOR-LESTE
ARAFURA SEA
TIMOR SEA
CORAL SEA
SOLOMON SEA
TASMAN SEA
PACIFIC OCEAN
INDIAN OCEAN
AUSTRALIA
WESTERN AUSTRALIA
NORTHERN TERRITORY
QUEENSLAND
SOUTH AUSTRALIA
NEW SOUTH WALES
VICTORIA
A.C.T.
TASMANIA
NEW ZEALAND
North Island
South Island
Great Barrier Reef
Great Dividing Range
Great Artesian Basin
Great Sandy Desert
Gibson Desert
Great Victoria Desert
Tanami Desert
Simpson Desert
Sturt Stony Desert
Nullarbor Plain
Great Australian Bight
Kimberley Plateau
Arnhem Land
Barkly Tableland
Cape York Peninsula
Gulf of Carpentaria
Eyre Peninsula
Bass Strait
Torres Strait
Cook Strait
Foveaux Strait
Darwin
Brisbane
Sydney
Canberra
Melbourne
Hobart
Adelaide
Perth
Auckland
Wellington
Uluru (Ayers Rock) 2,831 ft. 863 m.
Mt. Kosciuszko 7,313 ft. 2,229 m.
Bartle Frere 5,322 ft. 1,622 m.
Mt. Ossa 5,305 ft. 1,617 m.
Mt. Woodroffe 4,708 ft. 1,435 m.
Mt. Liebig 4,180 ft. 1,274 m.
Mt. Meharry 4,111 ft. 1,253 m.
Mt. Ruapehu 9,177 ft. 2,797 m.
Aoraki (Mt. Cook) 12,316 ft. 3,754 m.
Southern Alps
Darling Range
Hamersley Range
MacDonnell Ranges
Lake Eyre North
Lake Torrens
Lake Gairdner
Lake Amadeus
Lake Mackay
Murray
Darling
Tropic of Capricorn
© Rand McNally
Made in U.S.A.
M-101109-1

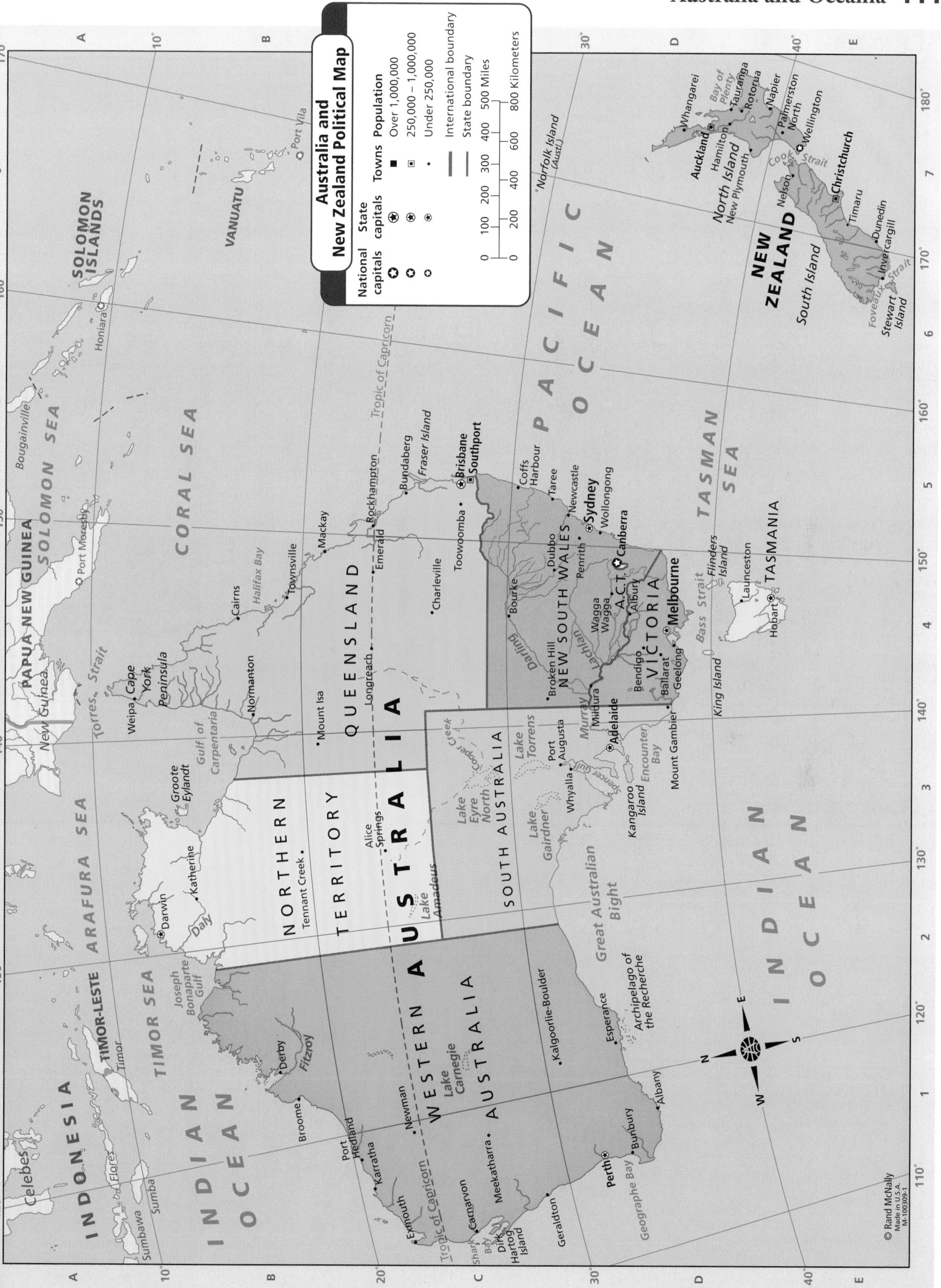
Australia and New Zealand Political Map
National capitals
State capitals
Towns
Population
Over 1,000,000
250,000 – 1,000,000
Under 250,000
International boundary
State boundary
0 100 200 300 400 500 Miles
0 200 400 600 800 Kilometers
AUSTRALIA
WESTERN AUSTRALIA
NORTHERN TERRITORY
QUEENSLAND
SOUTH AUSTRALIA
NEW SOUTH WALES
VICTORIA
A.C.T.
TASMANIA
NEW ZEALAND
North Island
South Island
PAPUA NEW GUINEA
SOLOMON ISLANDS
VANUATU
INDONESIA
TIMOR-LESTE
INDIAN OCEAN
PACIFIC OCEAN
TASMAN SEA
CORAL SEA
SOLOMON SEA
ARAFURA SEA
TIMOR SEA
Great Australian Bight
Gulf of Carpentaria
Joseph Bonaparte Gulf
Halifax Bay
Torres Strait
Bass Strait
Cook Strait
Foveaux Strait
Bay of Plenty
Spencer Gulf
Encounter Bay
Geographe Bay
Shark Bay
Tropic of Capricorn
Cape York Peninsula
Lake Eyre North
Lake Torrens
Lake Gairdner
Lake Amadeus
Lake Carnegie
Cooper Creek
Darling
Lachlan
Murray
Fitzroy
Daly
Canberra
Sydney
Melbourne
Brisbane
Adelaide
Perth
Darwin
Hobart
Southport
Newcastle
Wollongong
Geelong
Toowoomba
Townsville
Cairns
Mackay
Rockhampton
Bundaberg
Coffs Harbour
Taree
Dubbo
Penrith
Bourke
Broken Hill
Wagga Wagga
Albury
Mildura
Bendigo
Ballarat
Mount Gambier
Port Augusta
Whyalla
Alice Springs
Tennant Creek
Katherine
Mount Isa
Normanton
Weipa
Longreach
Charleville
Emerald
Launceston
Kalgoorlie-Boulder
Esperance
Albany
Bunbury
Geraldton
Carnarvon
Exmouth
Karratha
Port Hedland
Broome
Derby
Newman
Meekatharra
Groote Eylandt
Fraser Island
Kangaroo Island
King Island
Flinders Island
Dirk Hartog Island
Archipelago of the Recherche
Norfolk Island (Austl.)
Port Moresby
Honiara
Port Vila
Bougainville
New Guinea
Celebes
Flores
Sumba
Sumbawa
Timor
Wellington
Auckland
Christchurch
Hamilton
Tauranga
Rotorua
Napier
Palmerston North
New Plymouth
Whangarei
Nelson
Timaru
Dunedin
Invercargill
Stewart Island
N
S
E
W
A
B
C
D
E
1
2
3
4
5
6
7
110°
120°
130°
140°
150°
160°
170°
180°
10°
20°
30°
40°
© Rand McNally
Made in U.S.A.
M-100309-1

Climate

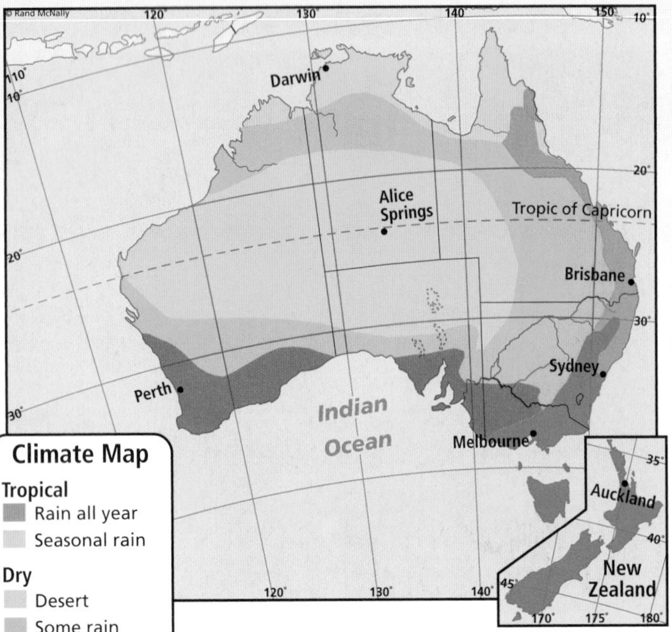

Transportation

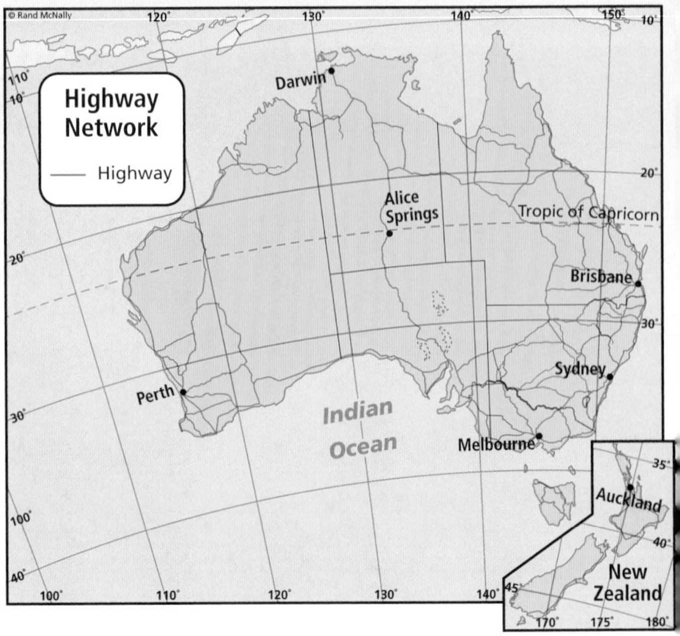

Australia's highways provide important links between widely separated towns and cities, especially in the Outback.

Did You Know?

Australia has more snow-covered land than Switzerland. Most snow falls in southeastern Australia.

Environments

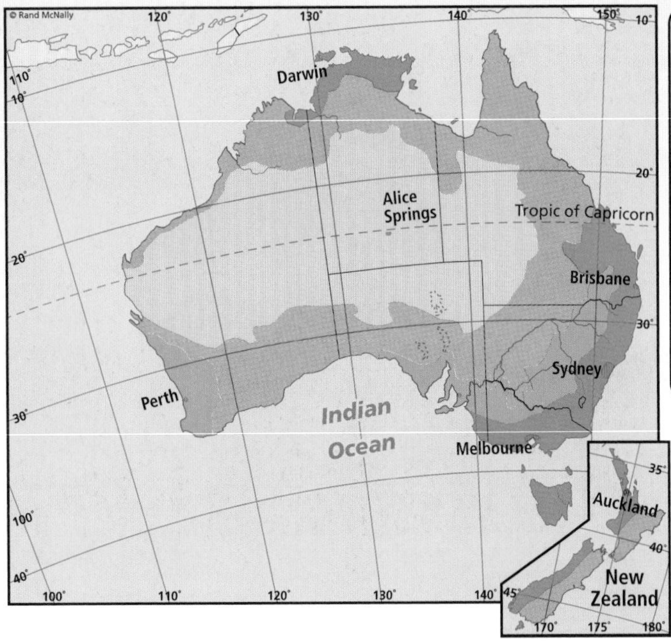

Pinnacles Desert in Nambung National Park, Western Australia, Australia

Grassland in Northern Territory, Australia

Rain forest in Queensland, Australia.

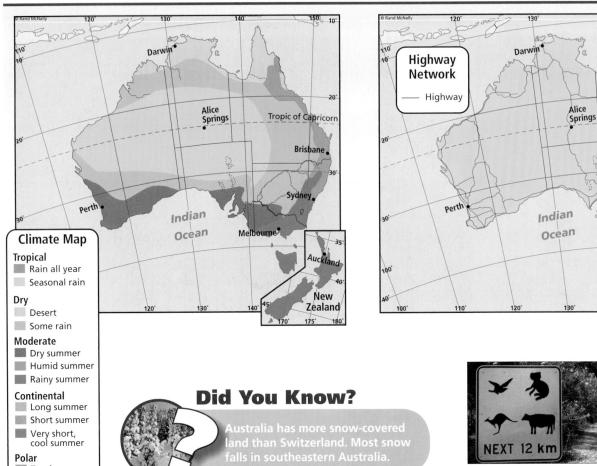

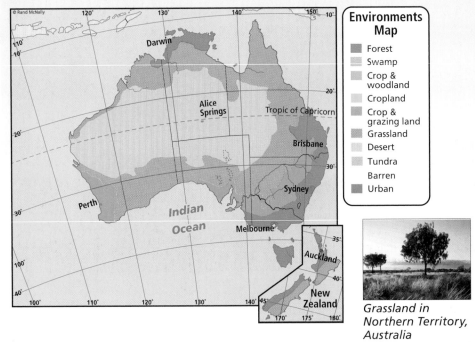

Grazing cattle and sheep, South Island, New Zealand.

Economic Activities

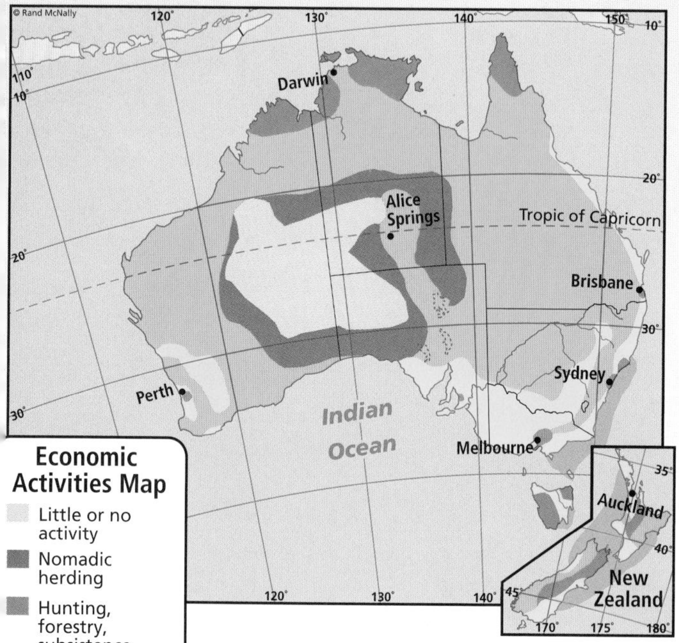

In Australia, sheep outnumber humans seven to one. In New Zealand, the ratio is 14 to one. Together, the two countries produce nearly 50% of the world's wool.

Population

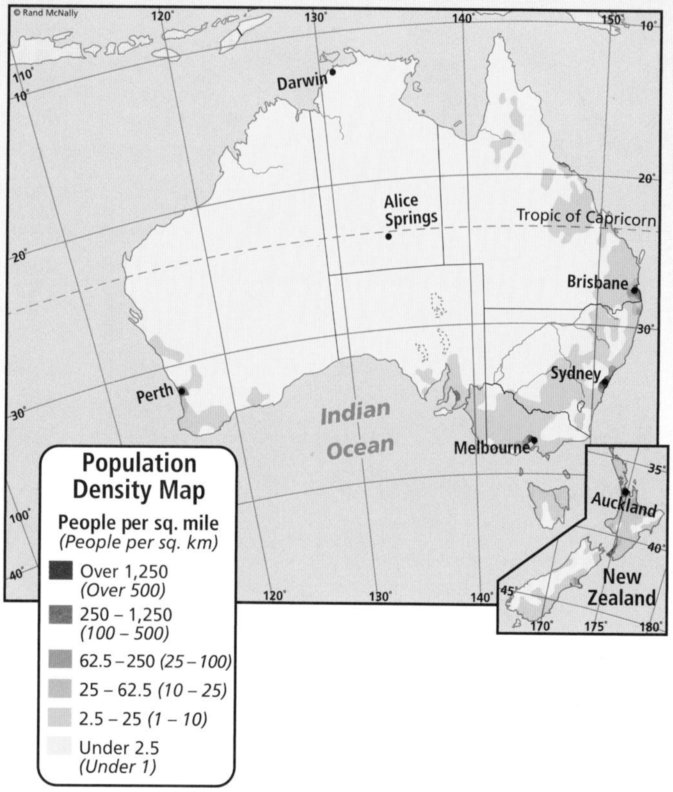

What If?

If all of Australia received plenty of rain, how might the population distribution be different?

The Great Barrier Reef

The Great Barrier Reef stretches for roughly 1,250 miles (2,000 km) along the northeast coast of Queensland, Australia. It is made up of more than 2,600 separate coral reefs. Together, they cover 80,000 square miles (207,200 square kilometers). The Great Barrier Reef is the largest group of coral reefs and islands in the world.

Scientists believe that the reef began forming millions of years ago. More than 400 different types of coral, in a great variety of colors, form the reef. In addition, about 1,500 species of fish live in the warm waters around the reef. Scientists warn that some human activities are causing serious damage to the reef.

An odd-looking fish called a Maori wrasse

A whale shark

Acropora plate coral

More than 600 islands are found along the Great Barrier Reef. Some of them have been developed as tourist resorts, but many are uninhabited.

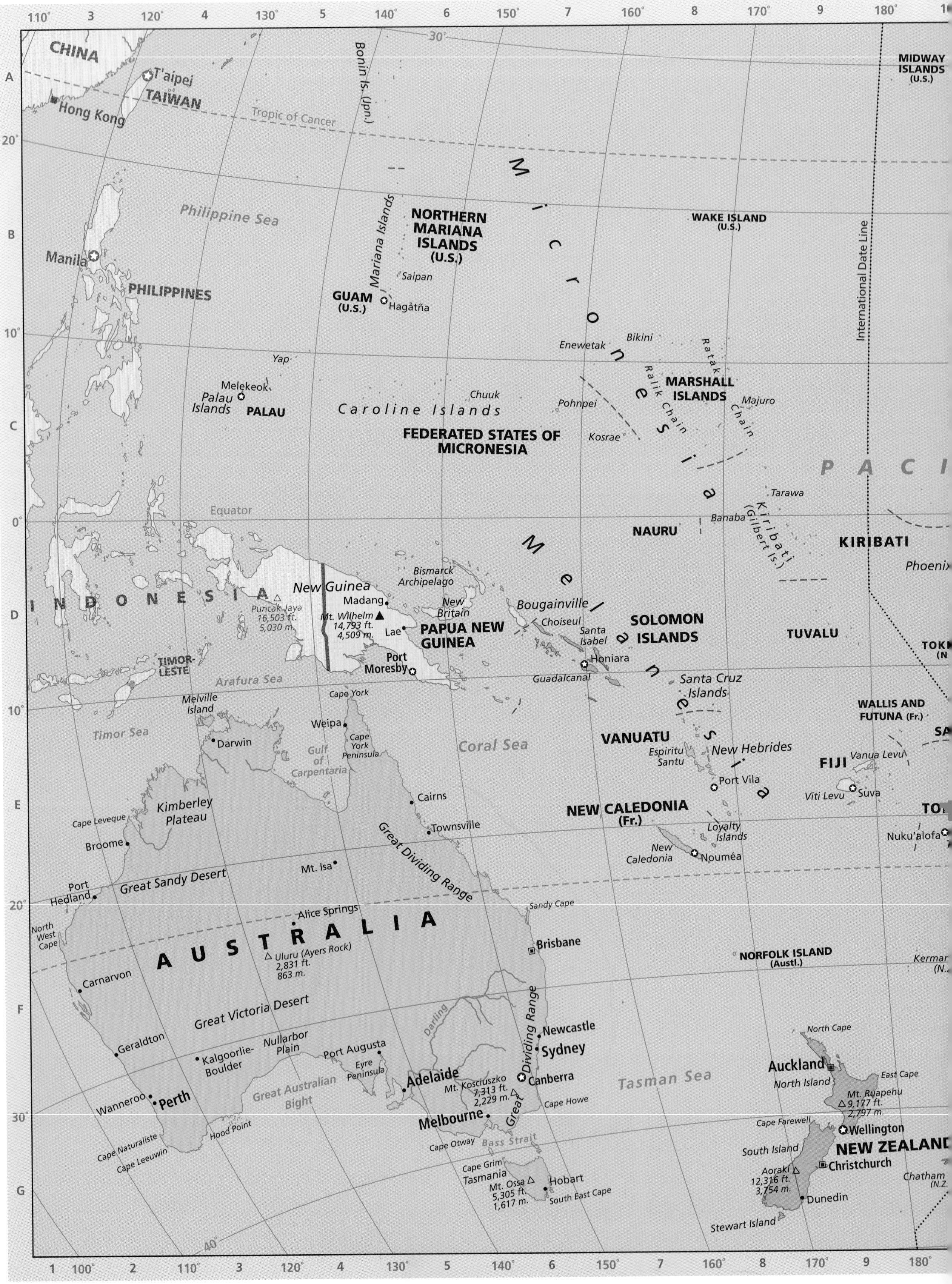
CHINA
T'aipei
TAIWAN
Hong Kong
Tropic of Cancer
Bonin Is. (Jpn.)
MIDWAY ISLANDS (U.S.)
Philippine Sea
Micronesia
Mariana Islands
NORTHERN MARIANA ISLANDS (U.S.)
Saipan
GUAM (U.S.)
Hagåtña
WAKE ISLAND (U.S.)
International Date Line
Manila
PHILIPPINES
Bikini
Enewetak
Ratak Chain
Ralik Chain
Yap
MARSHALL ISLANDS
Majuro
Melekeok
Palau Islands
PALAU
Chuuk
Caroline Islands
Pohnpei
Kosrae
FEDERATED STATES OF MICRONESIA
PACI
Tarawa
Equator
Banaba
Kiribati (Gilbert Is.)
NAURU
KIRIBATI
Phoenix
Melanesia
INDONESIA
New Guinea
Bismarck Archipelago
Puncak Jaya 16,503 ft. 5,030 m.
Madang
Mt. Wilhelm 14,793 ft. 4,509 m.
New Britain
Bougainville
Choiseul
Santa Isabel
SOLOMON ISLANDS
TUVALU
Lae
PAPUA NEW GUINEA
Port Moresby
Honiara
Guadalcanal
TIMOR-LESTE
Arafura Sea
Santa Cruz Islands
Cape York
Melville Island
WALLIS AND FUTUNA (Fr.)
Weipa
Timor Sea
Darwin
Cape York Peninsula
Gulf of Carpentaria
Coral Sea
VANUATU
Espiritu Santu
New Hebrides
FIJI
Vanua Levu
Port Vila
Cairns
Viti Levu
Suva
Kimberley Plateau
Cape Leveque
Townsville
NEW CALEDONIA (Fr.)
Loyalty Islands
Nuku'alofa
Broome
Great Dividing Range
New Caledonia
Nouméa
Mt. Isa
Port Hedland
Great Sandy Desert
Sandy Cape
Alice Springs
North West Cape
AUSTRALIA
Brisbane
Uluru (Ayers Rock) 2,831 ft. 863 m.
NORFOLK ISLAND (Austl.)
Kermar (N.
Carnarvon
Great Victoria Desert
Darling
Dividing Range
Newcastle
Sydney
North Cape
Geraldton
Kalgoorlie-Boulder
Nullarbor Plain
Port Augusta
Eyre Peninsula
Auckland
East Cape
North Island
Adelaide
Canberra
Tasman Sea
Mt. Kosciuszko 7,313 ft. 2,229 m.
Mt. Ruapehu 9,177 ft. 2,797 m.
Great Australian Bight
Wanneroo
Perth
Great
Cape Howe
Melbourne
Cape Farewell
Wellington
Cape Naturaliste
Hood Point
Cape Otway
Bass Strait
South Island
NEW ZEALAND
Cape Leeuwin
Cape Grim
Tasmania
Christchurch
Mt. Ossa 5,305 ft. 1,617 m.
Hobart
Aoraki 12,316 ft. 3,754 m.
Chatham (N.Z.)
South East Cape
Dunedin
Stewart Island

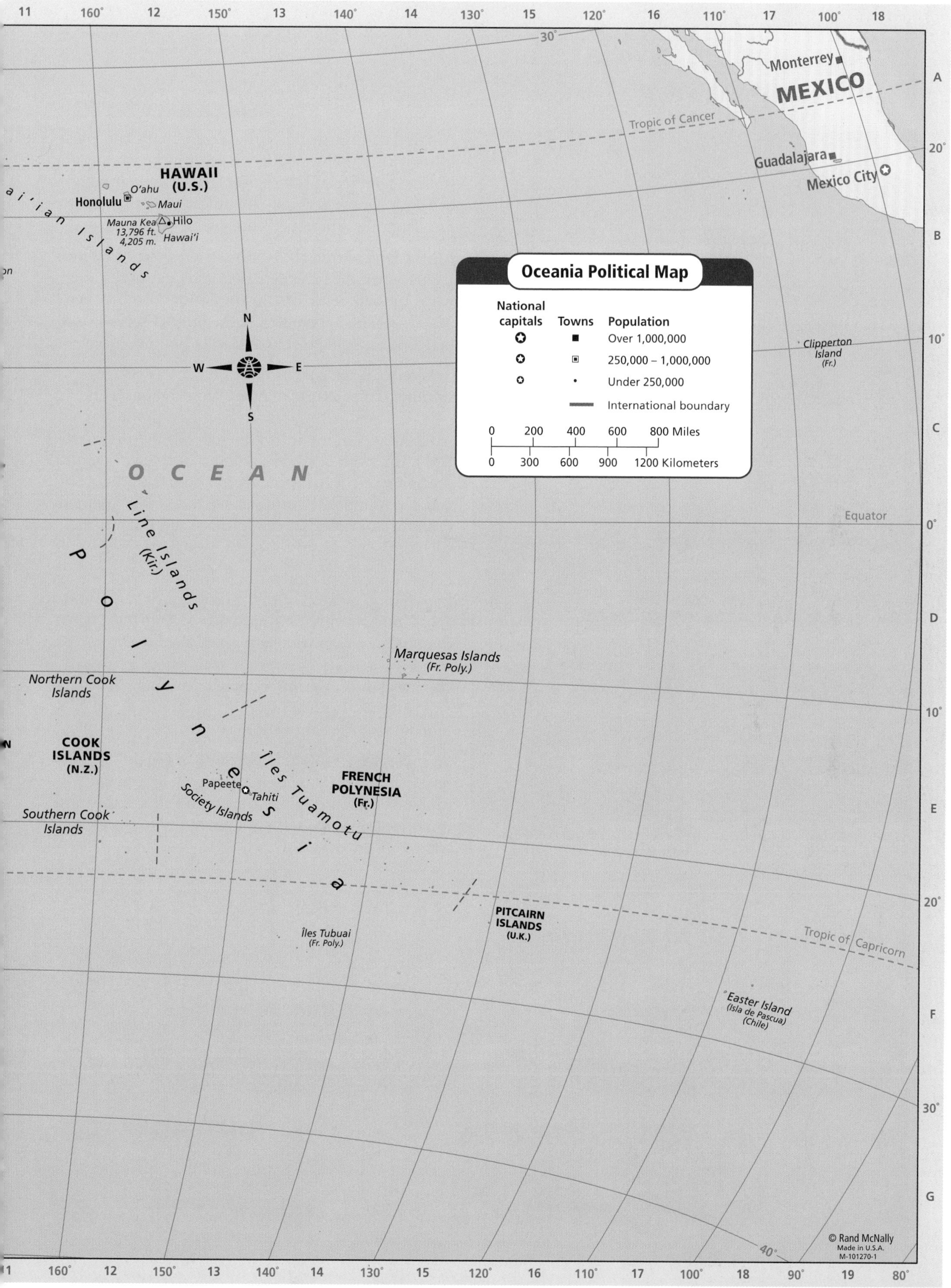

Oceania Political Map

National capitals	Towns	Population
✪	■	Over 1,000,000
✪	▣	250,000 – 1,000,000
✪	•	Under 250,000
	—	International boundary

0 200 400 600 800 Miles

0 300 600 900 1200 Kilometers

MEXICO

Monterrey ■

Tropic of Cancer

Guadalajara ■

20°

Mexico City ✪

HAWAII (U.S.)

O'ahu

Honolulu ▣

Maui

Mauna Kea △ Hilo
13,796 ft.
4,205 m. Hawai'i

B

Clipperton
Island
(Fr.)

10°

Hawaiian Islands

N
W E
S

OCEAN

Equator 0°

Line Islands
(Kir.)

C

P O L Y N

Marquesas Islands
(Fr. Poly.)

10°

Northern Cook
Islands

COOK
ISLANDS
(N.Z.)

Îles Tuamotu

FRENCH
POLYNESIA
(Fr.)

Papeete ✪ Tahiti

Society Islands

Southern Cook
Islands

E

20°

PITCAIRN
ISLANDS
(U.K.)

Tropic of Capricorn

Îles Tubuai
(Fr. Poly.)

Easter Island
(Isla de Pascua)
(Chile)

F

30°

G

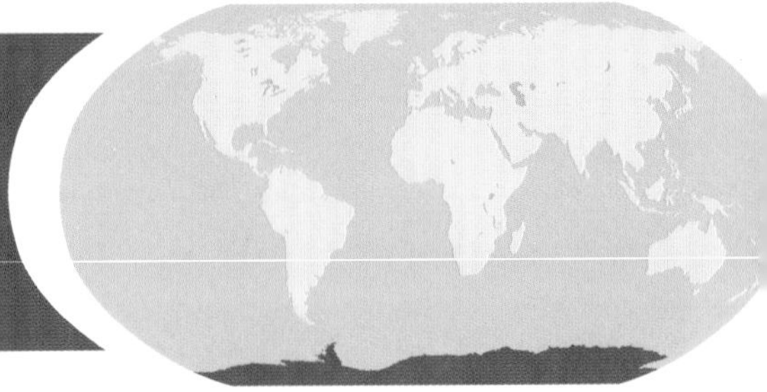

Antarctica

Kayaking in sea ice along the Antarctic coast.

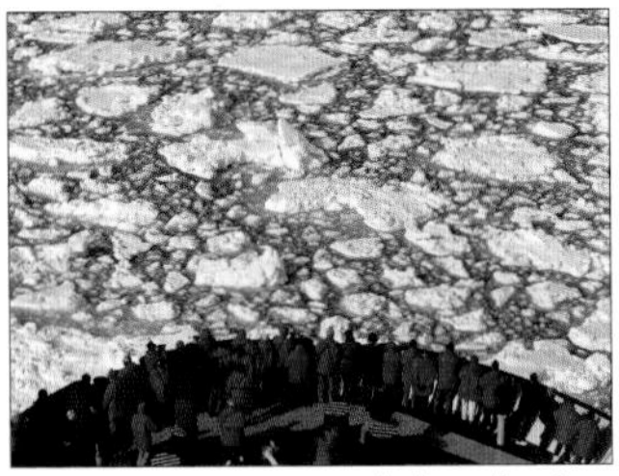

Passengers crowd the deck of an icebreaker ship as it plows through pack ice.

Exploring a huge crevasse on Ross Island.

Antarctica is the world's fifth-largest continent. Most of it lies within the Antarctic Circle. It is the world's most isolated landmass. The nearest land is the southern tip of South America, about 700 miles (more than 1,100 km) from the Antarctic Peninsula.

All the land within the Antarctic Circle has days in winter when the sun never rises and days in summer when the sun never sets. At the South Pole, between March 20 and September 21 the sun never rises, and between September 21 and March 20 it never sets.

Antarctica is the coldest place on earth. Average summer temperatures may reach only about 0° F (-18° C). Such a cold, frozen landmass produces cold winds that collide with warmer air around the coast and form a belt of storms. Antarctica receives very little precipitation. What precipitation does fall produces ice, which accumulates into thick ice sheets that gradually push toward the coast and form ice shelves over the edge of the land.

People discovered Antarctica only about 200 years ago. Exploration on land started a little more than 100 years ago. No people live on Antarctica permanently. More than a dozen countries have established scientific stations where scientists study such things as global climate change, the atmosphere's thinning ozone layer, and plant and animal life. A growing number of tourists visit the continent each year.

Scientists know that the continent has such resources as coal, but an international agreement prohibits exploiting these resources. Perhaps the most important resource is the abundant life in the cold waters off the coast.

A Historical Look At Antarctica

1819–1821
Fabian von Bellingshausen, a Russian, is the first European to see Antarctica.

1894
A Norwegian expedition is the first to land on Victoria Land.

1911
Roald Amundsen is the first person to reach the South Pole.

1929
Richard Byrd flies over the South Pole.

Scientific Stations in Antarctica

Frozen and isolated as it is, Antarctica offers some important advantages for researchers. Its darkness makes it a good place to study the stars. Its clean air allows studies of air quality. Scientists can see the effects of human activity. Antarctica has no borders—although seven countries have made territorial claims—so scientists from different countries can share the information they find.

A scientific station operated by Argentina.

Telecommunications equipment at a scientific station.

Palmer Station
The only U.S. station north of the Antarctic Circle.

Argentina
Brazil
Chile
China
Korea
Poland
Russia
Uruguay

United States
Ukraine
United Kingdom
Chile
Argentina
Argentina
Argentina

Halley Station
The site of important ozone research.

Argentina
United Kingdom

Germany

South Africa

McMurdo Station
Home to Antarctica's largest community—up to 1,100 people.

United States
New Zealand

United States
South Pole

Amundsen-Scott South Pole Station
Located about 1,150 feet (350 m) from the geographic South Pole.

India

Russia

SANAE IV
Built on poles, since 60-80 inches (150 to 200 cm) of snow piles up in winter.

ANTARCTICA

Russia

France

Japan

China
Russia

Russia

Dumont d'Urville Station
Built in 1956 to replace a station that burned down.

Vostok Station
The coldest recorded temperature on Earth, -128° F. (-89.2° C), was measured here on July 21, 1983.

Australia

Australia

Mawson Station
The oldest continuously inhabited station south of the Antarctic Circle.

Australia

Russia

Davis Station
The southernmost Australian station.

Mirnyy Station
Built in 1971-72 to replace an earlier station now under 6 feet (2 m) of ice.

Animals in Antarctica

Orcas, also known as killer whales

Wandering albatross

Emperor penguins

Leopard seal

1957–1958
The International Geophysical Year (IGY) focuses on the scientific study of Antarctica.

1991
The Wellington Agreement bans commercial mining operations in Antarctica.

The Antarctic Treaty provides for peaceful scientific cooperation in Antarctica.

1961

An iceberg 170 miles long and 25 miles wide breaks off the Ross Ice Shelf.

2000

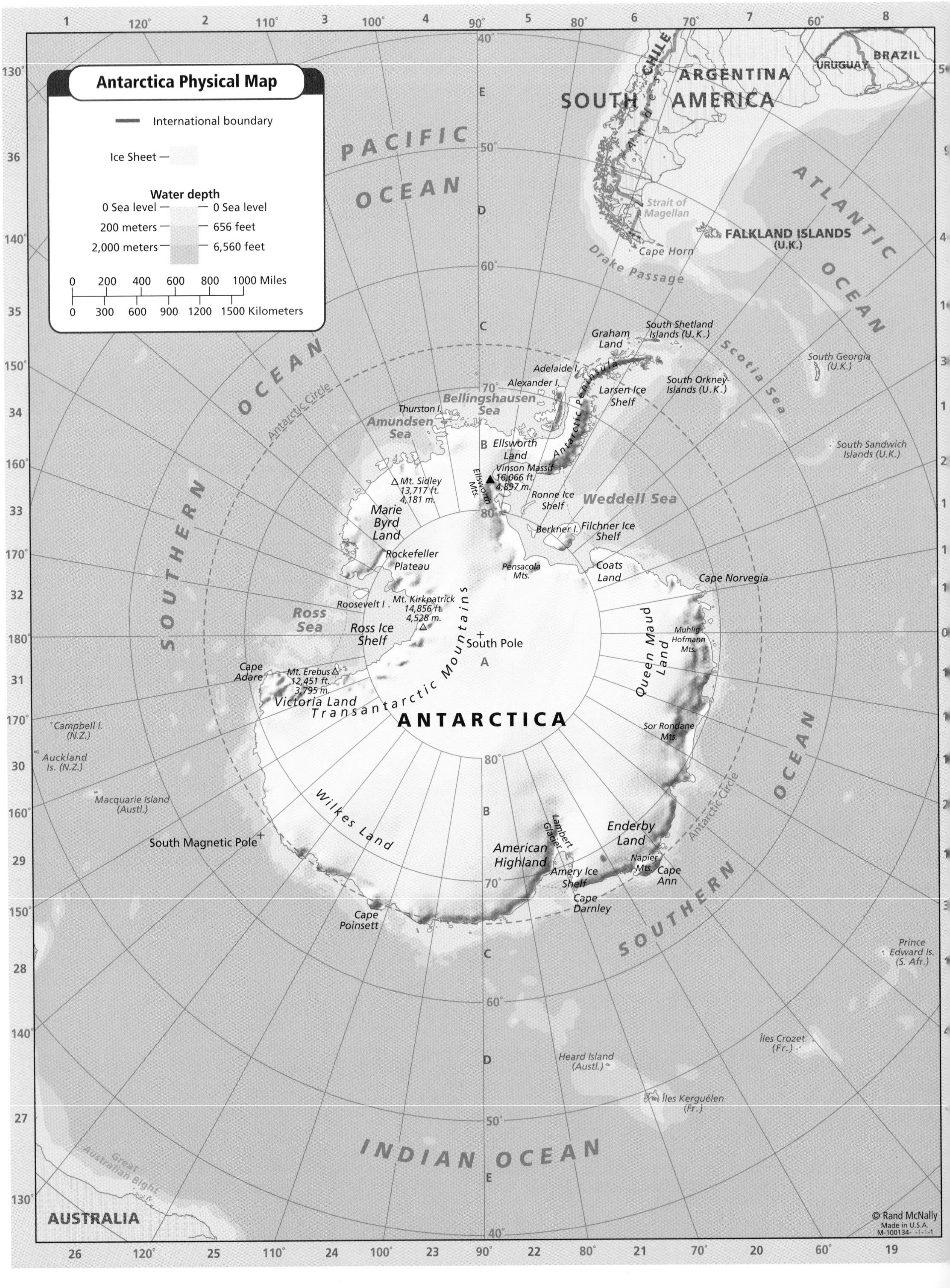
Antarctica Physical Map
International boundary
Ice Sheet
Water depth
0 Sea level — 0 Sea level
200 meters — 656 feet
2,000 meters — 6,560 feet
0 200 400 600 800 1000 Miles
0 300 600 900 1200 1500 Kilometers
PACIFIC OCEAN
SOUTHERN OCEAN
ATLANTIC OCEAN
INDIAN OCEAN
SOUTH AMERICA
ARGENTINA
CHILE
URUGUAY
BRAZIL
Andes
Strait of Magellan
FALKLAND ISLANDS (U.K.)
Cape Horn
Drake Passage
South Shetland Islands (U.K.)
Graham Land
Scotia Sea
South Georgia (U.K.)
South Orkney Islands (U.K.)
South Sandwich Islands (U.K.)
Adelaide I.
Alexander I.
Antarctic Peninsula
Larsen Ice Shelf
Bellingshausen Sea
Thurston I.
Amundsen Sea
Antarctic Circle
Ellsworth Land
Vinson Massif 16,066 ft. 4,897 m.
Ellsworth Mts.
Ronne Ice Shelf
Weddell Sea
Berkner I.
Filchner Ice Shelf
Mt. Sidley 13,717 ft. 4,181 m.
Marie Byrd Land
Rockefeller Plateau
Pensacola Mts.
Coats Land
Cape Norvegia
Roosevelt I.
Mt. Kirkpatrick 14,856 ft. 4,528 m.
Ross Sea
Ross Ice Shelf
Transantarctic Mountains
South Pole
Queen Maud Land
Muhlig-Hofmann Mts.
Cape Adare
Mt. Erebus 12,451 ft. 3,795 m.
Victoria Land
ANTARCTICA
Campbell I. (N.Z.)
Auckland Is. (N.Z.)
Sor Rondane Mts.
Macquarie Island (Austl.)
Wilkes Land
South Magnetic Pole
Lambert Glacier
American Highland
Enderby Land
Napier Mts.
Cape Ann
Amery Ice Shelf
Cape Darnley
Cape Poinsett
Prince Edward Is. (S. Afr.)
Îles Crozet (Fr.)
Heard Island (Austl.)
Îles Kerguélen (Fr.)
Great Australian Bight
AUSTRALIA
© Rand McNally
Made in U.S.A.
M-100134- -1-1-1

hematic Content Index

his index makes it easy to compare different continents and regions of the world in terms of climate, conomies, and other major themes covered in the atlas.

Index of Abbreviations

The following abbreviations are used in the index.

Afr.	Africa	**dist.**	district	**Terr.**	Territory or Territori
Austr.	Australia	**Eur.**	Europe	**S.A.**	South Americ
cap.	capital	**Mex.**	Mexico	**U.A.E.**	United Arab Emirat
Can.	Canada	**mts.**	mountains	**U.K.**	United Kingdo
dep.	dependency	**N.A.**	North America	**U.S.**	United Stat

Index

Review "How to Use the Atlas" pages 4 and 5 for information on using an index.

L

M